WINE COUNTRY

HOW TO USE THIS GUIDEBOOK

This guidebook is divided into five chapters: *An Introduction to the Wine Country, The Story of California Wine, Napa Valley, Sonoma Valley,* and *The Russian River Region.*

The first two chapters comprise essays, designed to provide you with facts on the area.

In the next three chapters we explore the Wine Country, with a detailed, geographical breakdown of the area. Each chapter contains an *essay* section, listings and descriptions of all the wineries in the area, and a *practical information* section which is designed to provide you with a ready reference to the area's accommodations, restaurants, recreational facilities, seasonal events, places of interest, etc., with hours, prices, addresses and phone numbers.

A quick and easy way into this book is the *Index* at the end.

Titles in this Series

The Complete Gold Country Guidebook
The Complete Lake Tahoe Guidebook
The Complete Monterey Peninsula Guidebook
The Complete San Diego Guidebook
The Complete San Francisco Guidebook
The Complete Santa Barbara Guidebook
The Complete Wine Country Guidebook
Farm Tours of Northern California
Vacation Towns of California

Indian Chief Travel Guides are available from your local bookstore or Indian Chief Publishing House, P.O. Box 5205, Tahoe City, CA 95730.

The Complete
WINE COUNTRY
Guidebook

Published by Indian Chief Publishing House
Tahoe City, California

Area Editor: **B. SANGWAN**
Editorial Associate: **PHILLIPPA J. SAVAGE**
Photographs: **Joseph Woods, B. Sangwan**

ISBN 0-916841-18-9

Printed in the U.S.A.

CONTENTS

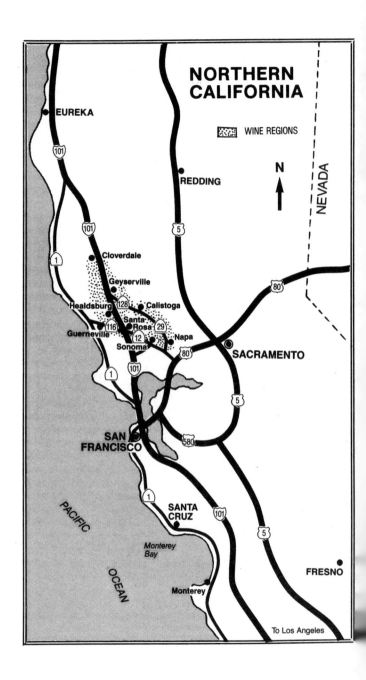

AN INTRODUCTION TO THE WINE COUNTRY

World Famous Wine Regions

The California wine country is world famous. It has the climate and soil types to rival the great wine regions of Europe. It has its grand old wine estates—such as The Christian Brothers, Inglenook, Beringer, Charles Krug and Buena Vista—which have endured for over a century. It has lured to its vineyards and cellars the wine greats of the world—among them the late Baron Phillipe de Rothschild, the French wine houses of Möet-Hennessy and Piper-Heidsieck, and Spain's Freixenet.

California, in fact, boasts nearly 700,000 acres of planted vineyards, at least fifty different appellations, and hundreds of microclimates. It produces approximately 400 million gallons of wine in an average year, with wine types ranging from varietals and generics to sparkling, appetizer and dessert wines. There are, besides, over 770 bonded wineries in California, nearly half of them in the Napa and Sonoma valleys and the Russian River region—which comprise the essential "wine country," with the greatest tourist interest. In the Napa Valley alone there are some 200 wineries, small and large, most with visitor facilities; and in Sonoma County's Russian River region and the Sonoma Valley are another 100 or so, mostly smaller, family owned and operated establishments.

The California wine country is also one of the state's foremost tourist regions. Napa Valley, typically, receives nearly 2 million visitors each year, with at least as many visitors to be found in the valley on any given weekend during the peak, harvest season (October-November), as in Southern California's Disneyland. The Sonoma Valley and Russian River region are no less popular with wine enthusiasts. Most wineries, too, are, by and large, visitor oriented, offering tours of their facilities, complimentary wine tasting, and on-the-premises wine and gift shops and picnic areas. Some of the wineries even feature restaurants and art galleries, or schedule music concerts, cooking schools, or other wine-related events in the summer months.

The wine country, in addition, has scores of excellent restaurants and bed and breakfast lodgings, several notable galleries and gift and import shops, and an array of recreational facilities, including bicycling, hot-air ballooning, soaring, golf, horseback riding, hiking, boating, camping, and riverboat cruises. And to add to this, the wine country has four distinct, and most interesting seasons—spring, summer, fall and winter—each unique in its colors and flavors.

The California wine country lies largely to the northeast of San Francisco, some 45 to 90 miles distant, ideally suited to day or overnight trips from the city.

THE STORY OF
CALIFORNIA WINE

Wine was first introduced to California by Spanish missionaries, who established in 1769 the first of California's 21 Franciscan missions, at San Diego. In the mission lands the missionaries planted the primitive Criolla winegrape; the harvest they crushed in their ox-skins, to produce a wine that was largely unexceptional but which nevertheless reminded them of the Old World.

As the mission trail moved northward, so did mission wine, foreshadowing, with uncanny accuracy, the great California wine regions of today. As missions were built, vineyards were planted and tended—mostly with native Indian labor—the grapes crushed and fermented, and the wines stored in the mission cellars. Of the 21 California missions, at least 16 are known to have had successful vineyards and aging cellars, the largest of them at the San Juan Capistrano Mission.

In 1823, however, the mission trail finally ended at Sonoma, where the last and northernmost of the California missions was established, as well as one of the most successful of the mission vineyards. But this, quite ironically, also signaled the end of an era: dominion of California passed from the hands of the Spanish to the Mexican Empire.

By the 1830s, the Spanish missions had been largely secularized, and with the departure of the brown-robed Franciscan monks, the mission vineyards fell into neglect and quickly deteriorated. But in the 1830s, too, General Mariano Guadalupe Vallejo, Mexican governer of California, arrived at Sonoma, and took over the Sonoma Mission vineyards. He revived the vineyards and tended his vines with enthusiasm, making wine in much the same manner as the Franciscans had done before him.

Some years later, in the early 1850s, Agoston Haraszthy — a Hungarian adventurer and "count" of sorts — arrived upon the scene, destined for greatness as the "father" of California viticulture. He planted some 16 acres of Criolla vines in the Sonoma Valley, close to Vallejo's vineyards, and over the next few years expanded his vineyard holdings to over 6,000 acres, to include what was then described as one of the largest vineyards in the world, with approximately 110,000 vines. In 1857, Haraszthy founded the Buena Vista Winery — which remains the oldest winery in California today. But his greatest triumph was yet to come: In 1861, he made his well-publicized pilgrimage to the famous wine regions of Europe, returning to California with over 100,000 cuttings of some 300 wine varieties from those fabled regions. He planted the cuttings in his Sonoma Valley vineyards and experimented with them, giving California viticulturists access to more than just the mission grape. This was, in many ways, the beginning of California's wine industry.

Meanwhile, in the adjoining Napa Valley another wine story was unfolding. The valley's first vineyard had been planted in 1838 by George C. Yount, an early American settler, in his 12,000-acre Caymus land grant in the Yountville area; and in the following years, others, including Dr. Edward Turner Bale, received land grants in the Napa Valley, resulting in more small acreages being devoted to winegrapes. But it was not until the 1860s and 1870s that wineries — the great glories of the Napa Valley — began springing up by the score throughout the valley. German immigrant, Charles Krug, who made the first wine in the Napa Valley using a grape press in 1858, established his winery in 1861; Jacob Schram, another pioneer vintner, established Schramsberg Cellars in the upper valley in 1862; Frederich and Jacob Beringer founded Beringer Vineyards at St. Helena in 1876; and in 1879, Gustave Niebaum, a Finnish sea captain, built Inglenook in the Rutherford area in the Napa Valley. In all, by 1889, Napa Valley boasted 142 wineries, producing over 3 million gallons of wine.

In the late 1800s and early 1900s, too, an Italian wine district was developing in the Russian River region, to the north of the Napa and Sonoma valleys, largely concentrated in the Healdsburg area. Brothers Pietro and Guiseppe Simi, among the first in the area, built their stone cellar just to the north of Healdsburg in 1876; and in 1896, John Foppiano founded his family winery just to the south of town. Among others, Edoardo Seghesio founded a winery in the area in 1902; Constante Pastori founded one in 1914; and Giovanni Pedroncelli acquired a winery in 1927, originally founded in 1904. North still, at Asti, directly below the town of Cloverdale, Andrea Sbaboro, an Italian-Swiss immigrant banker, built the sprawling Italian Swiss Colony, producing California bubbly, as a make-work project for his fellow countrymen. Also in the area, in 1881, the Korbel brothers — natives of Czechoslovakia — built their grand old champagne cellars, overlooking the Russian River, just to the east of the Russian River town of Guerneville.

The late 1800s, however, also witnessed one of the darkest periods in the brief history of the budding California wine industry. Over some 10 years, in the 1880s and 1890s, the *phylloxera vastatrix* root-louse — which feeds on grapevine roots, ultimately destroying them — ravaged the European wine districts, then virtually destroyed California viticulture, almost overnight. The root-louse was first discovered in a Sonoma County vineyard, but it quickly spread, devouring vineyards throughout Napa and Sonoma counties. Years of research and experimentation followed — even a state viticulture board was established — and eventually a phylloxera-resistant rootstock was developed — grafting the European *vitis vinifera* onto native American vine roots.

In the early 1900s, another disaster struck. The Prohibition of 1919 brought the California wine industry to a grinding halt. Wineries, many of them in their infancy, were forced to close, and vineyards were torn out and replanted to pears, apples and prunes. The only winemakers to survive were those making sacramental wine for the Church, such as Napa Valley's Beringer Vineyards — which remains today the valley's oldest winery in continuous operation.

When Prohibition was finally repealed in 1933, fewer than 200 acres of Cabernet Sauvignon remained in the entire state, and virtually none of Chardonnay. Most of California's vineyards had either decayed or been converted into fruit orchards, and what little acreage of winegrapes there was, had turned to common grapes. Demand for California wine, too, had by then plummeted: in the year 1934, reportedly, wine consumption in the U.S. fell to below a pint per capita.

In the mid-1900s, even as the demand for wine continued to lag, largely due to American drinking habits, great strides were made in the sciences of enology and viticulture; and in the Napa Valley — California's foremost wine region — vintners were discovering anew the noble Cabernet Sauvignon grape. In fact, by 1941 Napa accounted for more than half of the state's entire Cabernet acreage, and, at about the same time, Andre Tshelistcheff, a Russian-born winemaker at Napa Valley's Beaulieu Vineyard, brought to prominence Cabernet Sauvignon as the "Queen of California wines." And yet, a bottle of well-aged Napa Valley Cabernet sold for as little as $1.09 at cellar doors...on into the 1950s, and even into the early 1960s.

The 1970s, however, ushered in a new era. Social habits changed, wine became fashionable again, and U.S. consumption jumped to 1.5 gallons per head in 1972, then rose again, in 1984, to around 2.35 gallons. Americans were now enjoying wine to the tune of nearly 400 million gallons a year — much of it California wine. The state's vineyard acreages, too, increased several-fold, creeping into the coast ranges and north into Mendocino and Lake counties.

The 1970s and 1980s also witnessed waves of new investment in the California wine country, much of it in the Napa and Sonoma areas. First were the corporate investors: Swiss multi-national Nestlé bought the

ancient Beringer Vineyards; the Heublein Corporation acquired In-
glenook and Beaulieu; Sterling Vineyards was sold to the Coca-Cola
Company in 1977, then sold again, in 1983, to Canadian distiller
Seagrams; and Almaden, the bulk wine producer, was purchased by
National Distillers.

Next came such well-known names as Francis Ford Coppola,
movie-maker, who bought the old Niebaum Mansion in Rutherford in
1978 and established the Niebaum-Coppola Estate; and coffee-king
Austin Hills, who staked his claim in the Grigich-Hills winery, also in
the Napa Valley. Among others, Mrs. Walt Disney bought into the
Silverado Vineyards in Napa; comedians Tom and Dick Smothers
opened their tasting room in the Sonoma Valley, offering wines from
their Santa Cruz and Sonoma County vineyards; and Pat Paulsen, of
TV's "Laugh In" fame, built his winery at Asti, at the northern end of
the Russian River region.

In the latter years, of course, came the foreign invasion. The late
Baron Philippe de Rothschild—who in 1971 was quoted as saying,
"California wines are like Coca-Cola—they all taste the same"—
forged a partnership with Napa Valley's Robert Mondavi in the early
1980s, to produce Bordeaux-style proprietary red wines. French-based
Möet-Hennessy built a $30-million sparkling wine facility, Domaine
Chandon, near Yountville in 1973, and in 1980 the French winemaker
also purchased the prestigious Simi Winery at Healdsburg. Piper-
Heidsieck, also of France, built in 1980 the Piper Sonoma Cellars in the
Russian River Valley, specializing in *méthode champenoise* sparkling
wines; and Rémy Martin, the well-known French cognac producer, is
currently making brandies in the cognac style in a joint venture with
Napa Valley's Schramsberg Cellars. Also, Freixenet of Spain, the
world's largest sparkling wine producer, opened in 1986 its $12-million
Gloria Ferrer Champagne Caves just south of Sonoma.

Other foreign interests include the historic Buena Vista Winery and
Napa's Franciscan Vineyards, owned by the West German firms of A.
Racke and Peter Eckes Co., respectively; and Cuvaison, located near
Calistoga, owned by Inselhold of Switzerland. Also, the well-regarded
Chateau St. Jean Winery of Sonoma Valley was acquired in 1984 by
Japan's whiskey distiller, Suntory Ltd., for a reported $40 million; and
Domaine St. George, formerly Cambiaso, is now owned by the Four
Seas Corporation of Thailand. And then there are others.

But besides the "Who's Who" of the California wine industry, it is
California wine that continues to draw the greatest acclaim. In 1976, at
the famous "Paris Tasting," California wines first set the wine world on
its ear: a 1973 Chateau Montelana Chardonnay came in first among
twelve highly-regarded French and California offerings, and a 1973
Stag's Leap Cabernet Sauvignon won top honors in its category, ahead
of a 1970 Mouton-Rothschild. In the years since, California wines have
continued to dominate the wine scene, at international, national and
regional competitions, reaffirming for the California winemaker the
parochial boast— "every year is a vintage year!"

NAPA VALLEY

Grand Estates and Boutique Wineries

Napa Valley is practically synomymous with the California wine country—and with good reason. There are over 150 wineries in the valley, large and small, strung along a narrow stretch of some of the most fertile wine-growing land in the world. Famous wine estates such as The Christian Brothers, Inglenook, Beaulieu, Beringer and Charles Krug have been here for over a century. Newer establishments such as the French-owned Domaine Chandon and the elaborate Mediterranean-style Robert Mondavi Winery have also made their homes in the Napa Valley. And then there are the small, "boutique" wineries, popping up by the score all across the valley, all producing premium Napa wine.

Geographically, the valley runs southeast-northwest, flanked by the Mayacamas Mountain range on the west and smaller, low-lying hills on the east. The valley itself is approximately 29 miles long and 4 miles across at its widest point, comprising some 32,000 acres of planted vineyards. It is made up, primarily, of five major areas—the Napa area, the Yountville area, Rutherford and Oakville, the St. Helena area, and Calistoga at the very top end. There are, besides, two major routes that run the length of the valley—the St. Helena Highway (Route 29) and the Silverado Trail—with several smaller crossroads dashing off between the two, enabling the visitor to either journey up one of the major routes and down the other, or criss-cross up the valley, exploring wineries both along and between the St. Helena Highway and the Silverado Trail.

The Napa Valley, of course, can be reached by taking Highway 101 north from San Francisco, then 37 and 121 northeastward to the City of Napa, situated at the southern end of the valley. Alternatively, if you are traveling from Sacramento in the east, follow Interstate 80 to Vallejo, then north on 29 to Napa.

NAPA

We suggest you begin your tour of the Napa Valley where the valley itself begins—at Napa. Napa is situated at the southern end of the Napa Valley, some 10 miles or so above San Pablo Bay. It is the largest town in the area—with a population of approximately 55,000, fully one half of the total population of Napa County—and an important supply center for the valley to its northwest. There are also good, abundant accommodations and restaurants here, and modern shops, making this an ideal base from which to explore the rest of the valley.

Napa, it must also be said, is an historic town. It was originally founded in 1848, but grew largely in the 1850s as a center for miners from the Sierra goldfields and, again, from the silver mines in the eastern hills of the Napa Valley. In the mid-1800s, of course, the valley's wine industry had begun to develop, and several wealthy merchants and personages of the day built their grand old mansions in Napa. A fair number of these splendid Victorians can still be seen here, mostly restored, and many of them converted into charming bed and breakfast establishments, such as the Coombs Residence, Goodman House and Gallery Osgood, among others. Several more historic and lovely buildings, among them the old City Hall and the Napa County Courthouse, can also be toured on the city's "Landmark Walks"—a tour organized by Napa's Community Redevelopment Agency. For more information, and schedules, call the agency at (707) 255-7836.

Also of interest in Napa are the Napa County Historical Society Museum on First Street, housed in the elegant, dressed-stone Goodman Library Building, dating from 1901; and the Skyline Park on Fourth and Imola avenues, which has hiking, fishing, bicycling and equestrian events, and from where, on clear days, you can see the San Francisco skyline. Worth investigating, too, is the Napa Valley Marina, situated on the west side of the Napa River, between the Cuttings Wharf launch ramp and Edgerly Island, and from where you can take boat cruises up the Napa River—the second longest navigable river in California—on an authentic Mississippi riverboat-style paddlewheeler, *City of Napa*, operated by the Napa Riverboat Company (707 226-2628).

For wine buffs, of course, besides the Napa Valley to the northeast, the Napa township itself has a handful of interesting little wineries, among them the family owned and operated Tulocay, located on Coombsville Road; and the Napa Valley Port Works, on Napa's Main Street. Another winery in the area, especially interesting to the visitor, is Quail Ridge, located just to the north of Napa, along Highway 121 and Atlas Peak Road. Quail Ridge dates from 1885, housed in an historic, ivy-covered building, and with some 300 square feet or so of ancient hillside caves and tunnels where wines are still aged. On Atlas Peak Road, too, directly above Quail Ridge, is the well-known Silverado Country Club, with two 18-hole championship golf courses, 20 tennis courts, two gourmet restaurants, and nearly 400 luxury guest accommodations.

Also of interest, north of Napa, are the historic Trefethen Vineyards on Oak Knoll Avenue, with the winery housed in an 1886 building designed by Captain Hamden McIntyre, designer of the Christian Brothers' Greystone Cellars and Inglenook; and Monticello Cellars, situated on Big Ranch Road, and with its $3-million visitor center housed in a masterful replica of Thomas Jefferson's home in Monticello, Virginia, from which the winery, in fact, derives its name. Both Trefethen and Monticello offer primarily estate-grown varietal wines; Monticello, in addition, schedules wine-related events, such as cooking classes and wine seminars, as well as some comparative tastings.

Farther north of Napa on the Silverado Trail, and well worth visiting, are the European-style Clos du Val winery and Stag's Leap Wine Cellars, both situated on the east side of the trail in the Stag's Leap area—a microclimate famous for its Cabernet Sauvignon wines. Some other small wineries located in the area on the Silverado Trail include Stag's Leap Winery, Shafer Vineyards, Altamura, Pine Ridge, Silverado Vineyards—which are owned in part by Mrs. Walt Disney— and the S. Anderson Vineyard, which is actually located just below the Yountville Crossroad, and which features an astonishing, recently-excavated cave, with 18-foot-high ceilings.

On Highway 29—the well-traveled St. Helena Highway—are yet other wineries of interest, among them the Lakespring Winery, offering varietal wines from both Napa Valley and San Luis Obispo County grapes; and Chateau Chevre, a small, family owned winery which derives its name from the former use of the vineyard property—a goat farm. Three more small, owner-operated wineries here include Alatera Vineyards, Newlan, and Costello Vineyards; all are open to visitors by appointment.

Napa also has two or three worthwhile detours for wine country visitors. Just to the southwest of town, for instance, is the Los Carneros region, one of Napa's newest viticultural areas, characterized by its rolling, vine-covered hills, and reached by way of the Old Sonoma Road and Highway 12. Los Carneros, typically, has cooler growing conditions than Napa Valley, ideally suited to the early-ripening Chardonnay, Gewurztraminer, Pinot Noir and Johannisberg Riesling varieties. It also has in it a handful of small wineries, including the Carneros Creek winery on Dealy Lane, and Mont St. John, situated on the Old Sonoma Road. Three others, the Acacia Winery, Bouchaine and Saintsbury, are situated just to the south on Las Amigas Road, Buchli Station Road and Los Carneros Avenue, respectively. All offer wines from the Carneros region.

Another detour, northwestward from the Napa township, is on Redwood Road, which has on it the Christian Brothers' monastic Mont La Salle Cellars (not open to the public), the Hess Collection—a winery that opened to the public only recently, in 1989—and the tiny Artisan Winery, a producer of Cabernet Sauvignon and Chardonnay primarily. From Redwood Road, too, just south of Mont La Salle and the Hess Collection, Mount Veeder Road peels northward and into the small, lofty viticultural area of the same name, Mount Veeder, with roughly 200 acres or so of planted vineyards. On Mount Veeder Road, of course, is the small, family-owned Mount Veeder Winery, specializing in Cabernet Sauvignon; and a little farther, on Lakoya Road are the

Mayacamas Vineyards—named for the Mayacamas Mountain range, in which the Mount Veeder area itself is located—and Sky Vineyards, offering estate-grown Zinfandel from their hillside vineyards.

Yet another detour, south from Napa on Highway 29 and east on 37, leads to the 160-acre wild animal park, Marine World Africa USA — perhaps not of particular interest to wine buffs, but nevertheless a great tourist attraction. Marine World is actually located just on the outskirts of Vallejo, at the corner of Highway 37 and Interstate 80, and it features killer whales and dolphins, performing all sorts of feats in aquatic shows, and tigers, elephants and other wildlife, including more than 100 species of wild birds. There are also restaurants and snack bars here, and picnic areas and children's playgrounds.

YOUNTVILLE

North from Napa, some 4 miles up the valley on Highway 29, is Yountville, a small, historic town, founded in 1853 by pioneer settler George C. Yount, for whom it is named. Yount's grave can still be seen in the Yountville cemetary just to the north of town, and near to it is the site of his old blockhouse, also with a historic marker.

Yountville's chief attraction, however, is its "Vintage 1870"—a surprising red-brick complex, formerly the Gottlieb Goezinger Winery, dating from 1870 and once claimed to be the largest winery in the Napa Valley. Vintage 1870 now houses some 50 specialty and import shops, gourmet restaurants, and art galleries. It also has in it two hot-air balloon companies, offering scenic flights over the Napa Valley, and the Keith Rosenthal Theatre which features some unique audio-visual programs depicting the changing seasons and colors of Napa Valley.

Other places of interest in Yountville, close to "Vintage 1870," include Washington Square, which also has some interesting shops and restaurants, and the Napa Valley Railway Inn where nine refurbished, turn-of-the-century rail cars—including three cabooses—offer luxury hotel accommodations to visitors. Try to also see the Bordeaux and Burgundy houses on Washington Street—two superb country inns— the latter housed in a charming, native-stone, two-story brandy distillery dating from 1874. Also to be recommended is a saunter down the Yountville Crossroad, passing through one of the loveliest stretches in the Napa Valley, where you can catch glimpses of an untouched part of the valley, much as it appeared before the vineyardists arrived in the mid-1800s.

Another great glory of Yountville, just west of town on California Drive, which goes off the highway (29), is Domaine Chandon, the best-known *méthode champenoise* sparkling wine producer in the Napa Valley, owned by Möet Hennessy of France, makers of Champagne Möet & Chandon and Hennessy Cognac. The winery, of course, is housed in a striking, architect-designed modern structure, built into the hillside, and with beautiful, landscaped grounds, featuring large shade trees, a stream crossing, and duck ponds. There is also a delightful little

Christian Brothers' Mont La Salle Vineyards, nestled in the
Mayacamas foothills

Balloons above the Napa Valley

gourmet French restaurant here, and a patio for tasting wines. Besides which, Domaine Chandon offers an excellent tour of its facility, on which you can learn, step by step, the entire champagne-making process.

Near to Domaine Chandon, and also of interest, is the Veterans' Home of California, built in 1884 to house veterans of foreign wars. The Veterans' Home has in it a worthwhile museum with displays of rare military artifacts, many of them dating from the early 1900s. The museum is open to public viewing.

OAKVILLE AND RUTHERFORD

Oakville, 3 miles above Yountville, and Rutherford, another 2 miles north of Oakville, are areas of intense grape growing activity. In fact, some of Napa Valley's best Cabernet Sauvignon vineyards are located here, along the benchlands at the western edge of the valley floor, including the famous Martha's Vineyard, from which Heitz Cellars produces its widely-heralded Cabernet Sauvignon.

There are also several important wineries in the area. In Oakville, for instance, on Highway 29, is the rambling Robert Mondavi Winery, housed in an impressive, Mediterranean-style stucco building, with manicured lawns and one or two modern sculptures. The winery has guided tours, an art gallery featuring works of California artists, and a wine and gift shop. It also schedules music concerts and other events, such as cooking schools conducted by internationally-acclaimed chefs, in the summer months.

Another winery worth visiting here, just south of Mondavi on the main highway, is DeMoor—formerly Napa Cellars—housed in a unique geodesic dome which has in it the entire winemaking apparatus as well as a visitor center. On the Oakville Crossroad, too, are the Cakebread Cellars and Silver Oak Vineyards, the latter a Cabernet Sauvignon specialist, situated on the site of an old Oakville dairy, with some of the former dairy buildings still in use. Also of interest, more or less across the street from Silver Oak, is historic Villa Mount St. Eden, originally established in 1881, and situated amid estate vineyards planted largely to Cabernet Sauvignon and Chardonnay.

Among other wineries in the area are the family-owned Girard Winery, situated on an oak-studded knoll at the corner of Silverado Trail and the Oakville Crossroad; and the Robert Pepi and Sequoia Grove wineries, both located on Highway 29, the latter housed in a restored barn nestled in a grove of towering sequoias.

For first-time visitors to the area, a worthwhile detour from Oakville is westward on the Oakville Grade, passing by two mountain wineries—Vichon and Vose, the latter actually located in the Mount Veeder area—then descending steeply into the adjoining Sonoma County wine country. The drive is in fact some 10 miles long, with the Oakville Grade changing into Dry Creek Road and, again, into Trinity Road; but it offers the motorist some spectacular mountain scenery, and some rare moments of solitude.

In any case, returning to the Napa Valley, north of Oakville, in Rutherford are the famous Inglenook and Beaulieu wineries, both with supreme tourist interest. Beaulieu Vineyard, founded by Georges de Latour in 1900, has an excellent public tour of its facility, highlighting the winery's open-tank fermentation method; it also has an audio-visual program, as part of the orientation. At Inglenook, which is situated just off the highway, westward on Niebaum Lane, you can tour an historic, ivy-covered, Gothic stone chateau, built in 1887 by the winery's founder Gustave Niebaum, a Finnish sea captain who made his fortune in furs in Alaska. The winery also has a guided tour, which takes in the winery's aging caves, and a wine museum with displays of antique winemaking equipment, vintage wine bottles and glasses, and historic photographs. Inglenook, besides, has a wine and gift shop and picnicking possiblities.

Other wineries in the area, situated on the St. Helena Highway, include Grgich Hills Cellars, housed in a Spanish-style building, and owned in part by coffee-maker Austin Hills; Rutherford Vintners, a modest-sized winery situated on a 30-acre vineyard estate; and White-hall Lane, the newest of all, established in 1980, offering primarily estate-grown varietal wines. Also with visitor interest, across the highway from Rutherford Vintners and Whitehall Lane, is Franciscan Vineyards, with its visitor center housed in a large redwood structure. Franciscan offers visitors a brief course in the sensory evaluation of wines, and it has on display at its visitor center an antique corkscrew collection and an 18th-century German grape press.

Two valley crossroads connecting the St. Helena Highway to the Silverado Trail, namely Conn Creek Road and Zinfandel Lane, have upon them the Conn Creek Winery and Raymond Cellars, both housed in relatively modern facilities, and open to the public for wine sales. Also on Conn Creek Road are the small Louis Honig Cellars, specializing in Sauvignon Blanc, and Caymus Vineyards; and just to the north of the Conn Creek Road-Silverado Trail intersection, off on the tiny Rutherford Hill Road, there is the Rutherford Hill Winery, which has daily tours of its state-of-the-art facility, with a visit to its recently-excavated, 30,000 square feet or so of aging caves. Another, the Joseph Phelps Winery, situated just to the north, also on the east side of Silverado Trail, on Taplin Road, is housed in a most interesting wood-frame structure comprising two separate pavillions, joined together by an enclosed bridge. The winery dates from 1973, and is situated on a 220-acre vineyard estate.

For a detour eastward from the Rutherford area, continue on Conn Creek Road which, after crossing over Silverado Trail, becomes Sage Canyon Road (and Highway 128), dashing off into the eastern hills of the Napa Valley, skirting Lake Hennessy to the south and descending into the small Chiles Valley area, where you can visit, by appointment, a handful of interesting little wineries, among them Sage Canyon, Chappellet and Long Vineyards. Farther still, on 128 east, are the historic Nichelini Vineyards, with an antique Roman grape press on display. The winery is still owned and operated by descendants of the founding Nichelini family. Nichelini dates from 1890.

ST. HELENA

Two miles or so above Rutherford, more or less at the heart of the Napa Valley, sits St. Helena, surrounded by no fewer than 40 premium Napa wineries. St. Helena itself is an historic wine town, founded in the 1850s by pioneer vintners, and with an especially charming main street, lined with antique street lamps dating from 1915, and several old and lovely native-stone buildings, also from the late 1800s and early 1900s. The town's great glory, of course, is its Wine Library, housed in the public library building on Library Lane — just off Main Street — and containing some 3,000 volumes on wine and wine-related subjects, believed to be the largest such collection of wine literature on the West Coast. Also on Library Lane, and of equal interest, is the Silverado Museum, devoted entirely to the life and works of celebrated Scottish writer Robert Louis Stevenson, who honeymooned at nearby Mount St. Helena in the spring of 1880, gathering, too, notes for his Napa Valley classic, *The Silverado Squatters*. The museum has over 7,800 items of Stevenson memorabilia — including first editions of the author's books, original manuscripts and letters, paintings, sculptures and photographs of the author, and several of his personal and work-related items — believed to be one of the world's largest such collections of Stevensoniana. The museum is open to the public between 12 and 4 p.m., Tuesday-Sunday.

Besides the immediate town, however, St. Helena has much to offer the wine country visitor. Here, for instance, just to the north of town on Highway 29 is the historic Beringer Winery, one of the oldest wineries in continuous operation in the Napa Valley, which remained open during Prohibition, making sacramental wine for the Church. Beringer's chief attraction — and few would argue otherwise — is its majestic Rhine House, an elegantly restored European-style mansion, originally built in 1876 as the home of Frederick Beringer, co-founder of the winery, and now housing two tasting rooms, with superb period decor, and a well-stocked wine-cum-gift shop. The winery also has guided tours of its facility, which include a visit to the winery's 1,000 feet or so of ancient limestone caves and tunnels, dug into the hillside by hand in the 1880s, and where fine wines are still aged.

A little farther on, at the end of an avenue of splendid shade trees that line the highway, is the grand old Christian Brothers' Greystone Cellar, one of Napa Valley's most prominent landmarks, which only recently reopened to the public, in 1987, after undergoing extensive structural repairs. The winery's castle-like greystone building itself dates from 1889, originally built by mining magnate William Bowers Bourne, who, quite notably, also built the Filoli Mansion (featured on TV's *Dynasty*) at Woodside, California. The winery now offers public tours, as well as wine tasting and a wine and gift shop.

Close by, and also worth visiting, is the historic Charles Krug Winery, claimed to be the oldest winery in the valley. It was originally founded by German immigrant Charles Krug, who, we are told, was the first in the Napa Valley to make wine using a grape press, rather than by the traditional means of crushing grapes by stomping by foot. The winery has public tours, wine tasting and sales. There is also a gift shop on the premises.

North, still, on the highway are the historic, 19th-century Markham Winery, which offers a "sensory evaluation" course to visitors; and Freemark Abbey, which has a tasting room in a small complex with two delightful restaurants and an unusual gift shop. Other wineries here include the Round Hill Cellars, housed in a modest facility on Lodi Lane, which goes off the highway eastward; and Folie a Deux, a small, family owned and operated winery, situated on a knoll overlooking estate vineyards. Also, just above Folie a Deux, on the west side of the highway, is the Vintners Village, which not only has in it shops and galleries and a restaurant or two, but also a unique tasting facility where you can taste premium wines from several different valley wineries. There are also picnic facilities at the village, and a deli offering picnic lunches.

Farther north, on Larkmead Lane which goes east off Highway 29, are the Hanns Kornell Champagne Cellars, established in 1952 by Champagne Master Hanns Kornell, a native of Germany. Kornell offers a superb winery tour on which visitors can view, first hand, the champagne-making process. The tour also includes a visit to the winery's ancient aging caves, where you can see the original Victorian cupola, dating from 1901.

Southeast of Hanns Kornell are yet other wineries of interest: on the Big Tree Crossroad are the tiny, family-owned Tudal and Charles F. Shaw wineries, the latter specializing in estate-bottled Napa Gamay; and on Silverado Trail are the small, French-style Duckhorn Vineyards, Casa Neustra, and Chateau Boswell which is housed in a most attractive replica of an old French chateau, complete with a turreted tower.

Just south of the St. Helena township, too, on Highway 29 are a handful of historic and well-known wineries, well worth visiting, among them Louis M. Martini, Sutter Home, and Heitz Cellars, a delightful little family-owned-and-operated winery, noted increasingly for its Martha's Vineyard Cabernet Sauvignon. Sutter Home, too, has a distinction; it is the largest of Napa Valley's historic wineries built entirely from wood, besides which it is also one of the best known and largest producers of Zinfandel in California. Sutter Home dates from 1874, and Louis M. Martini from 1922.

Try to also visit the tourist-alluring, native-stone V. Sattui Winery just to the south of Heitz Cellars on the main highway, originally established in 1885 by immigrant Vittorio Sattui, and now owned and operated by Vittorio's great-grandson, Daryl Sattui. The winery has a large picnic area for visitors, a fully-stocked delicatessen, and wine and gourmet shops. Sattui offers primarily varietal wines from its estate vineyards, sold only at the winery.

Also to be recommended to visitors to St. Helena is a detour to the adjoining Spring Mountain area—a small, well-regarded winegrowing region, located high in the Mayacamas Mountain Range, to the west of St. Helena, and with a dozen or so picturesque little wineries situated there. It can be reached by way of Madrona Road west off the highway (29), from just south of St. Helena, then Spring Mountain Road northwest off Madrona. On Spring Mountain Road itself are the historic

Spring Mountain Vineyards, housed in a superbly restored, 1880s Victorian mansion, with beautiful stained-glass windows and a hand-hewn tunnel for aging wines, and famous, too, as the setting for the TV drama, *Falcon Crest*. Tours of Spring Mountain Vineyards are available by appointment, and the winery, besides, offers a line of "Falcon Crest" wines for tasting.

Another interesting winery in the Spring Mountain area is Chateau Chevalier, situated on an historic, 1891 Spring Mountain estate, with the winery housed in a lovely, three-story stone chateau, with turreted towers. Also, north of there, still on Spring Mountain Road, are the Robert Keenan, Yverdon, Smith-Madrone and Ritchie Creek wineries; and just to the southwest on Langtry Road are the Cain Cellars, situated on a large, 542-acre site, with panoramic views of the Napa Valley.

East from St. Helena there is yet another detour to delight the Napa Valley visitor. Deer Park Road, which goes east off the St. Helena Highway, crossing over Silverado Trail and dashing off into the eastern hills of Napa, has upon it, situated high above the valley floor, the historic, native-stone Deer Park Winery, dating from 1891, and Burgess Cellars, also housed in a stone structure, and situated on the site of an 1880s vineyard, overlooking Napa Valley. Farther still, Deer Park Road merges with Howell Mountain Road and, again, with Pope Valley Road, finally descending into the small, lesser-known viticultural area of Pope Valley, which has in it a family owned and operated winery of the same name, the Pope Valley Winery, originally built in the late 1800s.

CALISTOGA

North of St. Helena, of course, some 6 miles or so on Highway 29, lies the small resort town of Calistoga. But before reaching Calistoga, on the highway itself, there are two places of special interest to first-time visitors. The first, the Bale Grist Mill, a long-standing Napa Valley landmark, originally built in 1846 by Dr. Edward Turner Bale, one of the valley's first settlers, is located some 3 or 4 miles above St. Helena. The mill, recently restored, is now part of the Bale Grist Mill State Historic Park, and it has in it a small museum with old photographs depicting the building of the mill. Just to the north of the grist mill, another mile or so, is the larger Bothe-Napa Valley State Park, comprising some 1,800 acres of unspoiled wilderness; it has hiking and picnicking possibilities, and a swimming pool for day use.

Finally, there is Calistoga, situated at the top end of the Napa Valley, where the valley, in fact, fans out to its widest point —approximately 4 miles—before the Mayacamas and Howell mountains close it off. Calistoga enjoys an especially lovely setting, with the ancient Mount St. Helena—frequently picture-perfect—to its north, and lush vineyards to its south, planted largely to Zinfandel and Cabernet Sauvignon, and in typically warmer growing conditions than the rest of the Napa Valley farther to the south.

Calistoga itself is a lively little town, notable increasingly for its hot springs and spa resorts. It was originally founded in 1868 by Sam Brannan, one of California's first millionaires, who established here the first of the area's spa resorts, and named it "Calistoga"—which, we are told, is derived from confusing the words "California" and "Saratoga." In any case, the town has in it no fewer than eight full-fledged spa resorts, offering visitors a wide range of health and beauty treatments, and all sorts of exotic baths—steam, mud, mineral, herbal, sulphur.

The town also has a colorful little main street (Lincoln Avenue), lined with old and lovely buildings, dating from the late 1800s and early 1900s, mostly restored, and now housing modern shops and restaurants. Toward the upper end of the main street, of course, is the Old Calistoga Depot, one of the chief attractions of the town, dating from 1868 and claimed to be the oldest railroad depot in existence in California. The depot has been largely restored, and converted into a small shopping arcade, with gift shops, a wine shop, delicatessen and a well-liked cafe. Alongside the depot, on the railroad tracks are a half-dozen old Southern Pacific rail cars, refurbished and converted, again, into unique shops, specializing in rare gifts and old-fashioned candy. The Calistoga-based Once-in-a-Lifetime hot-air balloon company also has its offices here.

Another place of supreme tourist interest is the Sharpsteen Museum on Washington Street, a block or so east off the main street, where you can view some excellent displays of Calistoga's pioneer history, including three or four superb dioramas, one of which features Brannan's original hot springs resort and the town as it appeared in the 1860s. Adjoining the museum—and, in fact, with its entrance through the museum—is Brannan's old cottage, built in 1866 and now beautifully restored with original 19th-century furnishings and decor. The museum and cottage are open on weekdays, 10-4.

Also, not to be missed is Calistoga's "Old Faithful" geyser, located just to the north of town on Tubbs Lane. It is one of the area's oldest and most famous geysers, claimed to be among only three regularly erupting geysers in the world: it erupts approximately every 50 minutes, gushing forth in a fountain of boiling water and steam, some 60 feet or so directly into the air. There is a small picnic area at the site, and an admission fee is charged.

For wine buffs, too, Calistoga has much of interest. There are, in fact, in and around Calistoga, at least a half-dozen or so well-known wineries, some of them indeed quite historic. Just to the south of town, for instance, on a small side road off Highway 29 are the celebrated Schramsberg Vineyards, founded in 1862 by pioneer vintner Jacob Schram, and memorialized, in 1880, by noted author Robert Louis Stevenson in his book, *The Silverado Squatters*. Schramsberg makes bottle-fermented champagne primarily.

Two other wineries worth visiting, located on Dunaweal Lane which goes off the highway, eastward, are Stonegate and Sterling Vineyards. The latter is especially to be recommended to first-time visitors to the area, housed in a splendid, white Mediterranean-style building, perched on a hilltop overlooking valley vineyards. The only way up to the winery is by way of an aerial tram, which, again, has superb views of the valley.

At the winery there is an excellent, self-guided tour of the winemaking facility, quite interesting to wine enthusiasts who can study, at their own pace, the winemaking process. There is also a comfortable tasting room here, and a delightful patio with panoramic views, where you can sample Sterling wines. A gift-cum-wine shop on the premises retails Sterling wines, as well as wine-related books, gifts and other paraphernalia.

Among other interesting wineries in the Calistoga area are the Robert Pecota Winery, just north of town, and Cuvaison which is situated at the top end of the Silverado Trail and housed in a lovely Spanish-style building. Chateau Montelena, also north of Calistoga, on a side road that dashes off Tubbs Lane, is housed in a picturesque, French chateau-style stone castle, overlooking the artificially-created, yet beautiful, Jade Lake, with its small, Oriental bridges and red lacquered pavillions, and a real Chinese junk beached at one end of the lake. Chateau Montelena and Cuvaison have good visitor facilities, and offer primarily varietal wines from the Napa Valley.

Two worthwhile detours from Calistoga, much to be recommended to visitors, are the 4,000-acre Robert Louis Stevenson State Park just to the north on Highway 29, which has in it the majestic Mount St. Helena, with a foot-trail leading to its summit; and the ancient Petrified Forest, reached on the Petrified Forest Road, west from Calistoga, and where you can view giant redwoods, uprooted during the volcanic period millions of years ago, and, over a period of time, turned to stone. There is an admission fee charged for the Petrified Forest.

From Calistoga, too, it is possible to journey over the Mayacamas ridge on Highway 128 northwest, past the small viticultural area of Knights Valley — where Beringer and Sterling own vineyards — and into Sonoma County's Alexander Valley (part of the celebrated Russian River region), which has in it some 40 or so notable wineries, most with visitor interest.

NAPA VALLEY WINERIES

ACACIA WINERY. 2750 Las Amigas Road, Napa; (707) 226-9991. Visitors by appointment only.
☐ Small Napa winery, established in 1979. The winery produces vintage-dated Chardonnay, Pinot Noir and Merlot from grapes grown in the Los Carneros region. Wines are also bottled under a second label, Caviste.

ALATERA VINEYARDS. 2170 Hoffman Lane, Napa; (707) 944-2620. Visitors by appointment.
☐ Alatera Vineyards offers premium estate-bottled Cabernet Sauvignon, Chardonnay, Gewurztztraminer, and a Late Harvest Johannisberg Riesling. The winery was founded in 1977.

ALTAMURA VINEYARDS & WINERY. 4240 Silverado Trail, Napa; (707) 253-2000. Tasting and sales daily 10-4; tours by appointment.
□ Small, owner-operated winery, specializing in estate-grown varietal Chardonnay. The winery was established in 1986 by present owner Frank Altamura.

AMIZETTA VINEYARD AND WINERY. 1099 Greenfield Road, St. Helena; (707) 963-1053. Winery visits by appointment only.
□ Amizetta is a small, owner-operated winery, situated in the heart of the Napa Valley. It offers two types of vintage-dated varietal wines, Chardonnay and Sauvignon Blanc, both made from grapes grown on its 54-acre estate vineyard located in the Napa region.

S. ANDERSON VINEYARD. 1473 Yountville Crossroad, Yountville; (707) 944-8642. Visitors by appointment.
□ S. Anderson Vineyard enjoys a lovely hillside setting, overlooking estate vineyards. Wines produced include an estate-bottled Chardonnay and six *méthode champenoise* sparkling wines—Blanc de Blanc, Blanc de Noirs, Brut, Rosé, Tivoli and Cuvée de La Cave Chardonnay. The winery also features a recently-excavated cave, where Anderson wines are available for tasting. The winery was established in 1974.

VINCENT ARROYO WINERY. 2361 Greenwood Ave., Calistoga; (707) 942-6995. Open for tours, tasting and sales by appointment only.
□ Small, Napa Valley winery, established in 1984 by the Arroyo family, present owners, who have been in the wine growing business for a long time. The Arroyos produce primarily estate-grown, varietal wines from their 45-acre vineyard located in the valley. Offerings include Petite Sirah, Gamay, Chardonnay and Cabernet Sauvignon. Picnic area on premises.

DAVID ARTHUR WINERY. 1521 Sage Canyon Rd., St. Helena; (707) 963-5190. Winery visits by appointment.
□ Small, owner-operated winery, established in 1985 by the David Arthur Long family. The winery produces primarily Napa County wines from its 20-acre vineyard located in the Napa Valley.

ARTISAN WINES. 5301 Redwood Road, Napa; (707) 252-6666. Visitors by appointment only.
□ Artisan was founded in 1984 by winemaker Michael Fallow and graphic artist Jefferey Caldeway. The winery currently produces varietal Cabernet Sauvignon and Chardonnay, bottled under four different labels—Michael's, Ultravino, Cruvinet, and Cru Artisan. The winery is situated on a 125-acre estate in the Mt. Veeder area.

BEAULIEU VINEYARD. 1960 St. Helena Hwy., Rutherford; (707) 963-2411. Open for tours, tasting and sales, 10-4 daily; last tour at 3 p.m.
□ Beaulieu is one of the best-known large wineries in the Napa Valley, with approximately 1,500 acres of estate vineyards located in the central part of the valley. The winery itself is housed in an ivy-covered brick and concrete building, dating from 1885. It was, however, founded in 1900, by a Frenchman named Georges de Latour, and brought to prominence in the early 1900s by Russian-born winemaker Andre Tshelistcheff, who is also credited with establishing Cabernet Sauvignon as the "Queen of California wines." The winery produces over 400,000 cases of wine annually, primarily red table wines, made by the open-tank fermentation method. Beaulieu was acquired by the Heublein

Corporation in 1969.

BERGFELD CELLARS. 401 St. Helena Hwy., St. Helena; (707) 963-7293. Tasting and sales by appointment, 10-4.30 daily.
☐ Small Napa winery, offering primarily Napa Valley Appellation wines. Gift shop on premises.

BERINGER VINEYARDS. 2000 Main Street, St. Helena; (707) 963-7115/963-4812. Open daily 9.30-4.45; summer hours: 10-6.
☐ Beringer is Napa Valley's oldest winery in continuous operation, originally founded in 1876 by Jacob and Frederich Beringer, and which, during Prohibition, remained open, selling sacramental wine to the Church. Frederich Beringer's majestic 19th-century mansion, the Rhine House, is now a visitor center; besides which, the winery also features 1,000 feet or so of ancient tunnels and aging caves, dug into the hillside by hand in the 1880s. The winery produces primarily varietal wines from its 1,400 acres of vineyards in the Napa and Knights valleys. Small lots of dessert wines are also bottled under the Beringer label, and generic and jug wines are bottled under a secondary label, Los Hermanos. Beringer is now owned by the Swiss multi-national, Nestlé.

BUEHLER VINEYARDS. 820 Greenfield Road, St. Helena; (707) 963-2155. Visitors by appointment only.
☐ Buehler is a small, family-owned winery, established in 1964. It produces 100% varietal wines from its 60-acre vineyard located in the eastern Napa hills. Offerings include Cabernet Sauvignon, Zinfandel and White Zinfandel; tiny lots of Muscat Blanc and Pinot Blanc are also produced.

BURGESS CELLARS. 1108 Deer Park Road, St. Helena; (707) 963-4766. Open for sales daily 10-4; tours by appointment.
☐ Burgess Cellars was originally founded in 1889, on the site of an 1880s vineyard, located high above Napa Valley in the hills just to the east of the valley floor. The winery produces two types of Cabernet Sauvignon, a Chardonnay, and a Zinfandel. Some wines are also bottled under the Bell Canyon label.

CAIN CELLARS. 3800 Langtry Road, St. Helena; (707) 963-1616/(800) 422-1111. Visitors welcome by appointment, daily 10-4.
☐ Cain Cellars is situated on an historic, 542-acre ranch in the Spring Mountain area, with good views of St. Helena. It produces primarily vintage-dated Sauvignon Blanc, Malbec, Chardonnay, Merlot and Cabernet Sauvignon. The winery was established in 1981 by Jerry and Joyce Cain.

CAKEBREAD CELLARS. 8300 St. Helena Hwy., Rutherford; (707) 963-5221. Open for sales 10-4 daily; tours by appointment.
☐ Small, family-owned winery, established in 1973. Cakebread offers vintage-dated varietals from its 65-acre vineyard located adjacent to the winery. Offerings include Cabernet Sauvignon, Sauvignon Blanc and Chardonnay. Wines are aged in French oak barrels.

CALAFIA CELLARS. 629 Fulton Lane, St. Helena; (707) 963-0114. Sales by mailing list only; tours by appointment. Call the winery for more information.
☐ Calafia is a small, 1,500-case winery, founded in 1979. It specializes in vineyard-designated varietal wines: Cabernet Sauvignon, Cabernet Franc, Sauvignon Blanc, Zinfandel, Merlot and Chardonnay. The winery derives its name from Queen Calafia of the Amazons, whose wealth was guarded by

griffins; hence the winery label features a griffin.

CARNEROS CREEK WINERY. 1285 Dealy Lane, Napa; (707) 253-9463. Open for sales Wed.-Sun. 9-5; tours by appointment.
□ Founded in 1972, Carneros Creek is a typical small, modern Napa winery, with 20 acres of estate vineyards located adjacent to the winery in the Carneros district. The winery produces vintage-dated varietal Cabernet Sauvignon, Pinot Noir, Merlot, Chardonnay, and Sauvignon Blanc. Picnic area on premises.

CASA NUESTRA WINERY. 3473 Silverado Trail, St. Helena; (707) 963-4684. Wine tasting and sales, Mon., Thurs. and Fri. 12-5; Sat.-Sun. 10-5.
□ Small, 1,000-case winery, established in 1980. The winery produces Dry Chenin Blanc and Cabernet Sauvignon from its 10-acre vineyard located at the winery. It also makes tiny lots of blended red wines, including a proprietary Napa Gamay Tinto. Picnic area on premises.

CAYMUS VINEYARDS. 8700 Conn Creek Road, Rutherford; (707) 963-5683/963-4204. Open for tasting and sales daily, 10-12 and 1-4; tasting fee.
□ Premium Napa winery, established in 1972 by present owners, the Wagners. The winery's expanding line of high-quality varietals includes a Reserve Cabernet Sauvignon, a Reserve Pinot Noir, Chardonnay, Sauvignon Blanc, Zinfandel and Pinot Noir Blanc. Caymus bottles wines under two labels: Caymus Vineyards and Liberty School.

CHAPPELLET VINEYARDS. Pritchard Hill, St. Helena; (707) 963-7136. Tours and tasting by appointment; call the winery for hours.
□ Chappellet Vineyards features primarily vintage-dated varietal wines, including Cabernet Sauvignon, Chardonnay, a dry-styled Chenin Blanc, and Johannisberg Riesling—all made from grapes grown on its 110 acres of vineyards located on the eastern side of the Napa Valley. The winery was founded in 1969 by Donn Chappellet, present owner.

CHATEAU BOSWELL. 3468 Silverado Trail, St. Helena; (707) 963-5472. Tasting and sales Wed.-Sun. 10.30-5.30. Picnic area.
□ Chateau Boswell is housed in a picturesque replica of an Old World chateau, situated on a hillside just east of the valley floor, with views of rolling vineyards and wooded scenery. The winery produces small lots of Cabernet Sauvignon, aged in French oak barrels. The winery was founded in 1979.

CHATEAU BOUCHAINE. 1075 Buchli Station Road, Napa; (707) 252-9065/(800) 451-WINE. Open for sales Mon.-Fri. 10-4.
□ Bouchaine is housed in a large winemaking facility in the Los Carneros district. It produces primarily vintage-dated varietal Chardonnay, Pinot Noir and Sauvignon Blanc from its 38-acre vineyard located at the winery, as well as some 70 acres or so in the Santa Rosa area. The winery was originally founded in 1899 as the Garetto Winery, and re-established in 1980.

CHATEAU CHEVALIER WINERY. 3101 Spring Mountain Road, St. Helena; (707) 963-2342. Call the winery for hours and visitor information.
□ Chateau Chevalier is housed in a lovely, three-story stone chateau with turreted towers, situated on an historic, 1891 Spring Mountain estate. The winery was revived in 1972 with the planting of approximately 60 acres of

vineyards. It now offers premium, estate-bottled Chardonnay and Cabernet Sauvignon from its hillside vineyards. Small lots of Pinot Noir, Merlot and Riesling are also produced. The winery was sold to the owners of Far Niente Cellars in 1984.

CHATEAU CHEVRE. 2030 Hoffman Lane, Yountville; (707) 944-2184. Visitors by appointment only.

☐ Small, family-owned, 2,000-case winery, established in 1979. The winery specializes in Napa Valley Merlot and Sauvignon Blanc, made from grapes grown on its 10-acre vineyard located at the winery. Chateau Chevre, interestingly, derives its name from the original use of the property—a goat farm.

CHATEAU MONTELENA. 1429 Tubbs Lane, Calistoga; (707) 942-5105. Tasting and sales daily 10-4; tours by appointment.

☐ Chateau Montelena is housed in a French-architect-designed native-stone castle, dating from 1882. The castle is built into a hillside overlooking picturesque Jade Lake, with its tiny islands and red lacquered pavillions, and little arched bridges connecting the islands. The winery is of course noted for its superb 1973 Chardonnay, which won top honors at the 1976 Paris Tasting, ahead of 12 California and French offerings. The winery also produces two Cabernets, one each from Napa and Sonoma counties, a Zinfandel, and a Johannisberg Riesling which is sold only at the winery.

CHATEAU NAPA BEAUCANON. 1695 St. Helena Hwy., St. Helena; (707) 963-1896. Tasting and sales daily 10-4.30; tours by appointment.

☐ French-style Napa Valley winery, founded in 1987 by the DeConinck family of France's Bordeaux region, who have been in the wine business since 1740. The winery is housed in an architect-designed, Bordeaux-style facility, characteristic in its large, vaulted ceiling. Wines produced are varietal, vintage-dated Cabernet Sauvignon, Merlot, Chardonnay, and Chenin Blanc, all made from grapes grown on the estate's 65 acres of vineyards, located adjacent to the winery in Rutherford, and in Napa.

CHIMNEY ROCK WINERY. 5320 Silverado Trail, Napa; (707) 257-2641. Tasting and sales daily 10-4; tours by appointment.

☐ New Napa winery, founded by Hack and Stella Wilson, avid golfers, who rebuilt their 18-hole golf course, converting it into a 9-hole course, and planting a 75-acre vineyard adjacent to it. The winery produces estate-bottled varietal Chardonnay and a dry-styled Sauvignon Blanc.

THE CHRISTIAN BROTHERS GREYSTONE CELLARS. 2555 Main St., St. Helena; (707) 967-3112. Tours, tasting and sales daily 10-4; barrel tastings by appointment.

☐ The Christian Brothers' historic Greystone Cellars is one of Napa Valley's great landmarks, originally built in 1889 by mining magnate William Bowers Bourne, Jr., who also built the famous Filoli Mansion (featured on TV's *Dynasty*) at Woodside, California. The winery recently underwent extensive structural repairs and reopened to the public in 1987. Christian Brothers now produces nearly 2 million cases of wine annually, both at its Napa Valley facility and at Mont La Salle, just to the south. A full line of vintage-dated varietal wines as well as some dessert wines and brandies are bottled under the Christian Brothers label. Generic and proprietary wines are also produced from the estate's Mont La Salle vineyards. Christian Brothers was purchased by the Heublein Corporation in 1989. Wine and gift shop on premises.

CLOS DU VAL WINE CO., LTD. 5330 Silverado Trail, Napa; (707) 252-6711. Tasting and sales daily 10-4; tours by appointment, at 10 a.m. and 2 p.m.

☐ Located in the Stag's Leap area of the Napa Valley, the winery was founded in 1972 by John Goelet and French winemaker Bernard Portet. Some 120 acres of Clos Du Val's estate vineyards are located near the winery, and another 160 acres or so are in the Carneros district. The winery specializes in European-style varietal and proprietary wines, including Cabernet Sauvignon, Sauvignon Blanc, Zinfandel, Muscat, Chardonnay, Semillon, Pinot Noir, an Early Harvest Johannisberg Riesling, and Calcaine and Fruitwood. Wines are also bottled under a second label, Gran Val. Some picnicking possibilities.

CLOS PEGASE. 1060 Dunaweal Lane, Calistoga; (707) 942-4981. Open for tours, tasting and sales, 10.30-4.30 daily; tours on the hour. Tasting fee.

☐ Clos Pegase houses its winemaking operations in a dramatic, Greco-Roman, architect-designed stucco ediface, built in 1986 as a tribute to wine, art and mythology. The winery is in fact named for the mythological flying horse Pegasus, featured on its wine label. Varietal, vintage-dated wines produced here are Chardonnay, Cabernet Sauvignon, Merlot, and Sauvignon Blanc.

CONN CREEK WINERY. 8711 Silverado Trail; St. Helena; (707) 963-9100. Wine sales daily 10-4; tasting and tours by appointment, weekends 11-3.

☐ Established in 1974, Conn Creek produces premium varietal wines from grapes grown on its two estate vineyards, totalling some 120 acres, located in the Napa Valley. Offerings include Cabernet Sauvignon, Chardonnay, Zinfandel and Chenin Blanc. The winery houses its operations in a relatively newly-constructed winemaking facility.

COSENTINO-CRYSTAL VALLEY CELLAR. 7415 St. Helena Hwy., Yountville; (707) 944-1220. Tasting and sales Mon.-Sat. 9.30-5.30, Sun. 10-5; tours by appointment.

☐ The Cosentino winery was founded in 1981 by present owner-winemaker Mitch Cosentino, who produces varietal, vintage-dated Chardonnay, Cabernet Sauvignon and Merlot from his 20-acre vineyard located in Stanislaus County. Some proprietary wines are also offered, and a line of sparkling wines is bottled under the Cosentino Selections label. Cosentino's second label is Cosentino Wine Company.

COSTELLO VINEYARDS. 1200 Orchard Ave., Napa; (707) 252-8483. Visitors by appointment only.

☐ Owner-winemaker John Costello makes varietal Chardonnay and Sauvignon Blanc from his 53-acre vineyard located at the winery. The winery was established in 1982, and the vineyard in 1979.

CUVAISON WINERY. 4550 Silverado Trail; Calistoga; (707) 942-6266. Tasting and sales daily 10-4; tours by appointment. Tasting fee. Picnic facilities.

☐ Cuvaison is housed in a splendid, white mission-style building, with landscaped grounds and picnic facilities. The winery produces primarily varietal Zinfandel, Chardonnay, Cabernet Sauvignon, Merlot, and small lots of Pinot Noir. The winery was founded in 1969, and is currently owned by A.G. Inselhold of Switzerland.

DEER PARK WINERY. 1000 Deer Park Road, Deer Park (3.5 miles northeast of St. Helena); (707) 963-5411. Open for sales Mon.-Sat. 10-4; tours and tasting by appointment.
☐ Historic stone winery, built in 1891, situated on a small, 7-acre foothill estate. The winery was closed in 1960, and purchased and reopened in 1979 by present owners Lila and Robert Knapp and David and Kinta Clark. Vintage-dated varietals featured here are Zinfandel, Sauvignon Blanc, and Chardonnay.

DE MOOR. 7481 St. Helena Hwy., Oakville; (707) 944-2565. Tours, tasting and sales, daily 10.30-5.30 in summer; 10-5 in winter.
☐ De Moor, formerly Napa Cellars, is housed in a unique geodesic dome which has in it the entire winemaking apparatus as well as a visitor center. The winery produces vintage-dated varietal Cabernet Sauvignon, Zinfandel, Chardonnay, and Sauvignon Blanc. The winery was originally esatblished in 1976, and is now owned by the DeSchepper-DeMoor family of Belgium. Picnic area on premises.

DIAMOND CREEK VINEYARDS. 1500 Diamond Mountain Road, Calistoga; (707) 942-6926. Open by invitation only (5 days each year).
☐ A small, Cabernet-only winery, Diamond Creek offers three different bottlings from its three adjoining vineyards — Volcanic Hill, Red Rock Terrace, and Gravelly Meadow. The winery was established in 1968 by present owner-winemaker Al Brownstein.

DOMAINE CHANDON. California Drive, Yountville; (707) 944-2280, restaurant phone (707) 944-2892. Tours, tasting and sales daily 11-6, May-Oct.; Wed.-Sun., Nov.-Apr. Fee for tasting.
☐ Domaine Chandon, is the best-known producer of *méthode champenoise* sparkling wine in the Napa Valley, and the first wholly French-owned winery in the U.S. It was established in 1973 by Möet-Hennessy of France, makers of Champagne Möet & Chandon, Hennessy Cognac and Dior perfumes. The winery is housed in a modern, architect-designed building, built into a hillside and surrounded by beautifully landscaped grounds with a duck pond and shaded picnic areas. Visitors can tour the facility and see the entire champagne-making process first-hand, as well as enjoy the winery's two principal offerings, Napa Valley Brut and Blanc de Noirs. The winery also produces a sweet, fortified wine under a second label, Panache. A small restaurant on the premises specializes in French gourmet cuisine; reservations are advised.

DOMAINE DE NAPA WINERY. 1155 Mee Lane, St. Helena; (707) 963-1666. Open for tours, tasting and sales, daily 10-5.
☐ Recently-established Napa Valley winery, specializing in varietal, vintage-dated Cabernet Sauvignon, Chardonnay and Sauvignon Blanc, all made from grapes grown in valley vineyards. The winery was founded in 1986.

DUCKHORN VINEYARDS. 3027 Silverado Trail, St. Helena; (707) 963-7108. Winery visits by appointment, Mon.-Fri. 9-4.30.
☐ Small, French-style winery, specializing in Napa Merlot and Cabernet Sauvignon. Varietal vintage-dated Sauvignon Blanc is also produced. The winery was established in 1976.

EHLERS LANE WINERY. 3222 Ehlers Lane, St. Helena; (707) 963-0144. Winery tours and retail sales by appointment only.
☐ Historic Napa winery, housed in an 1886 limestone building, located just north of St. Helena. The winery features varietal, vintage-dated Chardonnay,

Sauvignon Blanc, Cabernet Sauvignon and Semillon. The winery was re-established by present owners in 1983.

EVENSEN WINERY. 8254 St. Helena Hwy., Oakville; (707) 944-2396. Visitors by appointment.
☐ Small, 1,000-case winery, with 20 acres of estate-owned vineyards near Oakville in the Napa Valley. Vintage-dated Gewurztraminer is the only wine offered here.

FAR NIENTE WINERY. 1 Acacia Drive, Oakville; (707) 944-2861. No public tours, tasting or sales.
☐ Historic winery, originally founded in 1885, and restored and re-established in 1982. The winery offers primarily barrel-fermented Chardonnay and Cabernet Sauvignon, made from grapes grown on its 120-acre Napa Valley vineyards.

FLORA SPRINGS WINE CO. 1978 W. Zinfandel Lane; St. Helena; (707) 963-5711. Tours, tasting and sales by appointment, Mon.-Fri. 10-3.
☐ Flora Springs is housed in an 1880s stone building, located in the hills on the west side of the Napa Valley, on property that was first homesteaded by vintner Louis M. Martini. Varietal vintage-dated wines produced are Chardonnay, Sauvignon Blanc, Cabernet Sauvignon, and Merlot, all made from grapes grown on five estate-owned vineyards, totalling some 350 acres, located in the Napa Valley. The winery was founded in 1979.

FOLIE A DEUX WINERY. 3070 St. Helena Hwy., St. Helena; (707) 963-1160. Open for tours, tasting and sales, daily 11-5; group tours by appointment. Picnic area.
☐ Small, family owned and operated winery, situated on a knoll overlooking the estate's 10-acre vineyard. The winery produces limited quantities of varietal Cabernet Sauvignon, Chardonnay and Dry Chenin Blanc, all made from grapes purchased on a select-vineyard basis. The winery was established in 1981.

FORMAN VINEYARDS. 1501 Big Rock Rd., St. Helena; (707) 963-0234. Winery visits by appointment only.
☐ Owner-winemaker R.W. Forman specializes in varietal Chardonnay and Cabernet Sauvignon, made from grapes grown on his 6-acre vineyard located near Napa City. The winery was established in 1983, and the vineyard in 1979.

FRANCISCAN VINEYARDS. 1178 Galleron Road/Hwy. 29, St. Helena; (707) 963-7111. Tasting and sales daily 10-5.
☐ Franciscan houses its visitor center in a large, redwood structure on the highway, where an 18th-century German grape press and an antique corkscrew collection are on display. The winery produces in excess of 100,000 cases of wine annually, much of it devoted to estate-bottled varietals, including Cabernet Sauvignon, Chardonnay, Merlot, Zinfandel, Sauvignon Blanc and Johannisberg Riesling—all made from grapes grown on two 250-acre estate vineyards, one each in Oakville, Napa Valley and Sonoma County's Alexander Valley. The winery was originally established in 1972, and is now owned by the Peter Eckes Company of West Germany.

FREEMARK ABBEY WINERY. 3022 St. Helena Hwy., St. Helena; (707) 963-9694. Tasting and sales daily 10-4.30; winery tour at 2 p.m.
☐ Established in 1967, the winery is owned by a consortium of seven partners

who own large acreages of producing vineyards in Napa Valley's Rutherford area. Grapes for Freemark Abbey wines come largely from these vineyards; some grapes are also purchased on a select-vineyard basis. Varietal, vintage-dated wines offered at the winery include Cabernet Sauvignon, Cabernet Bosche, Chardonnay, White Riesling, and a Johannisberg Riesling, finished in a sweet style. The winery is housed in a 19th-century stone cellar, with a tasting room located in the small Freemark Abbey complex on the highway in St. Helena.

FROG'S LEAP WINERY. 3358 St. Helena Hwy., St. Helena; (707) 963-4704. Wine sales by appointment and mailing list only. Annual open house by invitation.
☐ Frog's Leap is a small, 2,500-case cottage winery, specializing in vintage-dated Sauvignon Blanc and Chardonnay. The winery is located in the upper Napa Valley, on the site of a former, turn-of-the-century frog farm—hence the name. The winery was established in 1981.

GIRARD WINERY. 7717 N. Silverado Trail, Oakville; (707) 944-8577. Open for sales daily 12-5, May-Oct.; tasting and tours by appointment only.
☐ Family-owned winery, established in 1980 by the Girard family. The winery is situated on an oak-studded knoll near the Oakville Crossroad, overlooking the family's 47-acre vineyard located at the winery. Estate-bottled varietal wines offered are Chardonnay, Cabernet Sauvignon and Sauvignon Blanc. A dry-styled Chenin Blanc is also produced. The winery's second label is Stephens Winery.

GOOSECROSS CELLARS. 1119 State Lane, Yountville; (707) 944-1986. Open daily 11-3 by appointment only.
☐ Small, family owned and operated winery, specializing in Napa Valley Chardonnay. The winery was founded by the Rey Gorsuch family, present owners.

GRAESER WINERY. 255 Petrified Forest Rd., Calistoga; (707) 942-4437. Open for sales Thurs.-Mon. 11-5. No tasting or tours.
☐ Owner-winemaker Richard Graeser produces premium Napa wines from his hillside vineyard located at the winery. The winery is housed in an historic home, built in 1886. Shaded picnic area.

GREEN & RED VINEYARD. 3208 Chiles-Pope Valley Road, St. Helena; (707) 965-2346. Sales by appointment only.
☐ Small, owner-operated winery, producing White Zinfandel and Chardonnay from its 16-acre hillside vineyard in Napa Valley's Chiles Canyon. The winery was established in 1977.

GRGICH HILLS CELLAR. 1829 St. Helena Hwy., Rutherford; (707) 963-2784. Tasting and sales daily, 9.30-4.30; tours by appointment.
☐ Grgich Hills Cellars was founded in 1977 by winemaker Miljenko Grgich—formerly of Chateau Montelana, and notable as the creator of the Chateau's famous 1973 Chardonnay which came in first at the 1976 Paris Tasting—and coffee-maker Austin Hills. The winery offers primarily estate-bottled varietal wines, including a Zinfandel from the Alexander Valley, a Late Harvest Johannisberg Riesling, and Chardonnay, Fumé Blanc and Cabernet Sauvignon. Grgich Hills wines are aged in French oak.

GROTH VINEYARDS & WINERY. P.O. Box 412, Oakville; (707) 255-7466. Tasting and retail sales by appointment.
□ Groth Vineyards was established in 1982 by Dennis and Judith Groth. The winery offers two varietal white wines, Chardonnay and Sauvignon Blanc, and a red varietal, Cabernet Sauvignon, all made from grapes grown on estate-owned vineyards in Oakville and Yountville.

HEITZ WINE CELLARS. 436 St. Helena Hwy. South, St. Helena; (707) 963-3542. Tasting and sales daily 11-4.30; tours by appointment.
□ Small, family owned and operated winery, established in 1961 by Joseph and Alice Heitz. The winery is notable primarily for its delightful Martha's Vineyard Cabernet Sauvignon, which comes from Tom and Martha May's vineyard near Oakville in the Napa Valley. The winery also produces another vineyard-designated varietal Cabernet Sauvignon, and Chardonnay, Johannisberg Riesling, Gewurztraminer, and an estate-bottled Grignolino Rosé. Two generics, Burgundy and Chablis, and some sparkling and dessert wines round out the Heitz roster.

HESS COLLECTION WINERY. 4411 Redwood Rd., Napa; (707) 255-1144. Wine tasting and sales by appointment, daily 10-4. Self-guided tours; art gallery on premises.
□ New winery, located in the Mount Veeder area, housed in a renovated, turn-of-the-century stone cellar. The winery offers premium Napa Chardonnay and Cabernet Sauvignon. The winery was established in 1989 by Swiss businessman Donald Hess.

WILLIAM HILL WINERY. 1775 Lincoln Ave., Napa; (707) 224-6555. Open for tasting and sales by appointment only, Mon.-Fri. 9-4.
Owner-winemaker William Hill offers primarily estate-grown varietal Chardonnay and Cabernet Sauvignon from his 1,000 acres of vineyards located in the Mount Veeder and Atlas Peak areas in Napa County. The winery was established in 1974.

LOUIS HONIG CELLARS. 850 Rutherford Rd., Rutherford; (707) 963-5618. Visitors by appointment only.
□ Small winery, housed in a relatively new facility, established in 1981. The winery produces primarily Sauvignon Blanc, from grapes grown on its 65-acre estate vineyard near Rutherford. Two other varietals, Chardonnay and Cabernet Sauvignon, are also produced.

INGLENOOK VINEYARDS. 1991 St. Helena Hwy. South, Rutherford; (707) 967-3363/967-3359. Open daily 10-4.45. Tours, tasting and sales; museum and wine library on premises.
□ Historic Napa Valley winery, founded in 1879 by Gustave Niebaum, a Finnish sea captain who made his fortune in furs in Alaska. The winery itself is housed in a splendid, ivy-covered, Gothic-style stone chateau, built in 1887, and surrounded by estate vineyards. Winery tours feature sensory evaluation of wines, and include a visit to the winery's historic aging cellars where you can view some antique winemaking equipment and old photographs depicting the history of the winery, as well as the "captain's" collection of wine glasses and goblets. Inglenook bottles a complete line of varietal and generic wines, and also jug wines, with its current annual output in the 1-million-case range — nearly three-quarters of which is produced at the winery's Central Valley facility. Inglenook Vineyards is owned by the Heublein Corporation.

Sterling Vineyards, situated on a knoll in the Napa Valley, overlooking estate vineyards

Tasting patio at the French-owned Domaine Chandon, Napa Valley

Harvest in the Napa Valley: migrant workers picking grapes

Vineyards in autumn, Russian River Valley

JOANNA VINEYARDS. 6795 Washington St., Yountville; (707) 944-9157. Tasting and sales daily 10.30-5.30.
□ Small, family owned and operated winery, founded in 1984. Wines produced are Cabernet Sauvignon, Sauvignon Blanc, Chardonnay and White Zinfandel, all made from grapes purchased on a select-vineyard basis. The winery is named for the co-owner Joanne Ryno's mother, Joanna.

JOHNSON TURNBULL VINEYARDS. 8210 St. Helena Hwy., Oakville; (707) 963-5839. Tours and tasting by appointment only.
□ Small, 2500-case winery, established by present owners Reverdy and Martha Johnson and William Turnbull, in 1979. Cabernet Sauvignon is the only wine produced here, made from grapes grown on the estate's 20-acre vineyard located just above Oakville.

ROBERT KEENAN WINERY. 3660 Spring Mountain Rd., St. Helena; (707) 963-9177. Tasting and sales Mon.-Sat. 9-4; tours by appointment. Picnic area.
□ Modest-sized winery, situated in the Spring Mountain area. The winery offers estate-grown Cabernet Sauvignon and Chardonnay from its 45-acre vineyard located at the winery. The winery was originally built in 1904, and remodeled and re-established by present owner Robert Keenan in 1977.

HANNS KORNELL CHAMPAGNE CELLARS. 1091 Larkmead Lane, St. Helena; (707) 963-1237. Tours, tasting and sales daily 10-4.30; last tour at 3.45 p.m.
□ Prestigious Napa Valley champagne producer, established in 1952 by Champagne Master Hanns Kornell, who arrived in Napa from his native Germany in 1940. Kornell offers seven different types of bottle-fermented champagne: Napa Brut, Extra Dry, Blanc de Blanc, Demi-Sec, Rosé, Rouge, Muscat Alexandria, and, finest of all, an award-winning Sehr Trocken. Winery tours highlight the champagne-making process, the history of the Kornell family, and the winery's historic aging cellars which were originally built in 1906 and which are now a designated historical site in the National Register.

CHARLES KRUG WINERY. 2800 St. Helena Hwy., St. Helena; (707) 963-5057. Tours, tasting and sales, daily 10-5; last tour at 4.00 p.m.
□ Charles Krug is the oldest operating winery in the Napa Valley, originally founded in 1861 by German immigrant Charles Krug, who was the first in the valley to make wine using a grape press rather than the traditional method of stomping by foot. Krug ran the winery until the 1890s, after which it changed hands several times, until in the 1940s it was finally acquired by the Peter Mondavi family, present owners. The winery offers a complete line of varietal and generic wines under the Charles Krug label, and jug wines under a second label, C.K. Mondavi. Gift and wine shop on premises.

LAKESPRING WINERY. 2055 Hoffman Lane; Napa; (707) 944-2475. Sales Mon.-Fri. 8-4.30; tasting and tours by appointment. Also open weekends in summer, 10-3.30.
□ Premium Napa winery, established in 1980. The winery offers vintage-dated varietal wines, including an estate-bottled Chardonnay and Cabernet Sauvignon from its 7-acre vineyard located at the winery, and Chenin Blanc, Merlot and Sauvignon Blanc. Wines are also made from grapes purchased from select vineyards in the Napa Valley and San Luis Obispo County.

NAPA VALLEY

(Note: Not all streets are represented)

□ WINERIES

Miles

0 ———— 5

Wineries on This Section of Map -

Beaulieu
Beringer
Burgess
Cain Cellars
Cakebread
Calafia
Casa Nuestra
Caymus
Charles Krug
Charles F. Shaw
Chateau Boswell
Chateau Chevalier
Chateau Montelena
Christian Brothers
Clos Pegase
Conn Creek
Cuvaison
Deer Park
Domaine de Napa
Duckhorn
Ehlers Lane
Flora Springs
Folie a Deux
Franciscan
Freemark Abbey
Frog's Leap
Green & Red
Grgich Hills
Hanns Kornell
Heitz
Inglenook

POPE VALLEY

CHILES & POPE VALLEY RD.

POPE VALLEY RD.

HOWELL MTN. RD.

ANGWIN

WHITE COTTAGE RD.

WELL MOUNTAIN RD.

Pope Valley □

CALISTOGA

Storybook Mountain □

Robert Pecota □

BENNETT LANE

TUBBS LANE

Napa River

PETRIFIED FOREST RD.

LINCOLN AVE.

Chateau Montelena

Traulsen □

SILVERADO TRAIL

Cuvaison □

Clos Pegase □

Sterling □

Stonegate □

DUNAWEAL

Diamond Creek □

DIAMOND MTN. RD.

SOUTH FORK

Schramsberg □

Napa River

LARKMEAD LANE

Hanns Kornell □

Wermuth □

SILVERADO TRAIL

BALE LANE

Charles F. Shaw □

Forman □

Tudal □

Frog's Leap □

Burgess □
RD.

Bothe-Napa State Park

Stony Hill □

Bale Grist Mill State Historic Park

Robert Keenan State Park

Ritchie Creek □

Smith-Madrone □

SPRING MOUNTAIN

Yverdon □

34

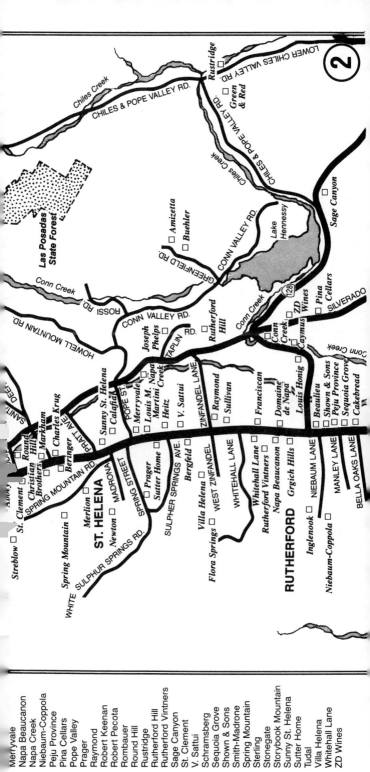

Merryvale
Napa Beaucanon
Napa Creek
Niebaum-Coppola
Peju Province
Pina Cellars
Pope Valley
Prager
Raymond
Robert Keenan
Robert Pecota
Rombauer
Round Hill
Rustridge
Rutherford Hill
Rutherford Vintners
Sage Canyon
St. Clement
V. Sattui
Schramsberg
Sequoia Grove
Shown & Sons
Smith-Madrone
Spring Mountain
Sterling
Stonegate
Storybook Mountain
Sunny St. Helena
Sutter Home
Tudal
Villa Helena
Whitehall Lane
ZD Wines

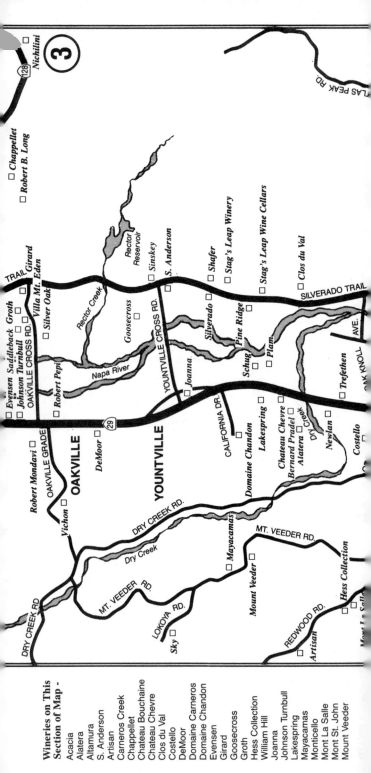

Wineries on This Section of Map -

Acacia
Alatera
Altamura
S. Anderson
Artisan
Carneros Creek
Chappellet
Chateau Bouchaine
Chateau Chevre
Clos du Val
Costello
DeMoor
Domaine Carneros
Domaine Chandon
Evensen
Girard
Goosecross
Groth
Hess Collection
William Hill
Joanna
Johnson Turnbull
Lakespring
Mayacamas
Monticello
Mont La Salle
Mont St. John
Mount Veeder

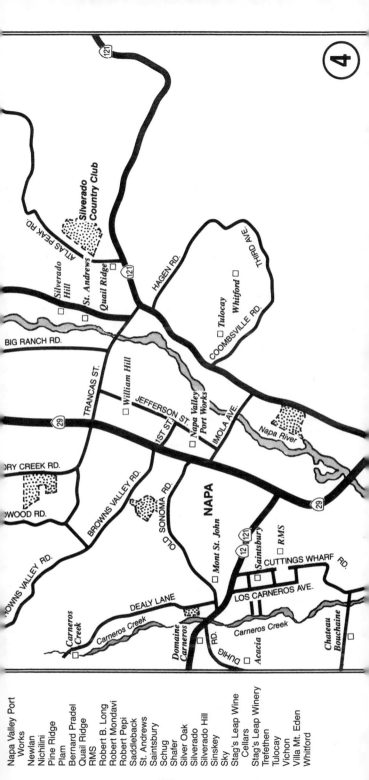

Map labels (on map):

121
Silverado Country Club
ATLAS PEAK RD.
Silverado Hill
St. Andrews
Quail Ridge
121
HAGEN RD.
THIRD AVE.
Tulocay
Whitford
COOMBSVILLE RD.
BIG RANCH RD.
TRANCAS ST.
William Hill
JEFFERSON ST.
Napa Valley Port Works
1ST ST.
IMOLA AVE.
Napa River
29
DRY CREEK RD.
BROWNS VALLEY RD.
OLD SONOMA RD.
NAPA
29
WOOD RD.
Mont St. John
12 121
Saintsbury
RMS
CUTTINGS WHARF RD.
TOWNS VALLEY RD.
DEALY LANE
LOS CARNEROS AVE.
Carneros Creek
Carneros Creek
Domaine Carneros
DUHIG RD.
Acacia
Carneros Creek
Chateau Bouchaine

LA VIEILLE MONTAGNE. 3851 Spring Mountain Rd., St. Helena; (707) 963-9059. Visitors by appointment only.
□ Small, owner-operated winery, offering estate-grown varietal Cabernet Sauvignon and Riesling from its 7-acre vineyard located in Napa County. Wines are also produced from grapes purchased on a select-vineyard basis. The winery was established in 1983, the vineyard in 1979.

LONG VINEYARDS. P.O. Box 50, St. Helena; (707) 963-2496. Visitors by appointment only.
□ Small, 2,000-case winery, established in 1978. Long Vineyards offers high quality, vintage-dated Chardonnay and Johannisberg Riesling from its 14-acre mountainside vineyard located at the winery. Retail sales are by mailing list.

MARKHAM WINERY. 2812 N. St. Helena Hwy., St. Helena; (707) 963-5292. Tasting and sales daily 11-4; tours Mon.-Fri. by appointment only.
□ Owner Bruce Markham acquired, restored and reopened this historic, 19th-century Napa winery in 1978. The winery currently bottles vintage-dated varietals from its 300 acres of vineyards located in the valley. Offerings include an award-winning Chardonnay and Merlot, and Cabernet Sauvignon, Gamay Blanc, Chenin Blanc, Muscat de Frontignan, and Johannisberg Riesling. Markham's second label is Vin Mark. The winery also offers a sensory evaluation course to visitors on weekdays.

MARSTON VINEYARD. 3600 White Sulphur Springs Rd., St. Helena; (707) 963-3069. Not open to the public. Sales by mailing list only.
□ Small Napa winery, founded in 1982. Marston offers primarily estate-grown, varietal Cabernet Sauvignon, Zinfandel, Petite Sirah, Grenache, Chardonnay and Pinot Blanc, all made from grapes grown in its 45-acre vineyard located in the Napa Valley. Small lots of Pinot Noir and sparkling wines are also produced. Wines are aged in oak.

LOUIS M. MARTINI WINERY. 254 St. Helena Hwy., St. Helena; (707) 963-2736. Tours, tasting and sales, daily 10-4.30.
□ Well-known Napa winery, originally established as the Louis M. Martini Grape Products Company in Kingsburg, California in 1922, and moved to its present location in St. Helena, by owner Louis M. Martini, in 1933. Martini currently owns in excess of 1,500 acres of planted vineyards in Napa, Sonoma and Lake counties, including substantial acreages in the Los Carneros district, the Mayacamas Mountains, Pope and Chiles valleys, and the Healdsburg area. The winery, of course, bottles a full line of estate varietal wines, with red table wines, aged in large cooperage, accounting for more than half of the winemaker's total annual output. Some generic and dessert wines are also produced, with emphasis on sherries.

MAYACAMAS VINEYARDS. 1155 Lokoya Rd., Napa; (707) 224-4030. Visitors by appointment only.
□ Family owned and operated winery, situated high in the Mayacamas Mountains, and named for its location. Mayacamas, in fact, is the Spanish adaption for an Indian word, meaning "howl of the mountain lion"; hence the winery label features two lions rampant. The winery offers two exceptional estate-bottled varietal wines, a Chardonnay and Cabernet Sauvignon, made from grapes grown on the estate-owned 47-acre hillside vineyard located at the winery. Small lots of Pinot Noir, Sauvignon Blanc, and some Late Harvest

Johannisberg Riesling are also offered. The winery was originally built in 1889, and restored and re-opened in 1941.

MERLION WINERY. 1224 Adams St., St. Helena; (707) 963-7100. Open daily, 10-5, for tours, tasting and sales.
☐ Small St. Helena winery, established in 1985. The winery bottles vintage-dated Cabernet Sauvignon, Chardonnay, Chevrier, Sauvrier—a blend of Sauvignon Blanc and Chevrier—and Coeur de Melon. Also produced is a dessert wine, Doux Blanc. The winery's second label is Piccolo.

MERRYVALE VINEYARDS. 1000 Main St., St. Helena; (707) 963-0397. Tasting and sales daily, 10-5.30; tours by appointment.
☐ A Chardonnay-only winery, housed in the old, restored Sunny St. Helena Winery—which Merryvale owns—in downtown St. Helena. Wines are made from grapes purchased on a select vineyard basis. The winery was founded in 1983.

MILAT VINEYARDS. 1091 St. Helena Hwy., St. Helena; (707) 963-0758. Tasting and sales, daily 10-6.
☐ Milat is a small, family winery, situated on a 22-acre vineyard estate in the heart of the Napa Valley, owned and operated by the Milat family. The winery offers estate-bottled varietal Chenin Blanc, White Zinfandel, and Cabernet Sauvignon. Wine sales are limited to the winery.

ROBERT MONDAVI WINERY. 7801 St. Helena Hwy., Oakville; (707) 963-9611. Tours, tasting and sales daily, 9-5 May-Oct., 10-4.30 Nov.-Apr. Tour reservations recommended.
☐ Highly-regarded Napa Valley winery, established in 1966 by Robert Mondavi, who left the family-owned Charles Krug Winery to make wine in his own style. The winery is housed in a striking Italian-Mediterranean stucco building, situated among estate vineyards. Mondavi produces primarily vintage-dated varietal wines from his 1,000 acres or so of estate vineyards, located in the Oak Knoll area along the Silverado Trail and at the foot of the Mayacamas Mountains, near the winery. Offerings including Cabernet Sauvignon—including a reserve bottling—Chardonnay, Fumé Blanc, Chenin Blanc, Johannisberg Riesling, Gamay Rosé, Napa Gamay, Pinot Noir, and Zinfandel. A Bordeaux-style proprietary red wine, "Opus One," is also produced in a joint venture with the late Baron Phillipe de Rothschild interests. The winery also features an art gallery and a wine and gift shop; and during summer, several jazz and other music concerts are scheduled, as well as the "Great Chefs of the World" series, where cooking schools are conducted by internationally-acclaimed chefs.

MONTICELLO CELLARS. 4242 Big Ranch Rd., Napa; (707) 253-2187. Tasting and sales daily 10-4.30; tours daily at 10.30 a.m., 12.30 and 2.30 p.m. Fee charged for tasting.
☐ Monticello was founded in 1980, and named for Thomas Jefferson's home in Monticello, Virginia—a replica of which was built here in 1985 and now houses the visitor center. The winery offers estate-grown Chardonnay, Sauvignon Blanc and Gewurztraminer from its 200 acres or so of planted vineyards located in the southern part of the valley; also produced are varietal vintage-dated Cabernet Sauvignon and Zinfandel. Monticello schedules wine-related events throughout the year, including cooking classes and seminars, and comparative tastings.

MONT ST. JOHN CELLARS. 5400 Old Sonoma Rd., Napa; (707) 255-8864. Tasting and sales daily 10-5; tours by appointment.

☐ Mont St. John is located in the Los Carneros region in Napa County. It was founded in 1979 by the Bartolucci family, who have been in the winegrowing business since 1934. The winery bottles primarily estate-grown Chardonnay, Pinot Noir, Johannisberg Riesling, Gewurztraminer, Cabernet Sauvignon, Zinfandel, and Petite Sirah. Gift shop on pemises; also creekside picnic area.

MOUNT VEEDER WINERY. 1999 Mt. Veeder Rd., Napa; (707) 224-4039. Open for tours and sales by appointment.

☐ Small winery, founded in 1972. Mount Veeder makes Cabernet Sauvignon from its 22-acre hillside vineyard located high on Mount Veeder, in Napa Valley's Mayacamas Mountains. Also featured are vintage-dated Chardonnay and Dry Chenin Blanc.

NAPA CREEK WINERY. 1001 Silverado Tr., St. Helena; (707) 963-9456. Tasting and sales daily 10.30-5.

☐ Founded in 1980, Napa Creek produces vintage-dated varietal wines from its 20-acre vineyard located at the winery. Offerings include Chardonnay, Sauvignon Blanc, Cabernet Sauvignon, Johannisberg Riesling, Gewurztraminer, and Dry Chenin Blanc. The winery, interestingly, is housed in a former meat-packing plant.

NAPA VALLEY PORT WORKS. 736 California Blvd., Napa; (707) 257-7777. Open for sales Fri.-Sat. 10-5; tours and tasting by appointment.

☐ Napa Valley Port Works specializes in vintage-dated Port, made from grapes purchased on a select-vineyard basis. The winery was founded in 1984 by owner-winemaker Shawn Denkler.

NAPA VALLEY WINE CO. 1721 Action Ave., Napa; (707) 255-9463. Visitors by appointment only.

☐ Owner-winemaker Don Charles Ross produces varietal Cabernet Sauvignon, Chardonnay, Sauvignon Blanc and Zinfandel from grapes purchased on a select-vineyard basis. Wines are also bottled under the Napa Vintners and Napa Valley Winery labels. The winery was established in 1976.

NEWLAN VINEYARDS & WINERY. 5225 St. Helena Hwy., Napa; (707) 944-2914. Winery not open to the public; wines may be tasted at the tasting room in Vintners Village, St. Helena.

☐ Small, owner-operated winery, established in 1981. Newlan offers estate-bottled Cabernet Sauvignon, Pinot Noir, Chardonnay, and Sauvignon Blanc from its 60-acre vineyard located in the Napa Valley.

NEWTON VINEYARD. 2555 Madrona Ave., St. Helena; (707) 963-9000. Tours and sales on weekdays by appointment.

☐ Built in 1979, the winery features sunken cellars, an observation tower, and a formal garden on the roof. The estate's 60-acre vineyard is located on the terraced slopes of Spring Mountain, high above Napa Valley. Varietal, vintage-dated wines produced here are Merlot, Cabernet Sauvignon, Chardonnay and Sauvignon Blanc.

NICHELINI VINEYARDS. 2349 Lower Chiles Valley Rd., St. Helena; (707) 963-3357. Open for tasting and sales, weekends and holidays 10-6, weekdays by appointment.

☐ Historic winery, located in the small Chiles Valley, east of Napa Valley, on the way to Lake Berryessa. The winery was originally founded in 1890 by Anton and Catrina Nichelini, and is now owned and operated by the third generation of the Nichelini family. The winery makes Sauvignon Vert, Chenin Blanc, Cabernet Sauvignon, Zinfandel, Semillon, Petite Sirah, and Gamay, mostly from grapes grown in the estate's 200-acre vineyard located just east of Rutherford in the Napa Valley. Picnic area at winery, and display of rare old Roman grape press.

NIEBAUM-COPPOLA ESTATE. 1460 Niebaum Lane, Rutherford; (707) 963-9435. Visitors by appointment only.

☐ In 1978, film-maker Francis Ford Coppola acquired the historic mansion of Gustave Niebaum, founder of Inglenook, and an adjacent 110-acre vineyard, and established his winery. The only wines produced are a red table wine—blended from Cabernet Sauvignon, Cabernet Franc and Merlot—and a Chardonnay. First vintage was released in the spring of 1984.

ROBERT PECOTA WINERY. P.O. Box 303, Calistoga; (707) 942-6625. Visitors by appointment, weekdays 9-5.

☐ Small, owner-operated winery, established in 1978. The winery offers vintage-dated varietal wines from the 40-acre estate vineyard located at the winery. Emphasis is on Cabernet Sauvignon and Sauvignon Blanc; other offerings include Grey Riesling, Gamay Beaujolais, and Muscat Di Andrea.

PEJU PROVINCE. 8466 St. Helena Hwy., Rutherford; (707) 963-3600. Tasting and sales daily 11-6 (11-5 Nov.-Feb.).

☐ Small, family owned and operated winery, founded in 1982 by Tony Peju. Peju offers an estate-bottled Cabernet Sauvignon from his 30-acre Napa vineyard. Also on the roster are vintage-dated varietal Sauvignon Blanc, Chardonnay and French Colombard, made from grapes purchased on a select-vineyard basis. Some wines are vineyard-designated.

ROBERT PEPI WINERY. St. Helena Hwy., Oakville; (707) 944-2807. Tasting and sales daily 11-4.30.

☐ Small, family winery, specializing in varietal Sauvignon Blanc. The winery is housed in a modern stone building, situated on a knoll overlooking family vineyards. The winery was established in 1981.

JOSEPH PHELPS VINEYARD. 200 Taplin Rd., St. Helena; (707) 963-2745. Open for tours, tasting and sales by appointment, Mon.-Sat. 9-4.

☐ Reputable Napa winery, situated on a 640-acre ranch at the eastern edge of the valley floor, with some 300 acres devoted to wine grapes. The winery houses its operations in a wood frame building comprising two separate pavillions, joined together by an enclosed bridge. Varietal, vintage-dated wines produced here are Chardonnay, Cabernet Sauvignon, Zinfandel, Sauvignon Blanc, Johannisberg Riesling, Gewurztraminer, Pinot Noir and Syrah. A blended red wine, Insignia, made from Cabernet Sauvignon, Cabernet Franc and Merlot, is also offered under the Phelps label. The winery was founded in 1973.

PINA CELLARS. 8050 Silverado Trail, Rutherford; (707) 944-2229. Open for retail sales only, Wed.-Sun. 10-4.

☐ Pina Cellars is owned and operated by the Pina family, a fifth generation Napa Valley winegrowing family. Vintage-dated Zinfandel and Chardonnay are the wines produced here. The winery was established in 1979.

PINE RIDGE WINERY. 5901 Silverado Trail, Yountville; (707)

253-7500. Tasting and sales, Tues.-Sun. 11-4; tours by appointment.

□ Small, owner-operated winery, established in 1978. The estate comprises an old building which was formerly the Luigi Domeniconi Winery, and a more modern structure in which the winery is currently housed. Approximately 50 acres of vineyards are located at the winery, and smaller acreages are in the Carneros district, the Stag's Leap and Oak Knoll areas, and Rutherford. Vintage-dated varietal wines produced are Chardonnay, Cabernet Sauvignon, Merlot, Sauvignon Blanc, and Chenin Blanc. Shaded picnic area on premises, and hiking trail to Pine Ridge.

PLAM VINEYARDS. 6200 St. Helena Hwy., Napa; (707) 944-1102. Open for sales daily 10-4; tours and tasting by appointment.

□ Small, owner-operated winery, established in 1984 by Kenneth and Valerie Plam. The winery bottles primarily vintage-dated varietal Chardonnay and Sauvignon Blanc. An occasional Merlot and Cabernet Sauvignon is also offered. Plam's 6-acre vineyard is located in the Napa Valley.

POPE VALLEY. 6613 Pope Valley Rd., Pope Valley; (707) 965-9463. Visitors by appointment only.

□ Originally built by a German blacksmith in the late 1800s, the winery was acquired and restored by the present owners, the Devitts, in 1972. The Devitts produce Chardonnay, Cabernet Sauvignon, and Pinot Noir, all from grapes purchased on a select-vineyard basis. The winery is located in the small Pope Valley, east of Napa Valley.

BERNARD PRADEL WINERY. 2100 Hoffman Lane, Yountville; (707) 944-8720. Tasting and sales by appointment only.

□ Small, owner-operated winery, producing varietal, vintage-dated Cabernet Sauvignon, Chardonnay, and a Late Harvest Sauvignon Blanc. The winery was founded by Bernard Pradel, present owner.

PRAGER WINERY & PORT WORKS. 1281 Lewelling Lane, St. Helena; (707) 963-3720. Wine sales daily 10.30-4.30; tours and tasting by appointment. Bed and breakfast suites available at winery.

□ Small, 3,000-case winery, family owned and operated, established in 1979 by Jim and Imogene Prager. The winery makes premium Port from 100% Cabernet Sauvignon grapes, which come primarily from Knights Valley. The winery also produces varietal, vintage-dated Cabernet Sauvignon, Chardonnay, and Zinfandel. Retail sales at winery and by mailing list. Picnic area on premises.

QUAIL RIDGE WINERY. 1055 Atlas Peak Rd., Napa; (707) 257-1712. Tours, tasting and sales by appointment, daily 10-4.

□ Quail Ridge is housed in the historic, 300-square-foot Hedgeside Cave, dug into the hillside by hand in 1885. The winery was of course re-established in 1978 by present owners Elaine Wellesley and Leon Santoro, who lend an Anglo-Italian flavor to the California wines they make. Wines produced are vintage-dated Chardonnay, Sauvignon Blanc, Cabernet Sauvignon, and French Colombard. The winery's 20-acre estate vineyard is located in the Mount Veeder area.

RAYMOND VINEYARD & CELLAR. 849 Zinfandel Lane, St. Helena; (707) 963-8511. Tasting and sales daily 10-4; tours by appointment.

□ Raymond Vineyard and Cellar was founed in 1974 by the Raymond family, who have been involved in winemaking in the Napa Valley since the 1870s, and are in fact directly related to the Beringer family of Beringer Vineyards. The winery itself is housed in a relatively new, frame structure, built in 1978. It produces premium vintage-dated varietal wines from its 90-acre vineyard located in the valley. Offerings include Chardonnay, Chenin Blanc, Cabernet Sauvignon, Zinfandel, Sauvignon Blanc, and Johannisberg Riesling.

RITCHIE CREEK VINEYARD. 4024 Spring Mountain Rd., St. Helena; (707) 963-4661. Visitors by appointment only.
□ Small, 1,000-case winery, with 8 acres of planted vineyards located in the Spring Mountain area at an elevation of 2,000 feet. Ritchie Creek offers vintage-dated Cabernet Sauvignon and Chardonnay. Wines are also bottled under a second label, Vineyard 1967. The winery was established in 1974.

RMS VINEYARDS. 1250 Cuttings Wharf Rd., Napa; (707) 253-9055. Open for sales Mon.-Sat. 9-4; tours Mon.-Fri., at 10.30 a.m. and 2.30 p.m.
□ RMS specializes in California Alambic Brandy, made in the old, European tradition, using handmade copper stills and Limousin oak barrels. The winery was established only recently, in 1989, by Rémy Martin of France, maker of cognac and fine brandies.

ROMBAUER VINEYARDS. 3522 Silverado Trail, St. Helena; (707) 963-5170. Wine sales Mon.-Fri., 9-4; tours and tasting by appointment.
□ Family owned and operated winery, housed in a 24,000-square-foot facility which is partially underground. The winery was founded in 1982 by present owners Koerner and Joan Rombauer. Premium vintage-dated Chardonnay and Cabernet Sauvignon are the only wines produced here.

ROUND HILL CELLARS. 1097 Lodi Lane, St. Helena; (707) 963-5251. Wine sales daily 10-5; tours by appointment.
□ Established in 1977, Round Hill is housed in a modest facility just north of St. Helena. The winery primarily buys wine in bulk and finishes it in its own facility. It also bottles a full line of varietal vintage-dated wines under its own label, with emphasis on Napa Valley Chardonnay, Gewurztraminer, Cabernet Sauvignon, and Zinfandel. Some generics are also offered. The winery's second label is Rutherford Ranch.

RUSTRIDGE WINERY. 2910 Lower Chiles Valley Rd., St. Helena; (707) 965-2871. Winery visits by appointment only.
□ Owner-operated winery, founded in 1985. The winery produces estate-grown Chardonnay, Johannisberg Riesling and Zinfandel from its 52-acre vineyard located in the Napa Valley. Small lots of Sweet Botrytised Johannisberg Riesling are also offered. Picnic area on premises.

RUTHERFORD HILL WINERY. 200 Rutherford Hill Rd., Rutherford; (707) 963-9694. Open for tours, tasting and sales, daily 10.30-4.30; tours at 11.30 a.m. and 2.30 p.m. Picnic area.
□ Rutherford Hill is housed in a large facility located at the foot of the eastern hills of Napa Valley. It produces approximately 100,000 cases of estate-grown varietal wine from its 700 acres or so of vineyards located in the Rutherford area, utilizing some of the most modern winemaking equipment and technology. The winery also features some 30,000 square feet of hillside caves, recently excavated, where wines are aged in French oak barrels. Wines produced under

the Rutherford Hill label include varietal Cabernet Sauvignon, Merlot, Zinfandel, Pinot Noir, Chardonnay, Sauvignon Blanc and Gewurztraminer. The winery was established in 1976.

RUTHERFORD VINTNERS. 1673 St. Helena Hwy., Rutherford; (707) 963-4117. Tasting and sales daily 10-4.30.
□ Modest-sized winery, founded in 1977 by Frenchman Bernard Skoda. Skoda makes vintage-dated varietal wines from his 30-acre vineyard located at the winery, as well as from grapes purchased from the Alexander Valley and Fresno area. Cabernet Sauvignon, Merlot, Pinot Noir, Riesling, Chardonnay, and a sweet Muscat are the wines produced. Wines are also bottled under a second label, Chateau Rutherford. Gift shop at winery.

SADDLEBACK CELLARS. 7802 Money Rd., Oakville; (707) 963-4982. Tours, tasting and sales by appointment only.
□ Saddleback Cellars—named for the Saddleback Mountains just to the east of Oakville—was founded in 1982 by Robert Call and winemaker Nils Venge, formerly of Villa Mt. Eden. The winery produces primarily estate-grown varietal Chardonnay, Cabernet Sauvignon and Pinot Blanc, all made from grapes grown in its 17-acre vineyard located in the Napa Valley.

SAGE CANYON WINERY. 2153 Sage Canyon Rd., St. Helena; (707) 963-1491. Visitors by appointment only.
□ Small winery, specializing in Dry Chenin Blanc. Sage Canyon was founded in 1981.

ST. ANDREW'S WINERY. 2921 Silverado Trail, Napa; (707) 252-6748. Visitors by appointment.
□ Small Napa winery, established in 1980. St. Andrew's produces limited quantities of Chardonnay from its 22-acre vineyard located at the winery. Vintage-dated estate Cabernet Sauvignon and Sauvignon Blanc are also offered.

ST. CLEMENT VINEYARDS. 2867 St. Helena Hwy. North, St. Helena; (707) 963-7221. Winery visits by appointment only, Mon.-Fri. 10-4.
□ St. Clement Vineyards was established in 1975 by Dr. and Mrs. William Casey of San Francisco. The winery is housed in a handsome Victorian home dating from 1876, which is featured on the St. Clement wine label, and in the cellars of which the first wines of historic Spring Mountain Vineyards were made. The winery produces primarily varietal Chardonnay, Sauvignon Blanc and Cabernet Sauvignon from estate vineyards located at the winery in St. Helena, and in Rutherford and Yountville. Wines are also bottled under the Garrison Forest label.

SAINTSBURY. 1500 Los Carneros Ave., Napa; (707) 252-0592. Visitors by appointment only. Informal tours.
□ A relatively new winery, established in 1981. Saintsbury offers vintage-dated Chardonnay and Pinot Noir from grapes purchased on a select-vineyard basis. The winery is located in Napa County's Los Carneros district.

ST. SUPERY WINERY. 8440 St. Helena Hwy., 8440 St. Helena Hwy., Rutherford; (707) 963-4507. Tours, tasting and sales by appointment only, Mon.-Fri. 9.30-4.30.
□ St. Supery was established in 1982 by the present owners, the Robert Skalli family of France. The winery is housed in a modern facility, and near the

winery are a Napa Valley museum—housed in an historic Queen Anne Victorian—and an exhibition vineyard and wine production gallery, all open to public tours. The winery produces vintage-dated, varietal Cabernet Sauvignon, Chardonnay and Sauvignon Blanc from grapes grown in its 1500 acres of estate vineyards located in the valley. St. Supery is named for one of the original owners of the property, French winemaker Edward St. Supery.

V. SATTUI WINERY. Cnr. St. Helena Hwy. and White Lane, St. Helena; (707) 963-7774. Tasting and sales daily 9-5, tours by appointment.

☐ Tourist-alluring, historic Napa Valley winery, originally established in 1885 by Vittorio Sattui, and now owned and operated by Vittorio's great-grandson, Daryl Sattui. Sattui offers a full line of varietal, vintage-dated wines, both from its estate vineyards as well as from purchased grapes. Offerings include Cabernet Sauvignon, Sauvignon Blanc, Gamay Rosé, Johannisberg Riesling, Chardonnay, Zinfandel, Muscat, and a sweet, 20-year-old Madiera. The winery also has a fully-stocked deli, a gift shop, and a large picnic area. Wine sales are limited to the winery.

SCHRAMSBERG VINEYARDS. Schramsberg Rd., Calistoga; (707) 942-4558. Open for tours and sales by appointment.

☐ Schramsberg is a small, historic Napa Valley winery, originally established in 1862 by Jacob Schram, and visited in 1880 by Scottish writer Robert Louis Stevenson who wrote about it in his book, *The Silverado Squatters*. The winery enjoys a hillside setting, with some 40 acres of estate vineyards located at the winery, planted equally to Pinot Noir and Chardonnay. The winery produces primarily four types of *méthode champenoise* sparkling wines—Blanc de Blanc, Blanc de Noirs, Cuvée de Pinot, and Cremant. A fine brandy is also produced under the Schramsberg label, in a joint venture with Rémy Martin of France. Schramsberg Cellars is now a designated Historical Landmark.

SCHUG CELLARS. 6204 St. Helena Hwy., Napa; (707) 963-3169. Visitors by appointment only.

☐ German-born winemaker Walter Schug makes small lots of Pinot Noir, Chardonnay and Cabernet Sauvignon from three different vineyards: Heinemann Mountain in the Napa Valley, and Ahollinger and Beckstoffer Los Amigos in the Carneros district. Wines are bottled at the Storybook Mountain Vineyards in Calistoga, Napa Valley. The winery is owned by Walter and Gertrud Schug.

SEQUOIA GROVE VINEYARDS. 8338 St. Helena Hwy., Napa; (707) 944-2945. Tasting and sales daily 11-5; tours by appointment.

☐ Sequoia Grove is a small, family-owned winery, housed in a converted century-old barn, set among a grove of stately California redwoods. The winery specializes in vintage-dated Chardonnay and Cabernet Sauvignon, made from grapes grown on the estate's 24-acre vineyard located at the winery. The winery was established in 1980 by the Allen family, present owners.

SHADOW BROOK WINERY. 360 Zinfandel Lane, St. Helena; (707) 963-2000. Winery visits by appointment only. Picnic area.

☐ Small, owner-operated winery, housed in a converted turn-of-the-century barn. The winery specializes in varietal Chardonnay and Pinot Noir, made from grapes grown on the estate's 60-acre vineyard located in the Napa Valley. The winery was established in 1984 by Emil and Gary Hoffman, present owners.

SHAFER VINEYARDS. 6154 Silverado Trail, Napa; (707) 944-2877. Winery tours and wine sales by appointment only.
□ Small, family owned and operated winery, housed in a modern stone and redwood building, set amid estate-owned hillside vineyards. Varietal wines produced here include Cabernet Sauvignon, Chardonnay, Gewurztraminer, Merlot, and Zinfandel. Wines are also bottled under a second label, Chase Creek. The winery was founded in 1979.

CHARLES F. SHAW VINEYARD. 1010 Big Tree Rd., St. Helena; (707) 963-5459. Visitors by appointment. Tasting available at tasting room in Vintners Village, St. Helena.
□ Small, family operation, established in 1979. Charles F. Shaw specializes in Napa Gamay, made from his 47-acre vineyard located at the winery in St. Helena. Limited quantities of Chardonnay, Fumé Blanc, and Nouveau Beaujolais-style Gamay wines are also offered. The winery's second label is Bale Mill Cellars. Gift shop on premises.

SHOWN & SONS VINEYARDS. 8514 St. Helena Hwy., Rutherford; (707) 963-9004. Wine sales daily 10-4.
□ 15,000-case, family-owned winery, founded in 1979. Shown produces primarily estate-grown varietal wines, with emphasis on Cabernet Sauvignon. The family's 75-acre vineyard is located near Rutherford.

SILVERADO HILL CELLARS. 3103 Silverado Tr., Napa; (707) 253-9308. Open for sales Mon.-Fri. 10-4; tours and tasting by appointment only.
□ Producer of premium estate-grown Pinot Noir, Sauvignon Blanc, and Chardonnay. 35 acres of estate vineyards are located at the winery in the Napa Valley. The vineyards were originally established in 1977 by Louis K. Mihaly, present owner.

SILVER OAK CELLARS. 915 Oakville Crossroad, Oakville; (707) 944-8808. Sales and tasting Mon.-Fri. 9-4.30, Sat. 10-5; tours by appointment, weekdays at 1.30 p.m.
□ 15,000-case, Cabernet Sauvignon only winery, established in 1972. The winery is situated on the site of an old Oakville dairy, with some of the former dairy buildings still in use as part of the winemaking facility. The winery also features a wine library, housing every Silver Oak Cellars vintage.

SILVERADO VINEYARDS. 6121 Silverado Trail, Napa; (707) 257-1770. Open for wine sales, daily 11-4.
□ Silverado Vineyards was established in 1981, and is owned in part by Mrs. Walt Disney. It comprises two vineyards, totalling some 185 acres, located on either side of the Napa River on part of what was originally the Rancho Yajome Mexican land grant. Varietal wines produced here are Sauvignon Blanc, Chardonnay, and Cabernet Sauvignon.

SINSKEY VINEYARDS. 6320 Silverado Tr., Napa; (707) 944-9090. Open for tasting and sales 10-4.30; tours by appointment. Tasting fee.
□ Established in 1987 by Dr. Robert Sinskey, present owner. The winery offers vintage-dated varietal Chardonnay, Merlot and Pinot Noir, all made from grapes grown in its 40-acre Napa vineyard.

SKY VINEYARDS. 1500 Lokoya Rd., Napa; (707) 255-7421. Visitors by appointment only.

☐   Sky Vineyards offers vintage-dated varietal Zinfandel from its 20-acre Napa vineyard. The winery was established in 1973.

SMITH-MADRONE VINEYARDS. 4022 Spring Mountain Rd., St. Helena; (707) 963-2283. Visitors by appointment.
☐   Small, quality-minded winery, established in 1977. The winery offers estate-bottled varietal Cabernet Sauvignon, Chardonnay and Pinot Noir from its 40-acre vineyard located on Spring Mountain, at an elevation of 1,700 feet.

SPOTTSWOODE WINERY. 1401 Hudson Ave., St. Helena; (707) 963-0134. Visitors by appointment only.
☐   Established in 1982, Spottswoode offers varietal, estate-grown Cabernet Sauvignon and Sauvignon Blanc from its 30-acre vineyard located at the winery.

SPRING MOUNTAIN VINEYARDS. 2805 Spring Mountain Rd., St. Helena; (707) 963-5233. Wine sales daily 10-5; tours by appointment, Mon.-Fri. 10.30 a.m. and 2.30 p.m., Sat.-Sun. 10.30 a.m.
☐   Historic Napa winery, housed in an 1880s Victorian mansion, with beautiful stained-glass windows and a hand-hewn tunnel for aging wines. The winery was re-established in 1968, and the mansion restored in 1974. In the years since, new facilities have been added to the estate, all in the same Victorian style as the original mansion. The winery produces 100% varietal wines from its estate vineyards on Spring Mountain, in Rutherford, and near Napa. Offerings include Chardonnay, Sauvignon Blanc, Cabernet Sauvignon, and Pinot Noir; one or two proprietary wines are also featured. Spring Mountain Vineyards, by the way, is the setting for the TV drama, *Falcon Crest.*

STAG'S LEAP WINERY. 6150 Silverado Trail, Napa; (707) 944-1303. Visitors by appointment.
☐   Stag's Leap Winery was established in 1972, in Napa's Stag's Leap area, with 100 acres of estate vineyards located at the winery. Stag's Leap's list of estate-grown, vintage-dated varietal wines includes a Petite Sirah, Merlot, Cabernet Sauvignon, Pinot Noir, and Dry Chenin Blanc.

STAG'S LEAP WINE CELLARS. 5766 Silverado Trail, Napa; (707) 944-2020. Tasting and sales daily 10-4; tours by appointment.
☐   The Stag's Leap Wine Cellars are situated in Napa Valley's well-known Stag's Leap area—a microclimate noted for its fine Cabernet Sauvignon yields. The winery produces primarily varietal, vintage-dated wines from its 45-acre estate vineyard located a quarter-mile from the winery. Wines produced are Cabernet Sauvignon, Chardonnay, Johannisberg Riesling, Sauvignon Blanc, Gamay Beaujolais, Petite Sirah, and Merlot. The winery's most famous offering is of course its 1973 Cabernet Sauvignon, which won top honors at the 1976 Paris Tasting, ahead of a 1970 Mouton-Rothschild. The winery was founded in 1972 by present owner-winemaker Warren Winiarski.

STERLING VINEYARDS. 1111 Dunaweal Lane, Calistoga; (707) 942-5151. Open for tours, tasting and sales, daily 10.30-4.30. Aerial tram at winery; fee: $5.00.
☐   Spectacular, white Mediterranean-style winery, situated on a hilltop in upper Napa Valley, overlooking estate vineyards. The winery is reached by way of an aerial tram, which incurs a modest charge. The winery has an excellent self-guided tour of its facility; it also has a wine and gift shop on the premises, and a spacious tasting room and terrace with valley views. Sterling offers primarily vintage-dated varietal wines, including Chardonnay, Sauvignon

Blanc, Cabernet Blanc, Cabernet Sauvignon, and Merlot, made largely from grapes grown in the estate's 500 acres of vineyards located in the valley. Some sparkling wine is also produced in a joint venture with the French Mumm champagne interests. The winery was originally established in 1969, acquired by the Coca-Cola Company in 1977, and by Seagrams of Canada in 1983.

STONEGATE WINERY. 1183 Dunaweal Lane, Calistoga; (707) 942-6500. Wine sales daily 9-5, tasting 10.30-4.00; tours by appointment.
☐ Stonegate, located adjacent to Sterling Vineyards, is unique in that it first named the winery and designed its wine label featuring a stone gate, and then, some 10 years later, went about the task of building an actual stone gate to match the one on its label. The winery itself is small, family owned and operated, founded in 1973. It has 15 acres of estate vineyards located at the winery, and another 30 acres or so on a hillside above the town of Calistoga. Wines produced are Cabernet Sauvignon, Chardonnay, Sauvignon Blanc, and Merlot.

STONY HILL VINEYARD. P.O. Box 308, St. Helena; (707) 963-2636. Visitors by appointment only.
☐ Small winery, owned and operated by the McCrea family since 1943. The winery produces limited quantities of high-quality wines from its 35-acre estate vineyard located in the foothills just to the north of St. Helena. Estate-bottled varietals offered are Chardonnay, Riesling, Gewurztraminer, and Semillon de Soleil, a sweet dessert wine. Wines are aged in oak.

STORYBOOK MOUNTAIN VINEYARDS. 3835 Hwy. 128, Calistoga; (707) 942-5310. Tours, tasting and sales by appointment only.
☐ Historic winery, originally founded in the early 1880s by Adam and Jacob Grimm. The winery specializes in varietal Zinfandel, made from grapes grown on the estate-owned 36-acre vineyard located in the Napa Valley. The winery also features three wine caves, dug into the hillside more than a century ago, and still in use today, restored by present owner, Dr. Bernard Seps.

STRATFORD WINERY. 1472 Railroad Ave., St. Helena; (707) 963-3200. Winery visits by appointment only.
☐ 75,000-case winery, established in 1984. The winery produces primarily varietal Chardonnay, Cabernet Sauvignon, Merlot, and Sauvignon Blanc. Wines are also bottled under a second label, Canterbury Wines.

STREBLOW VINEYARDS. 2849 Spring Mountain Rd., St. Helena; (707) 963-5892. Visitors by appointment only.
☐ Small, family-owned winery, founded in 1985 by Jack and Patricia Streblow. The Streblows offer estate-grown Cabernet Sauvignon and Sauvignon Blanc from their 13-acre vineyard located at the winery. Wines are aged in oak.

SULLIVAN VINEYARDS WINERY. 1090 Galleron Lane, Rutherford; (707) 963-9646. Tours, tasting and sales by appointment only.
☐ Small, family owned and operated winery, founded in 1979. Sullivan Vineyards makes vintage-dated varietal wines from its 30-acre vineyard located at the winery.

SUNNY ST. HELENA WINERY. 1000 Main St., St. Helena; (707) 963-2225. Open for tasting and sales, daily 10-5.
☐ Historic St. Helena winery, in downtown location. Varietal, vintage-dated Cabernet Sauvignon and Chardonnay are the only wines produced here. The

Beringer Vineyards' stately Rhine House dates from 1876

Christian Brothers Greystone Cellars, Napa Valley

winery also has on display a collection of rare, turn-of-the-century oak casks. The winery was restored and re-established in 1986 by the partners of San Francisco-based Merryvale Vineyards.

SUTTER HOME WINERY. 277 St. Helena Hwy., St. Helena; (707) 963-3104. Wine tasting daily 10-4.30, sales 9-5. No tours.
☐ Sutter Home is the oldest winery in the Napa Valley built entirely from wood, originally established in 1874 by Swiss winemaker John Thomann. It was acquired by pioneer land baron John Sutter some years later, and subsequently renamed. In 1946, the Trinchero family, present owners, purchased the property. Sutter Home is now among the prominent Napa wineries, and one of the largest Zinfandel producers in the nation. The winery also bottles a Dessert Zinfandel, Muscat Amabile, and a proprietary Trinchero Triple Cream aperitif wine. Sutter Home's 15-acre estate vineyard is located in the Calistoga area.

PHILLIP TOGNI VINEYARD. 3870 Spring Mountain Rd., St. Helena; (707) 963-3731. Visitors by appointment only.
☐ Owner-operated winery, situated on an historic Spring Mountain vineyard estate, some 2,000 feet above Napa Valley, originally established in 1883. The winery was re-established by present owners Phillip and Brigitta Togni in 1985. Varietal, estate-grown wines produced are Sauvignon Blanc and Cabernet Sauvignon.

TRAULSEN VINEYARDS. 2250 Lake County Hwy., Calistoga; (707) 942-0283. Winery visits by appointment only.
☐ Small, 2,000-case Zinfandel specialist, family owned and operated, with a 2-acre vineyard located at the winery, planted to Zinfandel. The winery was established in 1980.

TREFETHEN VINEYARDS. 1160 Oak Knoll Ave., Napa; (707) 255-7700. Wine tasting and sales daily 10-4; tours by appointment.
☐ Historic Napa winery, originally founded in 1886 as part of the Eschol Ranch, and acquired by the Trefethen family in 1968. The old winery building was designed by Captain Hamden McIntyre, designer of the Christian Brothers' Greystone Cellars and the Inglenook Winery. Trefethen Vineyards offers estate-bottled varietal wines from its 600 acres of vineyards located in the Napa Valley. Offerings include Cabernet, Chardonnay, Riesling, and Pinot Noir. The winery also bottles a pair of proprietary wines, Red Eschol and White Eschol, both under the Eschol label.

TUDAL WINERY. 1015 Big Tree Rd., St. Helena; (707) 963-3947. Tours, tasting and sales by appointment only.
☐ Tudal is a small, family owned and operated, modern winery, producing primarily Cabernet Sauvignon from its 10-acre Napa vineyard, and a vintage-dated Chardonnay from purchased grapes. The winery was established in 1979.

TULOCAY WINERY. 1426 Coombsville Rd., Napa; (707) 255-4064. Winery visits by appointment.
☐ Founded in 1975, Tulocay is a small, 2,000-case winery, owned and operated by William Cadman. The winery features four barrel-aged Napa Valley varietals: Pinot Noir, Cabernet Sauvignon, Zinfandel, and Chardonnay. Wine sales are by mailing list.

VICHON WINERY. 1595 Oakville Grade, Oakville; (707) 944-2811. Wine tasting and sales daily 10-4.30; tours by appointment.

☐ Modern Napa winery, perched high on the Oakville Grade, overlooking Napa Valley vineyards. Cabernet Sauvignon, Chardonnay, and Chevrier, a blend of Semillon and Sauvignon Blanc, are the only wines produced here. The winery was originally founded in 1980, and is now owned by Robert Mondavi. Oak-shaded picnic area on premises.

VILLA HELENA WINERY. 1455 Inglewood Ave., St. Helena; (707) 963-4334. Winery visits by appointment, daily during summer.
☐ Owner-winemaker Donald McGrath makes vintage-dated Chardonnay at his small St. Helena winery. The winery was established in 1984.

VILLA MT. EDEN. 620 Oakville Crossroad, Oakville; (707) 944-2414. Tasting and sales daily 10-4; tours by appointment.
☐ Villa Mt. Eden was originally founded in the 1880s, and re-established in 1974. The winery is situated on a 87-acre vineyard estate which supplies the grapes for the winery's two principal offerings—Cabernet Sauvignon and Chardonnay. Small lots of Pinot Noir, Gewurztraminer, and Dry Chenin Blanc are also produced.

VOSE VINEYARDS. 4035 Mt. Veeder Rd., Oakville; (707) 944-2254. Winery visits by appointment only; tasting available at Vintners Village, St. Helena. Tasting fee.
☐ Established in 1970 by present owner Hamilton Vose III, the winery is located in the small Mount Veeder area, high above the Napa Valley. The winery offers primarily varietal Chardonnay, Cabernet Sauvignon and Zinfandel from its 22-acre estate vineyard, also on Mount Veeder. Some Gewurztraminer and a Late Harvest Johannisberg Riesling are also produced. Mountain picnic area on premises.

WERMUTH WINERY. 3942 Silverado Trail, Calistoga; (707) 942-5924. Tours, tasting and sales by appointment only.
☐ Small, owner-operated winery, established in 1983. Wermuth offers varietal French Colombard from its estate vineyard located at the winery. Vintage-dated Sauvignon Blanc, Cabernet Sauvignon and Cabernet Franc, are also produced.

WHITEHALL LANE WINERY. 1563 St. Helena Hwy., St. Helena; (707) 963-9454. Wine tasting and sales daily 11-5, tours by appointment.
☐ Whitehall Lane is a conventional winery, housed in a modern facility, with some 40 acres or so of estate vineyards located at the winery and an additional 4 acres in the Rutherford area, just to the south. The winery produces varietal vintage-dated Chardonnay, Sauvignon Blanc, Cabernet Sauvignon, Merlot, Blanc de Pinot Noir, Chenin Blanc, and one or two proprietary dinner wines. Wines are also bottled under a second label, Jacabels Cellars. The winery was founded in 1980 by winemaker Art Finkelstein and his brother Alan Steen.

WHITFORD CELLARS. 4047 East 3rd Ave., Napa; (707) 257-7065. Winery visits by appointment only.
☐ Small, family-owned winery, producing estate-grown Chardonnay from its 25-acre vineyard located in the Napa Valley. The winery was founded by Douglas and Patricia Haynes, present owners.

YVERDON VINEYARDS. 3787 Spring Mountain Rd., St. Helena; (707) 963-4270. Winery visits by appointment only.
☐ Small, owner-operated winery, located in the Spring Mountain area, above

St. Helena, and housed in a handsome stone building. Owner-winemaker Fred Aves actually designed and built the entire stone winery himself, and even coopered the oak casks in-house. He first established the winery in 1970, and has operated it intermittently since, producing primarily Cabernet Sauvignon and Chenin Blanc, and tiny lots of Riesling, Gewurztraminer, and Napa Gamay. Aves owns 12 acres of vineyards at the winery, and an additional 80 acres in upper Napa Valley.

ZD WINES. 8383 Silverado Trail, St. Helena; (707) 963-5188. Tours, tasting and sales by appointment, weekdays 8-12 a.m. and 1-4 p.m.
□ Small, 17,000-case, family owned and operated winery. Originally established in 1969 in Sonoma County, ZD Wines moved its operation to Napa in 1979, and two years later, in 1981, planted a 3-acre vineyard in the valley. The winery features a barrel-fermented Chardonnay, and Pinot Noir, Cabernet Sauvignon, Zinfandel, and a Late Harvest Gewurztraminer.

PRACTICAL INFORMATION FOR NAPA VALLEY

HOW TO GET THERE

Napa is situated at the bottom end of the Napa Valley, roughly 54 miles northeast of San Francisco. It can be reached by taking *Highway 101* directly north from San Francisco to Novato (26 miles), then *Highways 37* and *121* northeast to the city of Napa, another 27 miles. North of Napa, on *Highway 29* are Yountville (10 miles), Oakville (13 miles), Rutherford (15 miles), St. Helena (19 miles), and Calistoga (28 miles).

An alternative route is by way of *Interstate 80* east from San Francisco to Vallejo (31 miles), then *Highway 29* directly north to Napa, another 16 miles.

TOURIST INFORMATION

Napa Chamber of Commerce, 1556 First St., Napa; (707) 226-7455. Tourist literature for the Napa Valley wine country, including lodgings, restaurants, wineries, seasonal events and recreational facilities.

St. Helena Chamber of Commerce, 1508 Main St., St. Helena; (707) 963-4456. Tourist brochures, including restaurant and bed & breakfast listings; winery maps, and information on local events. Also, the *Bed & Breakfast Exchange,* 1118 Pine St., (707) 963-7756, offers a referral service for local inns; free brochure available upon request.

Calistoga Chamber of Commerce. Housed in the Old Depot, at 1458

Lincoln Ave., Calistoga; (707) 942-6333. Information on lodging, restaurants, spas and wineries; calendar of events. There is also a *Wine Country Bed & Breakfast Reservations* service in the Napa Valley area; call (707) 257-7757 for referrals and reservations.

ACCOMMODATIONS

Napa

Best Western Inn. *$75-$159.* 100 Soscol Ave., Napa; (707) 257-1930/(800) 528-1234. 68 rooms; TV, phones. Pool, spa, restaurant.

Chablis Lodge. *$59-89.* 3360 Solano Ave., Napa; (707) 257-1944/(800) 443-3490 in CA. 34 units, with TV, phones, refrigerators and wet bars; some whirlpool baths; some kitchenette units. Pool and jacuzzi.

The Chateau. *$95-$175.* 4195 Solano Ave., Napa; (707) 253-9300/(800) 253-NAPA in CA. 115 rooms, including 6 suites; TV, phones, pool and jacuzzi. Complimentary continental breakfast and evening wine; room service; valet service. Also hot-air balloon rides and private winery tours arranged.

Clarion Inn. *$105-$300.* 3425 Solano Ave., Napa; (707) 253-7433/(800) 362-6000. Full service hotel with 191 rooms and suites; TV, phones, some fireplaces. Pool, jacuzzi, tennis courts. Restaurant and cocktail lounge.

Embassy Suites. *$129-$139.* 1075 California Blvd., Napa; (707) 253-9540/(800) EMBASSY. 205 two-room suites, with wet bar, kitchenette, phones, TV. Indoor and outdoor pools, spa, sauna and steam rooms. Complimentary breakfast, evening cocktails. Restaurant.

John Muir Inn. *$60-$125.* 1998 Trower Ave., Napa; (707) 257-7220/(800) 522-8999 in CA. 60 rooms, many with wet bars, kitchenettes, and whirlpool spas. TV, phones; pool and spa. Complimentary continental breakfast and wine reception.

Napa Valley Travelodge. *$60-$70.* 853 Coombs & 2nd St., Napa; (707) 226-1871/(800) 255-3050. 44 units; TV, phones, pool. Some non-smoking rooms.

Silverado Country Club. *$130-$465.* 1600 Atlas Peak Rd., Napa; (707) 257-0200/(800) 532-0500. Luxury resort with 280 guest accommodations, ranging from studios to 3-room cottage suites with fireplaces. 2 Robert Trent Jones-designed 18-hole golf courses, 20 tennis courts, 8 pools; 3 gourmet restaurants.

Wine Valley Lodge. *$60-$75.* 200 South Coombs St., Napa; (707) 224-7911. 54 units; TV, phones, pool, tennis courts.

Yountville

Napa Valley Lodge. *$108-$140.* 2230 Madison St., Yountville; (707) 944-2468/(800) 368-2468. 55 units, overlooking valley vineyards; some rooms with fireplaces and balconies, some kitchenettes. Exercise room, pool, spa, sauna. Continental breakfast.

Napa Valley Railway Inn. *$95-$105.* 6503 Washington St., Yountville; (707) 944-2000. Located adjacent to Vintage 1870. 10 units with private baths, sitting rooms, skylights and bay windows, housed in elegantly-restored vintage railroad cars and cabooses. Complimentary continental breakfast. Vineyard views.

Vintage Inn. *$150-$180*. 6541 Washington St., Yountville; (707) 944-1112/(800) 351-1133 in CA/(800) 9-VALLEY in Continental USA. 80 spacious units, each with whirlpool spa, fireplace, bar and ceiling fans. Also pool, tennis courts, spa. Complimentary continental breakfast, featuring fresh fruit, pastries and champagne.

St. Helena

Harvest Inn. *$95-$300*. 1 Main St., St. Helena; (707) 963-9463. 32 individually-decorated rooms in Tudor-style inn. TV, phones, wet bars, fireplaces. Vineyard views.

Meadowood Resort. *$200-$310*. 900 Meadowood Lane, St. Helena; (707) 963-3646/(800) 458-8080. Luxury resort complex, set on 250 acres. 70 rooms and suites, 2 restaurants, golf course, tennis courts, croquet, pool.

Calistoga

Comfort Inn. *$68-$90*. 1865 Lincoln Ave., Calistoga; (707) 942-9400/(800) 228-5150. 55 units, with TV and phones; heated pool, mineral water whirlpool, steamroom and sauna. Complimentary continental breakfast.

Hideaway Cottages. *$44-$85*. 1412 Fairway, Calistoga; (707) 942-4108. 17 vintage housekeeping cottages, with TV and air-conditioning. Jacuzzi and mineral-water pool for guests. No children.

Pine Street Inn. *$65-$90*. 1202 Pine St., Calistoga; (707) 942-6829. 16 units, including some suites and kitchenettes. TV, air-conditioning, picnic and barbeque areas.

Mount View Hotel. *$90-$130*. 1475 Lincoln Ave., Calistoga; (707) 942-6877. Restored old hotel, with 24 rooms and 9 suites, all with private baths. Also pool, hot tub, restaurant and cocktail lounge; jazz music featured in restaurant on Sundays. Hotel rates include full breakfast.

BED & BREAKFAST INNS

Napa

Hennessey House. *$110-$140*. 1727 Main St., Napa; (707) 226-3774. Charming Eastlake-style Queen Anne Victorian home with carriage house, built in 1889. 5 guest rooms in the main house, with private baths, featherbeds and antique furnishings; 4 rooms in the carriage house, with private whirlpool baths and fireplaces. Full breakfast, afternoon wine tasting. Sauna.

Beazley House. *$105-$160*. 1910 First St., Napa; (707) 257-1649. 9 guest rooms, some with fireplaces and private spas. Breakfast features homemade muffins and fresh fruit.

Churchill Manor. *$75-$145*. 485 Brown St., Napa; (707) 253-7733. Elegant, antique-decorated 32-room mansion, dating from 1889. 8 guest rooms, with private baths; some with fireplaces; also music room, with grand piano. No children or pets.

Arbor Guest House. *$80-$120*. 1436 G St., Napa; (707) 252-8144. Colonial residence with carriage house, dating from 1906. 4 rooms with private baths; some fireplaces. Continental breakfast, served in formal dining room or on garden patio.

Coombs Residence, The Inn on the Park. *$80-$100*. 720 Seminary St., Napa; (707) 257-0789. Restored 1852 home, with 4 guest rooms. Antique furnishings, down comforters; pool and jacuzzi. Breakfast includes freshly-squeezed orange juice and homebaked breads and croissants; wine and cheese in the afternoon, served in the parlor. Bicycles available for guest use.

Goodman House. *$95-$130*. 1225 Division St., Napa; (707) 257-1166. Stately old Napa home, close to downtown. 4 guest rooms, each with private bath. Full breakfast.

La Residence. *$95-$150*. 4066 St. Helena Hwy., Napa; (707) 253-0337. Beautifully restored, antique-decorated home with lovely gardens, dating from the 1870s. 7 rooms in main house, some with private baths; 8 suites with fireplaces in the "barn." Spa.

Oakville Ranch. *$250-$300*. 7781 Silverado Tr., Napa; (707) 944-8612. Executive retreat, situated on a 332-acre wooded estate with vineyards and orchards, high above the Napa Valley. 3 luxuriously appointed rooms; tennis courts and library. Champagne breakfast, open bar.

Trubody Ranch. *$100-$120*. 5444 St. Helena Hwy., Napa; (707) 255-5907. Victorian home, built in 1872, surrounded by 120-acre vineyard. 2 rooms with private baths. Continental breakfast, featuring fresh fruit from the family orchard, and homemade breads.

Rutherford

Rancho Caymus Inn. *$95-$295*. 170 Rutherford Rd., Rutherford; (707) 963-1777. 26 guest rooms with fireplaces, stained glass windows and wrought iron accents. Continental breakfast, with homemade breads.

Auberge du Soleil. *$240-$390*. 180 Rutherford Rd., Rutherford; (707) 963-1211. Splendid French-country inn with valley views. 36 units, including 18 two-bedroom suites with kitchenette, deck, fireplace and private baths, and 18 one-bedroom suites. Pool, jacuzzi, tennis court. Continental breakfast.

Yountville

Bordeaux House. *$95-$135*. 6600 Washington St., Yountville; (707) 944-2855. 6 rooms with fireplaces and private baths; some with private patios or balconies. Continental breakfast.

Burgundy House. *$110-$120*. 6711 Washington St., Yountville; (707) 944-0889. Historic 2-story stone building, formerly a brandy distillery, dating from 1874. 6 guest rooms; garden patio. Continental breakfast.

Magnolia Hotel. *$89-$159*. 6529 Yount St., Yountville; (707) 944-2056. 12 rooms with private baths, in refurbished, antique-decorated old hotel. Country-style breakfast. Pool, jacuzzi.

St. Helena

Ambrose Bierce House. *$85-$125*. 1515 Main St.; (707) 963-3003. Luxury inn, formerly home of author Ambrose Bierce, built in 1872. 4 antique-furnished suites with brass beds and armoires; private baths, with claw foot tubs. Suites are named after notable 19th-century personages—Lily Langtree, Lillie Coit, Eadweard Muybridge, and Bierce. Country breakfast, comprising homemade pastries and fresh fruit. Bicycles available for guests' use.

Bartel's Ranch. *$125-$150.* 1200 Conn Valley Rd.; (707) 963-4001. Romantic country home on secluded 100-acre estate. 3 delightful guest rooms, with private baths. Jacuzzi, swimming pool and games room; complimentary wine and sherry, continental breakfast.

Bylund House. *$90-$100.* 2000 Howell Mountain Rd.; (707) 963-9073/963-1307. Secluded country estate, with two well-appointed guest rooms with private baths and balconies. Complimentary wine and hors d'oeuvres; hearty country breakfast.

Chestelson House. *$78-$98.* 1417 Kearney St.; (707) 963-2238. Centrally located, turn-of-the-century Victorian home; wide verandah, superb mountain views; 3 rooms. Delicious gourmet breakfast; complimentary wine.

The Cinnamon Bear. *$90-$115.* 1407 Kearney St.; (707) 963-4653. 3 guest rooms in small, comfortable home, dating from the early 1900s; antique quilts and toys, polished brass, private, old-fashioned baths. Full breakfast, served on the porch or in the dining room. Downtown location.

Deer Run Inn. *$70-$90.* 3995 Spring Mountain Rd.; (707) 963-3794. Secluded mountain retreat, tucked away in the forest on Spring Mountain. 3 guest rooms with private baths, 1 with a fireplace. Pool on premises.

Elsie's Conn Valley Inn. *$75-$95.* 726 Rossi Rd.; (707) 963-4614. Secluded country inn, 4 miles from St. Helena. 3 guest rooms, one with private bath. Country-style breakfast.

Erika's Hillside. *$85-$150.* 285 Fawn Park Rd.; (707) 963-2887. Century-old hillside chalet, situated on wooded 3-acre estate. 3 spacious rooms, with private entrances, hot tubs and fireplaces. Patio and garden room; continental breakfast, featuring German specialties.

Hotel St. Helena. *$85-$135.* 1309 Main St.; (707) 963-4388. Restored Victorian hotel in downtown St. Helena. 18 rooms, most with private baths. Sun deck; wine bar, continental breakfast. Close to shops and restaurants.

Ink House. *$95-$120.* 1575 St. Helena Hwy.; (707) 963-3890. 1884 Italianate Victorian home with 4 charming rooms, each decorated with period furnishings. Superb vineyard views. Continental breakfast served in the dining room. Antique pump organ in front parlor.

La Fleur. *$110-$130.* 1475 Inglewood Ave.; (707) 963-0233. Beautifully restored 100-year-old Victorian inn with solarium and 3 guest rooms featuring French decor. Breakfast comprises homemade pies and pastries.

Judy's Bed & Breakfast. *$85.* 2036 Madrona Ave.; (707) 963-3081. Charming country cottage set among vineyards in St. Helena. Large bedroom-cum-sitting room, with private bath, private entrance, fireplace, and TV; also pool on premises. Freshly baked pastries for breakfast; complimentary wine.

Oliver House. *$85-$195.* 2970 Silverado Trail; (707) 963-4089. Swiss chalet on private 4-acre estate in the hills above Napa Valley. 4 charming guest rooms, furnished with antiques and brass beds; large stone fireplace in parlor. Continental-style breakfast, comprising muffins, pastries and fresh fruit.

Prager Winery Bed & Breakfast. *$135-$150.* 1281 Lewelling St.; (707) 963-3720. 2 spacious suites, situated above the barrel aging cellar of Prager Winery. Fireplaces and private baths; verandah with mountain views and vineyard views. Breakfast served in suite.

Shady Oaks Country Inn. *$105-$125.* 399 Zinfandel Lane; (707) 963-1190. Delightful country inn, housed in 1920s home, and set among scenic vineyards on 2-acre estate. 3 antique-decorated rooms with private baths; complimentary wine. Homemade breakfast, served on the verandah or by the fireplace.

Villa St. Helena. *$150-$225*. 2727 Sulphur Springs Rd.; (707) 963-2514. Exclusive Mediterranean-style villa on private, 20-acre estate, nestled in the hills above St. Helena, with superb valley views. 3 luxurious guest rooms, period decor; courtyard pool, picnic area and walking trails. Continental breakfast, served in the solarium.

Wine Country House. *$100-$120*. 400 Meadowood Lane; (707) 963-0852. 2 guest rooms, each with private bath, in picturesque Victorian home in peaceful, wooded setting. Also private guest cottage beside the house, with kitchen, bath, sitting room and patio; decorated with pine and oak furnishings. Gourmet breakfast; complimentary wine.

Wine Country Inn. *$80-$160*. 1152 Lodi Lane; (707) 963-7077. 25 rooms, individually decorated with antiques and handmade quilts; some fireplaces and balconies; also pool, and spa. The inn is situated atop a knoll overlooking vineyards.

Calistoga

Brannan Cottage Inn. *$95-$135*. 109 Wapoo Ave.; (707) 942-4200. Award winning inn, housed in an historic cottage built by Sam Brannan in 1860. 6 guest rooms. Enchanting garden setting.

Calistoga Inn. *$40-$45*. 1250 Lincoln Ave.; (707) 942-4101. 17-room inn, housed in turn-of-the-century building in downtown Calistoga. Continental breakfast; restaurant and bar on premises. Shared baths.

Culver's. *$95-$105*. 1805 Foothill Blvd.; (707) 942-4535. Beautifully restored 1875 Victorian home, now an historical landmark, situated within easy walking distance of shops and restaurants. 6 guest rooms, individually decorated with period furnishings; panoramic views of Mount St. Helena. Sitting room with fireplace; spa, sauna.

The Elms. *$90-$115*. 1300 Cedar St.; (707) 942-9476. Elegant French-Victorian inn, built in 1871. 4 guest rooms, decorated with European antiques. Complimentary wine and cheese. Central location.

The Inn on Cedar Street. *$95*. 1307 Cedar St.; (707) 942-9244. Comfortable 3-bedroom Victorian cottage, located on tree-lined street near restaurants and park. Rooms decorated with patchwork quilts and period furnishings; claw foot tub in the bathroom. Spacious porch with swing.

Larkmead Country Inn. *$84-$88*. 1103 Larkmead St.; (707) 942-5360. Turn-of-the-century Victorian inn, surrounded by vineyards. 3 guest rooms, filled with antiques, Persian carpets and old paintings.

The Pink Mansion. *$65-$95*. 1415 Foothill Blvd.; (707) 942-0558. Charming 100-year-old Victorian mansion, nestled amid gardens on 3 wooded acres. 5 comfortable rooms with picture-postcard views of surrounding countryside. Also, heated indoor pool and game room. Gourmet breakfast.

Silver Rose Inn. *$95-$160*. 351 Rosedale Rd.; (707) 942-9581. Splendid setting among live oaks on a rocky outcropping overlooking Napa Valley vineyards. 5 guest rooms, with private baths and balconies. Pool, spa.

Trailside Inn. *$85-$100*. 4201 Silverado Trail; (707) 942-4106. Picturesque 1930s ranch house; 3 completely private suites, with private baths, living rooms with fireplaces, kitchenettes, and porches. Complimentary wine, and freshly-baked breads.

Wine Way Inn. *$65-$80*. 1019 Foothill Blvd.; (707) 942-0680. Built in 1915, this beautifully restored cottage has 6 antique-decorated guest rooms, some with private baths. Delicious homemade pastries for breakfast.

Zinfandel House. *$75-$95*. 1253 Tucker Rd.; (707) 942-0733. Country home in wooded setting, with commanding views of the Napa Valley. 2 beautifully furnished rooms; spacious deck. Country breakfast; complimentary wine.

SPA RESORTS

(Note: Mud bath prices usually include blanket wrap, steam room and whirlpool bath.)

Calistoga Spa Hot Springs, 1006 Washington St., Calistoga; (707) 942-6269. Family-style hot springs resort, with two outdoor hot mineral pools, one covered jet pool and one outdoor wading pool; also weight and workout rooms, and aerobic classes. Mud bath $27.00, with massage $45.00. 48 motel units on premises, with kitchenettes and air-conditioning; $66-$77.

Indian Springs, 1712 Lincoln Ave., Calistoga; (707) 942-4913. Oldest spa resort in Calistoga, established in 1862. Facilities include an outdoor hot mineral pool and sulphur steam cabinet. Mud bath $35.00, with massage $60.00. Also, 17 rental cottages on grounds, with TV, full kitchens, and housekeeping facilities; $85-$125.

Dr. Wilkinson's Hot Springs, 1507 Lincoln Ave., Calistoga; (707) 942-4102. Well-known spa, with good accommodations. Offers two warm outdoor mineral pools, one large indoor mineral whirlpool, and a swimming pool. Mud bath $33.00, with massage $49.00. Accommodations include 37 air-conditioned motel units, some with kitchenettes; also some cottages; $49-$85.

Golden Haven Spa, 1713 Lake St., Calistoga; (707) 942-6793. Facilities include a covered pool, hot mineral pools, an exercise room and sun deck. Mud bath $27.00, $44.00 with massage. Accommodations: 30 units, with air-conditioning; some kitchenettes, some private saunas and jacuzzis. $45-$95.

Roman Spa, 1300 Washington St., Calistoga; (707) 942-4441. Outdoor warm mineral pool and hot jacuzzi; also indoor hot mineral pool, S 1300 Washington St., Calistoga; (707) 942-4441. Outdoor warm mineral pool and hot jacuzzi; also indoor hot mineral pool, Swedish sauna, and large swimming pool. Mud baths, massage and other spa treatments available at adjacent International Spa (see listing below). Accommodations include 51 modern units with air-conditioning, TV, and kitchenettes; also some cottages; $60-$100.

International Spa, 1300 Washington St., Calistoga; (707) 942-6122. Specializing in Japanese enzyme baths; cost: $40.00, $60.00 with one-hour massage. Mud baths $29.00, with half-hour massage $47.00. Also variety of other spa treatments. Pools and accommodations available at the adjoining Roman Spa.

Le Spa Francais, 1880 Lincoln Ave., Calistoga; (707) 942-4636. Large outdoor pool, indoor hot mineral pool, sauna, jacuzzi, and full range of spa treatments. Mud bath $29.00, with massage $45.00. 42 lodging units; $60-$75.

Nance's Hot Springs, 1614 Lincoln Ave., Calistoga; (707) 942-6211. Family owned and operated spa resort, with hot mineral pool, whirlpool, hot sulphur and steam baths, and volcanic ash mud baths. Cost of mud bath $30.00, with massage $47.00. Also available are 24 lodging units, with TV, air-conditioning, and kitchenettes; $45-$65.

Lincoln Avenue Spa, 1339 Lincoln Ave., Calistoga; (707) 942-5296. Treatments offered here include mud wraps, herbal wraps, accupressure face-lifts and foot reflexology. Cost for mud wrap is $28.00, with massage $44.00; herbal wrap $28.00, with massage $44.00. No accommodations.

SEASONAL EVENTS

March. *Great Chefs Series.* Robert Mondavi Winery, Oakville; (707) 944-2866. Series of cooking schools, conducted by internationally-acclaimed chefs. Held during March and April.

April. *Great Chefs Series.* Robert Mondavi Winery, Oakville; (707) 944-2866.

June. *Concours d'Elegance.* Silverado Country Club, 1600 Atlas Peak Rd., Napa; (415) 652-9202. 1st weekend of the month. Popular annual event, usually featuring over 100 vintage cars. *Monday Night Concerts.* At the Domaine Chandon winery, Yountville. Features musical acts each Monday of the month. For a schedule, call the winery. (707) 944-2866. *Robert Mondavi Summer Festival.* At the Robert Mondavi Winery in Oakville, just south of St. Helena. Series of six jazz concerts, held on Sunday evenings, in June and July. Also wine and cheese tasting, featuring Rouge et Noir cheeses; informal picnics. Advance reservations required; for schedule and tickets, call the winery at (707) 963-JASS. *Napa Valley Wine Auction.* At the Meadowood Resort; last weekend of the month. Auction sponsored by Napa Valley Vintners Association to benefit local medical facilities. Candlelight banquet and dancing; barrel tastings, wine futures. For details, call (707) 963-5246.

July. *Napa County Fair.* Held at the Fairgrounds in Calistoga during the first week of the month. Activities include a carnival, horse show, wine show, exhibits and stage shows. (707) 942-6333. *Sharpsteen Annual Rummage Sale.* At the Sharpsteen Museum on Washington St., Calistoga; also during the first week of the month. (707) 942-6333. *Fourth of July Celebrations.* Lincoln Ave., Calistoga. Colorful parade down the main street of town, followed by fireworks at the Fairgrounds. (707) 942-6333. *4th of July Fireworks.* Kennedy Park, Napa; (707) 252-7800. *Fourth of July Celebration.* Domaine Chandon Winery, Yountville; (707) 944-2280. *Bastille Day Celebration.* Domaine Chandon Winery, Yountville; (707) 944-2280. Celebration of France's national holiday, held on July 14th.

August. *Napa Town & Country Fair.* Town & Country Fairgrounds, Napa. 1st week of the month. 5-day fair, with rodeo, wine show, livestock and agricultural exhibits; also art show, stage shows, and horse show. (707) 224-7951.

September. *Antique Show.* Town & Country Fairgrounds, Napa; (707) 265-5520. 3-day show, held during the first week of the month. Hundreds of dealers exhibit and sell antiques. *Wappo Indian Art Exhibit.* Held at the Vintage Hall, 473 Main St.; second week of the month. Annual event, featuring exhibits of the life and history of local Wappo Indians. (707) 963-7411.

October. *Oktoberfest.* Town & Country Fairgrounds, Napa; (707) 226-7455. German beer, food and music. *Yountville Days Festival.* Yountville; (707) 224-2937. Parade, arts and crafts show, entertainment and refreshments. *Great Chefs Series.* Robert Mondavi Winery, Oakville; (707) 944-2866. Series of cooking schools, conducted by internationally-acclaimed chefs. Held during October and November.

November. *Napa Valley Wine Festival.* Town & Country Fairgrounds, Napa; (707) 252-7122. 1st weekend of the month. Wine tasting and auction. *Gifts & Thyme.* Town & Country Fairgrounds, Napa. 3-day event during the 3rd week of the month. Arts and crafts exhibition and sale. *Great Chefs Series.* Robert Mondavi Winery, Oakville; (707) 944-2866.

PLACES OF INTEREST

Keith Rosenthal Theatre, Vintage 1870, Yountville; (707) 944-2525. 15-minute show featuring the four seasons in the Napa Valley and the Falcon Crest mansion. Shows daily 9.30-6.30 July-Oct., 10-5 Nov.-June. Admission $3.00 adults, $2.50 seniors, $1.00 children.

Vintage 1870, Washington St., Yountville; (707) 944-2451. Open daily 10-5.30. 40 shops and restaurants in 110-year-old winery buildings.

California Veteran's Home, Yountville; (707) 944-4000. Museum housed in the Armistice Chapel with displays honoring the veterans of foreign wars. Museum open to the public.

Lake Berryessa, Route 128 east; (707) 996-2111. Boating, fishing, water skiing, camping, picnicking and barbeque areas. Several resorts with RV hookups, accommodations and restaurants.

Lake Hennessy, Hwy. 128 (3 miles from Rutherford Cross Road), Rutherford. Picnic and barbeque areas, fishing.

Skyline Park, Imola and 4th Aves., Napa. Camping, hiking, picnicking, horseback riding.

Napa Valley Marina, west side of Napa River, off Milton Rd., Napa. Fishing, boat launching facilities, fishing and boating equipment sales.

Bale Grist Mill. 3 miles north of St. Helena on Hwy. 29. Historic, water-powered mill, built in 1846 by pioneer settler Dr. Edward Turner Bale, to grind corn. The mill is now owned and maintained by the State Parks Department, and is presently being restored. Mill building houses a small museum, with displays of old photographs and local-interest artifacts. Some walking possibilities in park. Open daily; admission for museum: $1.00.

Silverado Museum. 1490 Library Lane. Small museum, devoted to the collecting, preserving and exhibiting of artifacts pertaining to the life and works of Robert Louis Stevenson (author of *Kidnapped, Treasure Island* and *Doctor Jekyll and Mr. Hyde,* among others). Contains over 7,800 items of Stevenson memorabilia, believed to be the largest collection of Stevensoniana in the world. Exhibits include many first editions, letters, photographs, original manuscripts, personal and work-related items, and paintings and sculptures of the author. Free admission; open Tues.-Sun. 12-4.

Napa Valley Wine Library. Housed in the St. Helena Public Library Building, at 1492 Library Lane. Contains approximately 3,000 volumes on wine and wine-related subjects—including books, magazines, journals and special publications— claimed to be one of the largest such collections of wine literature on the West Coast. The library also schedules wine appreciation seminars and wine tastings during summer.

Bothe-Napa Valley State Park. Delightful 1800-acre park, with forests of redwood, fir, oak and madrone, and wildflowers in spring. Park facilities include camping, picnicking, hiking and swimming. Admission: $3.00 per car, $1.00 additional for use of pool. Open daily.

The Sharpsteen Museum, 1311 Washington St.; (707) 942-5911. Unique small museum, founded by Disney producer Ben Sharpsteen. Displays are of items of local historical interest, and include a superb scale model diorama of Calistoga as it appeared in 1865; other dioramas feature the Chinese quarter of town, railroad depot, and the life of Robert Louis Stevenson. Also, adjoining the museum is the old Brannan Cottage, dating from the 1860s and now restored to its former glory; it, too, can be visited. The museum is open daily 1-4 in summer, 12-4 in winter; no admission fee.

Robert Louis Stevenson State Park. Hwy. 29, 5 miles north of Calistoga;

(707) 942-4575. Undeveloped 4,000-acre park, containing Mount St. Helena. Novelist Robert Louis Stevenson spent his honeymoon here in 1880, in a cottage at the base of Mount St. Helena. A hiking trail now journeys to the top of the mountain, with sweeping valley views to be enjoyed from the summit. There are no facilities available at park; bring your own water. Free admission.

The Old Calistoga Depot. 1458 Lincoln Ave.; (707) 942-6332. Second oldest railroad depot in California, built in 1866. The Depot now houses a shopping arcade, with a restaurant and specialty shops; it also features a restored, 112-year-old passenger coach inside the arcade. Alongside the depot are six refurbished rail-cars, housing specialty shops featuring unique gifts and old-fashioned candy. Shops are open daily.

Old Faithful Geyser. 1299 Tubbs Lane (2 miles north of Calistoga, off Hwy. 128). Oldest and most famous of Calistoga's geysers, and one of only three regularly erupting geysers in the world; erupts approximately every 40 minutes, in a fountain of boiling hot water and steam, some 60 feet directly into the air. Picnic area at site. Admission $2.00 per person. Open daily, 9-6 in summer and 9-5 in winter.

The Petrified Forest. Petrified Forest Road, 6 miles northwest of Calistoga; (707) 942-6667. View giant redwoods in an ancient forest, all uprooted during the volcanic period millions of years ago, and turned to stone. The largest of these, the "Queen of the Forest," measures 80 feet in length and 8 feet in diameter. Picnic area, and museum and gift shop on premises. Admission: $4.00 adults, $2.50 children. Open daily 10-5.

Pioneer Cemetary. Foothill Blvd.. Historic cemetary, with graves of early settlers; some headstones date from 1885.

Also see **Spa Resorts** under *Accommodations*.

RECREATION

Ballooning. Hot-air ballooning is an increasingly popular recreational sport in the Napa Valley, with several different balloon companies offering scenic flights over valley vineyards, usually with a champagne reception or a champagne brunch to follow. Flight cost is around $155.00 per person. For more information, and flight reservations, contact any of the following: *Balloon Aviation of Napa Valley,* 2299 Third Street, Napa, (707) 252-7067; *Balloons Above The Valley,* P.O. Box 3838, Napa, (707) 253-2222/(800) 233-7681; *Bonaventura Balloon Company,* 133 Wall Road, Napa, (707) 944-2822; *Napa's Great Balloon Escape,* P.O. Box 4197, Napa, (707) 253-0860; *Above the West,* P.O. Box 2290, 6744 Washington St., Yountville; (707) 944-8638; *Adventures Aloft.* At Vintage 1870, Yountville; (707) 255-8688. *Napa Valley Balloons, Inc.,* Yountville, (707) 253-2224; *Once in a Lifetime Balloon Co.,* 1458 Lincoln Ave., #12, Calistoga, (707) 942-5641/(800) 722-6665.

Soaring. *Calistoga Soaring Center,* 1546 Lincoln Ave.; (707) 942-5592/(800) 262-SOAR. The Center offers half-hour scenic flights over the valley, as well as lessons, and sailplane rentals. Cost: $79.50 for a scenic flight for two people; $64.50 for a 20-minute introductory lesson; and $30-$42 for plane rentals.

Tours. *Napa Valley Excursions.* 1825 Lincoln Ave., Napa; (707) 252-6333. Tours of the Napa Valley. *California Wine Adventures.* 1459 Yountville Cross-road, Yountville; (707) 944-8468. Personalized tours of Napa wineries, conducted by residents of the Napa Valley. Group or individual tours. *Grape Line Tours,* Campbell; (408) 866-1400/(800) 675-7433. Bus tours of local wineries;

also shuttle service from the Bay Area to connect with the Wine Train.

Rail Tours. *Napa Valley Wine Train,* 1275 McKinstry Street, Napa; (707) 253-2111/(800) 522-4142. 32-mile tours aboard restored 1920s Pullman lounge cars. Train fare: $25.00 weekdays, $29.00 weekends; lunch and dinner available at additional cost. Call for reservations, schedules and more information.

Boat Cruises. *Napa Riverboat Company,* Napa Valley Marina, 1200 Milton Road, Napa; (707) 226-2628. Small, authentic sternwheeler, offering daily 90-minute historical excursions down the Napa River, as well as weekend sunset dinner cruises and Sunday brunch cruises. Reservations required.

Bicycling. The Napa Valley offers excellent bicycling possibilities, with several back-country roads criss-crossing between vineyards, all across the valley. Good bicycling areas are the *Lower Napa Valley, Yountville area, Los Carneros district, the Old Sonoma Road, Silverado Trail,* and *Mt. Veeder Road.* For bicycle rentals and service, contact either *St. Helena Cyclery,* 1156 Main St., St. Helena, (707) 963-7736; or *Jules Culver Bicycles,* at 1227-D Lincoln Ave., Calistoga, (707) 942-0421.

Tennis. *Napa High School.* 2475 Jefferson St., Napa; 6 courts, 2 with lights. *Redwood Middle School.* 3600 Oxford St., Napa; 4 courts. *Silverado Middle School.* 1133 Coombsville Rd., Napa; 8 courts, 4 with lights. *Temescal High School.* 2447 Old Sonoma Rd., Napa; 5 courts. *Vintage High School.* 1375 Trower Ave., Napa; 14 courts. *Crane Park,* Grayson Ave, St. Helena. 2 courts; no lights. *Robert Louis Stevenson School,* 1316 Hillview Place, St. Helena. 2 courts; no lights. *St. Helena High School,* 1401 Grayson Ave., St. Helena. 2 courts with lights. *Monhoff Center,* cnr. Stevenson and Grant Sts., Calistoga; (707) 942-5188. Facilities include 4 tennis courts and 2 raquetball courts; night lights.

Swimming. *Bothe-Napa Valley State Park,* 3601 St. Helena Hwy. North; (707) 942-4575. Admission $3.00 per car, $1.00 additional for pool use.

Horseback Riding. There are several stables in the area, offering horseback riding; horse rentals are generally $10-$15 per hour, and breakfast rides and dinner rides cost around $35.00 per person. For reservations and more information on horseback riding possibilities, contact any of the following area stables: *Oak Leaf Ranch,* 1066 Wyatt Ave., Napa, (707) 224-3977; *Silverado Trail Equestrian Center,* 4089 Silverado Trail, Napa, (707) 255-9606; *Wild Horse Valley Ranch,* Wild Horse Valley Road, Napa, (707) 224-0727; *Old West Riding Stables,* Skyline Wilderness Park, Fourth and Imola Sts., Napa, (707) 252-0481; *Oak Hill Stables,* 3485 Porter Creek Road, Santa Rosa (8 miles from Calistoga), (707) 528-6498.

GOLF

Chimney Rock Golf Course, 5320 Silverado Trail, Napa; (707) 255-3363. 9-hole public course; 3,386 yards, 36 Par. Golf carts and club rentals, pro shop, lessons. Coffee shop. Green fees: $10.00 weekdays, $13.00 weekends.

Napa Municipal Golf Course, 2295 Streblow Drive, Napa; (707) 255-4333. 18-hole public course; 6,480 yards, 72 Par. Golf cart and club rentals, pro shop, lessons, driving range and putting green. Coffee shop and cocktail lounge. Green fees: $10.00 weekdays, $17.00 weekends. Also twilight specials.

Napa Valley Country Club, Hagen Road (off Silverado Trail), Napa; (707) 252-1114. 9-hole private golf club. 2,909 yards, 36 Par. Electric carts, pro shop, restaurant. Green fees: $22.00.

Silverado Country Club, 1600 Atlas Peak Road, Napa; (707) 257-0200. Two 18-hole Robert Trent Jones-designed courses. The North Course is 6,896 yards, 72 Par; the South Course is 6,632 yards, 72 Par. Dining room, snack bar, pro shop. Green fees: $70.00 including cart (cart mandatory).

Meadowood Resort, 900 Meadowood Lane; (707) 963-3646. 9-hole private course, 4170 yards, Par 62; green fees: $20.00. Pro shop, hand-cart rentals, dining room and snack bar.

Mount St. Helena Golf Course. Located at the Fairgrounds in Calistoga; (707) 942-9966. 9-hole course, 2,700 yards, 34 Par; green fees: $7.00 weekdays, $8.00 weekends. Facilities include a clubhouse, coffee shop, rental of clubs and hand carts, pro shop, putting green, and practice fairway.

RESTAURANTS

(Restaurant prices—based on full course dinner, excluding drinks, tax and tips—are categorized as follows: *Deluxe*, over $30; *Expensive*, $20-$30; *Moderate*, $10-$20; *Inexpensive*, under $10.)

Napa

Royal Oak. *Expensive-Deluxe.* At the Silverado Country Club, 1600 Atlas Peak Rd., Napa; (707) 257-0200, ext. 5531. Comfortable gourmet restaurant, featuring hand-carved tables, open beams, and brick and copper accents. Emphasis on fresh seafood and prime steaks. Open for lunch and dinner Mon.-Sat., brunch on Sundays. Reservations required.

Vintners Court. *Expensive-Deluxe.* At the Silverado Country Club, 1600 Atlas Peak Rd., Napa; (707) 257- 0200. Elegant dining room, with chandelier and grand piano. Menu features California cuisine with fresh seafood, duck, venison and steak specialties. Open for dinner Wed.-Sat., brunch on Sundays. Also seafood buffet on Fridays. Reservations recommended.

The Penguin's Fish Grotto. *Moderate-Expensive.* 1533 Trancas St., Napa; (707) 252-4343. Fresh seafood, veal and charbroiled specialties. Open for lunch Mon.-Fri., dinner Mon.-Sat. Reservations recommended.

The Red Hen Cantina. *Moderate.* 5091 St. Helena Hwy., Napa; (707) 255-8125. Authentic Mexican cooking. Brick patio for outdoor dining. Lunch and dinner daily.

La Crepe Cafe. *Inexpensive.* 976 Pearl St., Napa; (707) 226-5642. Specializing in French crepes, including Crepe Suzette and a variety of dessert as well as vegetable, meat, and cheese crepes. Also salads, sandwiches and soups. Open Tues.-Sat. 10.30 a.m.-9 p.m., Sun. 10 a.m.-2 p.m.

Willett's Brewing Co. *Inexpensive-Moderate.* 902 Main St., Napa; (707) 258-2337. Pub-style restaurant, overlooking the Napa River. Barbequed and grilled specialties, and pastas, pizzas, sandwiches and salads. Also locally-brewed beer. Open for lunch and dinner Mon.-Sat.

Yountville

Domaine Chandon. *Expensive-Deluxe.* California Drive, Yountville; (707) 944-2892. Elegant little restaurant, located at the Domaine Chandon Winery, specializing in creative California and French cuisine. Secluded garden patio for outdoor dining in summer. Lunch and dinner daily daily (closed Mon. and Tues. in winter). Reservations recommended (2 weeks in advance).

Mustard's Grill. *Expensive.* 7399 St. Helena Hwy., Yountville; (707) 944-2424. Popular Napa Valley restaurant, located just north of Yountville. Mesquite-grilled seafood, American, Italian and Continental specialties, prepared in oakwood-burning oven. Also sandwiches. Open for lunch and dinner daily. Reservations suggested.

Mama Nina's. *Moderate.* 6772 Washington St., Yountville; (707) 944-2112. Italian cuisine, featuring fresh pastas prepared daily. House specialty is Fettucini al' Alfredo. Lunch and dinner daily; closed Wed. in winter. Reservations recommended.

Maison Rouge. *Expensive-Deluxe.* 6534 Washington St., Yountville; (707) 944-2521. French restaurant in downtown Yountville. Open for lunch and dinner Tues.-Sun. Reservations recommended.

Compadres Mexican Restaurant. *Expensive.* 6539 Washington St., Yountville; (707) 944-2406. Authentic Mexican cooking. Restaurant open for lunch and dinner daily.

California Cafe Bar & Grill. *Moderate.* Hwy. 29 and Madison St., Yountville; (707) 944-2330. Specializing in California cuisine; also homemade pastas and house-smoked foods, mesquite-grilled seafood and Cajun specialties. Menu changes daily. Extensive wine list. Open for lunch and dinner daily, and Sunday brunch.

Anestis. *Moderate.* 6518 Washington St., Yountville; (707) 944-1500. Specializing in Greek and American preparations; also burgers and steaks. Delightful patio with vineyard views. Open for lunch and dinner daily. Reservations suggested.

Rutherford

Auberge du Soleil. *Deluxe.* 180 Rutherford Hill Rd., Rutherford; (707) 963-1211. Elegant French restaurant, located high above the valley floor, with spectacular vineyard views. Prix fixe meals; menu changes daily. Extensive wine list. Open for lunch and dinner Thurs.-Tues. Reservations required.

St. Helena

The Starmont. *Expensive.* Meadowood Resort, 900 Meadowood Lane, St. Helena; (707) 963-3646. Elegant Napa Valley restaurant, overlooking golf course. Menu features California country cuisine, with emphasis on duck, venison and seafood preparations. Prix fixe dinners, from 6 p.m. daily; also Sunday brunch.

The Fairway Grill. *Moderate.* Meadowood Resort, 900 Meadowood Lane, St. Helena; (707) 963-3646. Salads, soups, sandwiches; also burgers and other grilled entrees. Casual bistro atmosphere; golf course setting. Open for breakfast, lunch and dinner.

The Spot. *Inexpensive.* 587 St. Helena Hwy., St. Helena; (707) 963-2844. Fifty's-style hamburger joint, authentic down to the jukebox and black and white checkered floor. Hamburgers, sandwiches, salad bar and pizza. Hours: 11.30 a.m.-9 p.m.

Spring Street. *Moderate.* 1245 Spring St. (cnr. of Oak), St. Helena; (707) 963-5578. Housed in delightful, early 1900s bungalow, with vine-covered patio. Homestyle dinners, featuring steaks, pasta, fish and barbequed specialties; also homemade desserts, and light luncheons. Open daily, 11 a.m.-2.30 p.m. and 5 p.m.-8.30. p.m.; brunch on weekends.

Knickerbockers. *Moderate.* 3010 N. St. Helena Hwy., St. Helena; (707) 967-9300. Casual restaurant, located adjacent to the Freemark Abbey Winery complex. Features salads, sandwiches, and a variety of creative California dishes. Napa Valley wines; patio for outdoor dining. Open for lunch Tues.-Sat., dinner Wed.-Sun.

Miramonte Restaurant. *Deluxe.* 1327 Railroad Ave., St. Helena; (707) 963-3970. French country-style and nouvelle cuisine, served in three cozy dining rooms. Prix fixe five-course dinners; reservations required. Closed Mon. and Tues.

The Vines. *Moderate.* 3111 N. St. Helena Hwy., St. Helena; (707) 963-8991. Continental and regional wine country cuisine. Deck for outdoor dining; vineyard views. Open for lunch and dinner daily.

Teng's Chinese Restaurant. *Inexpensive-Moderate.* 1113 Hunt Ave., St. Helena; (707) 963-1161. Specializing in Mandarin cuisine. Daily lunch specials; family dinners. 11.30 a.m.-3 p.m.; 4.30 p.m.-10 p.m.

Trilogy. *Moderate-Expensive.* 1234 Main St., St. Helena; (707) 963-5507. Small, intimate restaurant, offering French and California cuisine, with emphasis on fresh fish and poultry and local produce. Extensive wine list. Open for lunch and dinner Thurs.-Tues. Reservations recommended.

Freemark Abbey. *Moderate.* 3020 N. St. Helena Hwy., St. Helena; (707) 963-2706. Located in the Freemark Abbey Winery complex. Features Continental and contemporary California cuisine. Extensive wine list. Relaxed atmosphere. Lunch and dinner, Wed.-Sun.

Calistoga

Alex's. *Moderate-Expensive.* 1437 Lincoln Ave., Calistoga; (707) 942-6868. House specialties include prime rib and seafood. Fresh fruit daiquiris. Open for breakfast, lunch and dinner daily.

All Seasons Market and Cafe. *Inexpensive-Moderate.* 1400 Lincoln Ave., Calistoga; (707) 942-9111. Deli-cum-cafe, with a small restaurant, pastry shop, wine shop, delicatessen and market. Restaurant serves soups, sandwiches, salads, pate, and homemade croissants; also delicious pastries and ice cream. Napa Valley wines by the glass. Lunch daily; brunch and dinner on weekends.

Calistoga Inn. *Moderate.* 1250 Lincoln Ave., Calistoga; (707) 942-4101. Seafood and continental specialties, served in a relaxed, turn-of-the-century atmosphere; menu changes daily. Garden patio for outdoor dining. Extensive wine list; full bar. Dinners from 5.30 p.m. daily; lunch in summer. Reservations required.

Silverado Restaurant. *Moderate.* 1374 Lincoln Ave., Calistoga; (707) 942-6725. Spacious downtown restaurant, with a country charm. Features creative local and regional American cooking; specialties include Roast Duckling and homemade pasta. Award-winning wine list, with nearly 1,500 wine selections, mostly from small California wineries. Breakfast, lunch and dinner daily.

The Cinnabar Restaurant and Cafe. *Moderate.* 1440 Lincoln Ave., Calistoga; (707) 942-6989. Elegantly-furnished, established Calistoga restaurant serving omelettes, hot cakes, burgers and sandwiches; also fresh fish, broiled steaks, chicken and crepes. Wine by the glass, fresh fruit drinks and daiquiris; expresso bar. Open 7.30 a.m.-10 p.m. daily.

Soo Yuan Restaurant. *Inexpensive.* 1345 Lincoln Ave., Calistoga; (707) 942-9404. Mandarin and Szechuan cuisine. Open for lunch and dinner daily.

Bosko's Ristorante. *Moderate.* 1403 Lincoln Ave., Calistoga; (707) 942-9088. Delightful Italian restaurant, specializing in homemade pasta and Italian desserts. Expresso bar, wine bar. Casual atmosphere. Open for lunch and dinner daily.

Las Brasas. *Inexpensive-Moderate.* 1350 Lincoln Ave., Calistoga; (707)

942-4056. Mexican dishes, fresh seafood and mesquite grilled specialties; also combination platters. Lunch and dinner daily.

Mount View Hotel. *Moderate-Expensive.* 1475 Lincoln Ave., Calistoga; (707) 942-6877. Wine country cuisine, served in Art Deco-style dining room. House specialties include fresh fish and poultry, with locally-grown vegetables and fruit. Extensive wine list, featuring Napa and Sonoma county wines. Open for lunch and dinner daily; brunch on Sundays. Live jazz on weekends.

PICNIC FARE

The Fickle Pickle Delicatessen. 1222 Trancas St., Napa; (707) 252-0233. Sandwiches, cold cuts and cheeses; also salads.

Andrews Meat Co. & Delicatessen. 1245 Main Street, Napa; (707) 253-8311. Salads, cheeses, cold cuts and sandwiches.

Oakville Grocery Company. 7856 St. Helena Hwy., Oakville; (707) 944-8802. Sandwiches, meats and cheeses, freshly-baked sourdough French bread; wine cellar.

The Cottage Delicatessen. Rutherford Square, cnr. Hwy. 29 and Rutherford Crossroad, Rutherford; (707) 963-2317. Sandwiches, cheeses, cold cuts, home-made soups, quiche, wine and imported beer.

V. Sattui Winery Delicatessen. White Lane, St. Helena; (707) 963-7774. Salami, cheeses, homemade paté, oven-fresh French bread, cheesecake and fresh fruit. Also estate-bottled wine.

St. Helena Deli & Fine Foods. 61 Main St., St. Helena; (707) 963-3235. Croissants, pasta salad, homemade soups, sandwiches and cheeses. Excellent wine selection.

Karen Mitchell & Co. 1357 Main St., St. Helena; (707) 963-9731. Salads, cheeses, homemade patés, fresh baguettes, desserts.

Fellion's Delicatessen. 1359 Lincoln Ave., Calistoga; (707) 942-6144. Sandwiches, cheeses and meats, salads and wine.

SONOMA VALLEY

Ancient Vineyards and California History

Sonoma Valley—popularized by novelist Jack London as the "Valley of the Moon"—is one of the oldest wine-growing regions in the California wine country. Some of the vineyards in the valley date from the early 1820s, first planted by the Franciscans who built the Sonoma Mission; some date from the 1850s and 1860s, originally part of the historic Buena Vista estate founded by Count Agoston Haraszthy, the acknowledged "father" of California viticulture. There are also two dozen or so small to medium-sized wineries here, some of them indeed quite historic, among them Buena Vista, Sebastiani, Gundlach-Bundschu, and Valley of the Moon.

The Sonoma Valley itself is a narrow, north-south valley, some 20 miles long, flanked on its west by the Sonoma Mountain and on its east by the Mayacamas range—beyond which lies the celebrated Napa Valley. At the southern end of the valley, of course, sits the historic little town of Sonoma, and at its north end is the city of Santa Rosa. Two other towns of importance in the valley are Glen Ellen and Kenwood, both situated in the upper part of the valley.

The Sonoma Valley lies northeast of San Francisco, reached on Highway 101 north and 37 and 121 northeast. The valley can also be reached on Highway 121 westward from the nearby town of Napa, situated at the south end of the Napa Valley.

SONOMA

Clearly, the best starting point for a tour of the Sonoma Valley is the historic little town of Sonoma itself, situated at the bottom end of the valley and notable as the birthplace of the California Republic and of California's wine industry. Sonoma has in it a dozen or so small, delightful wineries, many of them dating from the 1800s, as well as some historic vineyards. It also has some good bed and breakfast accommodations, a fine selection of restaurants, and import and specialty shops and art galleries.

At the center of town, of course, is the famous Sonoma Plaza, the largest and most picturesque of California's Spanish-style plazas. Several historic and lovely buildings surround the plaza, among them the El Dorado, Sonoma and Swiss hotels, dating from the 1830s and 1840s, and all beautifully restored to their original splendor; and the Toscano Hotel, also dating from the 1840s, with its colorful display of flags that have flown over Sonoma—Russian, British, Spanish, Mexican Empire, Mexican Republic, Bear Flag, and Stars and Stripes. Also of interest are the old Casa Grande quarters where General Vallejo's Indian servants were once housed; and the Sonoma Barracks, dating from 1836, which have some worthwhile exhibits of the Indian, Mexican and early American periods, and where you can also see the original barracks compound, enclosed by thick adobe walls. The Sonoma Mission, directly across from the Sonoma Barracks, dates from 1823 and is notable as the last and northernmost of California's 21 Spanish missions; it, too, has some good historical displays, largely mission relics.

Among other places of visitor interest here are the El Paseo de Sonoma and Place des Pyrenees, two small, Spanish-style courtyard malls, containing a variety of interesting little shops and restaurants. Worth visiting, too, are the Sonoma French Bakery, noted for its Sourdough French Bread and baguettes; and the Sonoma Cheese Factory, the most famous of them all, home of the Sonoma Jack Cheese, and where you can enjoy ongoing tours of the factory, highlighting the cheese-making process. The Sonoma Cheese Factory also has a well-stocked deli, specializing in picnic lunches.

At the center of the plaza itself is a delightful park with picnic tables, duck ponds, flower bushes, an open-air theater, a children's play area, and a large bronze statue commemorating the Bear Flag Revolt—a memorable, historic event in which, in 1846, thirty American frontiersmen rode into town, took captive the Mexican commandante, General Mariano Vallejo, and declared here an independent Bear Flag Republic, raising a handmade "Bear Flag" which remains today the official flag of the State of California. Also try to visit the picturesque old Sonoma City Hall at the south end of the plaza park, built in 1905, using native stone and brick.

Other places worth visiting in Sonoma include the Depot Park on East First Street, just off the plaza, which has a railroad museum and children's play area; and the Train Town at the south end of town on

Broadway, where you can enjoy steam-train rides around a 10-acre landscaped park, featuring tunnels and bridges. Also, a little way to the west of the plaza, off Spain and West Third streets, is the splendid Vallejo Home, also known as Lachryma Montis (Spanish for "mountain tears"), named for the natural springs on the estate. The home dates from 1851, and is now part of the Sonoma State Historic Park, open to public viewing. There are some beautiful, shaded grounds here, with age-old trees and flower beds overflowing with seasonal color.

Besides the town and its plaza, however, Sonoma's great lure to visitors is its wineries—small, charming, and many of them quite historic. Closest, of course, is Sebastiani Vineyards, situated on East Spain Street, just to the west of the plaza. The winery dates from 1904, originally founded by Italian immigrant Samuele Sebastiani, and still owned and operated by the Sebastiani family. Public tours of the facility include the winery's aging cellars, where you can view one of the finest collections of hand-carved redwood casks in North America. The winery also has a comfortable tasting room, and a small picnic area at its front, where there is an antique grape press on display, with which, we are told, Samuele Sebastiani made his first wine in 1895.

A little farther, northeast on the Old Winery Road, is the historic Buena Vista Winery, dating from 1857 and housed in a picturesque old stone cellar. Buena Vista was originally founded by Count Agoston Haraszthy, the acknowledged "father" of the California wine industry, who imported into California in 1861 some 100,000 cuttings of 300 grape varieties from Europe's famed wine regions, giving the state's wine industry its start. The winery now has a superb tasting room, a large, shaded picnic area, nature trail, and self-guided tours of its wine museum and ancient aging caves where cream sherry is still aged in oak barrels. During the summer months, the winery features outdoor music concerts and other special events.

Two other wineries, well worth visiting, are the Hacienda Cellars and Gundlach-Bundschu Winery, located on Vineyard Lane and Thornberry Road (southeast of the Sonoma township), respectively. The first of these, Hacienda, is housed in a Spanish villa and is especially notable for its delightful picnic area, which overlooks the ancient, 50-acre Buena Vista Vineyard, originally established by Agoston Haraszthy in 1862, and now part of the Hacienda estate. Gundlach-Bundschu, founded in 1858, is also quite lovely, housed in an old native-stone building. It has wine tasting and retail sales, a picnic area, and a small reservoir adjacent to the winery. Both wineries offer primarily vintage-dated varietal wines from their Sonoma Valley vineyards.

Just to the north of Sonoma, and also with visitor interest, are the small, family-owned-and-operated Haywood Winery, situated on Gehricke Road, on the slopes of the little-known Chamizal Valley; and tiny Hanzell, a 3,000-case winery housed in a stone chateau, originally established in 1957 by the late Ambassador James Zellerbach. Hanzell, of course, is located on Lomita Avenue, north of Sonoma, and requires an appointment to visit.

Also in the Sonoma area, just to the south on Broadway, is

Ravenswood, another small winery, specializing in vineyard-designated, Sonoma County varietal wines which are fermented with wild yeast and aged in oak—in typical Ravenswood style! Another, the newly-opened Spanish-style Gloria Ferrer Champagne Caves, one of the newest and largest sparkling wine producers in the valley, is located some 3 or 4 miles south of Sonoma on Highway 121, near the tiny community of Schellville. Gloria Ferrer, in fact, represents a $12-million investment by Freixenet of Spain, the largest and best-known *méthode champenoise* sparkling wine producer in the world. The winery has public tours of its facility, which include a visit to its newly-excavated limestone caves, built into the hillside adjacent to the winery. There is also a delightful, spacious patio here, overlooking estate vineyards planted primarily to Chardonnay and Pinot Noir.

THE SONOMA VALLEY

The Sonoma Valley—the section from just above the town of Sonoma to the foot of the Santa Rosa hills in the north—is small, narrow, and approximately 15 miles long, flanked by the Mayacamas Mountain Range on its east—beyond which lies the celebrated Napa Valley—and the Sonoma Mountain on its west. The valley, quite notably, boasts more than a dozen appellations, and some 6,000 acres or so of vineyards, planted primarily to white varietal winegrapes. It also has in it seven or eight charming little wineries, some of them quite historic, and two equally lovely small towns, Kenwood and Glen Ellen.

The Sonoma Valley, it must also be fair to say, is really quite easy to tour, just staying on the main highway—12—which heads out north-westward from the town of Sonoma, through the tiny communities of Boyes Hot Springs, Fetters Hot Springs, Agua Caliente, and directly into the Sonoma Valley. Most of the wineries are located on the highway itself, with a brief detour leading westward to Glen Ellen, where you can visit two or three more wineries and a state historic park of much interest.

At the bottom of the tour, of course, southernmost in the valley is the historic Valley of the Moon Winery, dating from 1857 and originally part of the ancient Agua Caliente Mexican landgrant. The vineyard estate, in fact, was owned, at different times, by General "Fighting Joe Hooker" of Civil War fame, Eli Sheppard who served as the American Consul to China, and George Hearst, U.S. Senator and father of newspaper tycoon William Randolph Hearst. It is now owned by descendants of the Parducci family, associated with California wine for more than half a century. The winery produces largely jug wines, some generics, and a line of primarily estate-grown varietal wines.

A little to the north of the Valley of the Moon Winery, two miles or so, Arnold Drive branches off Highway 12, westward, to lead to Glen Ellen. But before Glen Ellen, off on the tiny Dunbar Road and Vintage Lane, is another historic winery, Grand Cru, located on the site of a 100-year-old wine cellar, but itself housed in a lovely, redwood A-frame building. The winery, in fact, offers a unique contrast between the old and new, utilizing the most modern, scientific equipment and wine-making techniques, together with some century-old stone and concrete fermentation tanks. Grand Cru produces primarily varietal wines from Sonoma Valley grapes.

Glen Ellen, a little farther on Arnold Drive, is a delightful little town nestled along the eastern slopes of the Sonoma Mountain. It has in it two or three splendid bed and breakfast inns and a worthwhile restaurant or two. But best of all, adjoining to the west of town, is the 800-acre Jack London State Historic Park, with its associations to famous American writer Jack London—author of *Call of the Wild* (1903), *White Fang* (1906) and *Burning Daylight* (1910), among others. The park actually comprises London's legendary "Beauty Ranch," where the author lived and worked during his latter years, until his death in 1916, and where you can now explore the charred remains of his dream mansion, the "Wolf House," and visit his grave, simply marked with a boulder. In the park, too, is "The House of Happy Walls," a lovely stone mansion built in 1919 by Jack London's wife, Charmain, and which now houses a museum with displays of furnishings and other items from London's original study as well as the Wolf House, and the author's collection of South Pacific art. The park also has some good hiking, picnicking and horseback riding possibilities.

Directly below the Jack London Park, and well worth visiting, is the historic Glen Ellen Winery, situated on property that was originally part of the 122-acre Rancho Petaluma Mexican landgrant, and itself dating from the 1860s. The winery has some good shaded areas for picnicking, and a tasting room housed in a restored 19th-century wood-frame building. The winery produces, for the large part, varietal wines from its estate.

From Glen Ellen, you can return via Arnold Drive to our original point of departure on the highway (12), some 5 miles north of which lies the small valley town of Kenwood, with a handful of shops, a cafe or two, and some important wineries. Just south of town, of course, are the Smothers Brothers' tasting room, housed in a small, Western-style building, and owned by the well-known comedians, Tom and Dick Smothers, who offer primarily varietal wines from their Santa Cruz County vineyards; and the Kenwood Winery, which is housed in a large wooden barn-like structure, dating from the turn of the century. The Kenwood Winery is one of the largest in the valley, with its annual production in excess of 40,000 cases, mostly devoted to varietal wines, but with one or two vintage-dated generics featured as well.

North of Kenwood, a half-mile or so, is Chateau St. Jean (pronounced, by the way, "Jean" and not "Jawn"), one of the valley's best known and most prestigious wineries. It is housed in a picturesque chateau-style building, complete with a turreted tower, and surrounded by well-kept landscaped grounds with picnic facilities. St. Jean is primarily a white varietal wine producer, with some sparkling wine bottled at a separate facility, some 25 miles from the winery. The winery also has an excellent, self-guided, educational tour of its facility, commencing in the fermentation cellar and ending in the tower, with beautiful views of estate and valley vineyards to be enjoyed from there.

Across the street from St. Jean is St. Francis, one of the newest wineries in the valley, founded in 1979. The winery is housed in a modern redwood building, situated on a 100-acre vineyard estate. St. Francis offers primarily estate-bottled varietal wines.

Two other places of interest in the Kenwood area, to the northeast in the Mayacamas foothills, are the Sugarloaf Ridge State Park, reached on the Adobe Canyon Road, and which has camping, picnicking, hiking and horseback riding; and the Adler Fels (German for "Eagle Rock") winery, named for a local landmark, and perched high above Sonoma Valley on the tiny Corrick Road. Adler Fels produces a line of Sonoma County appellation varietal wines, and a *méthode champenoise* sparkling wine known as "Melange A Deux"—a blend of Johannisberg Riesling and Gewurztraminer.

Northwest of Kenwood, of course, some 14 miles or so on Highway 12, is Santa Rosa, in many ways the northern terminus of the Sonoma Valley, and, equally importantly, the seat of Sonoma County. Santa Rosa is the largest population center in the county, with comfortable hotels and inns, and good restaurants and shopping possibilities. It also has in it two or three wineries, most notable among them the Matanzas Creek Winery, situated in the Santa Rosa hills, in the small Bennett Valley area, and reached on Bennett Valley Road itself. Matanzas Creek offers three varietals modeled after French wines: Sauvignon Blanc, Chardonnay and Merlot.

The great glory of Santa Rosa, however, is its historic and colorful Railroad Square, located just west of Highway 101 in the center of town, and with most of the buildings there dating from the late 1800s. Railroad Square comprises three city blocks, housing more than forty specialty and antique shops, restaurants, galleries, and even a small brewery. Another place of interest to visitors is the Robert L. Ripley (of TV's "Believe It Or Not" fame) Museum, housed in a famous church that dates from 1873 and was built from a single Russian River redwood tree, some 275 feet tall and 18 feet wide, which yielded nearly 78,000 board feet of lumber. The church and museum are situated in the Juilliard Park on Sonoma Avenue, more or less in the center of town. Museum artifacts and displays are centered on Ripley memorabilia.

Also try to visit the Luther Burbank Home and Gardens at the corner of Santa Rosa and Sonoma avenues, where the famed horticulturist lived and experimented with plant breeding, introducing over 800 new strains of fruits, vegetables, flowers and grasses. The Burbank Home and Gardens are open to the public 10-3.30, Wednesday-Sunday. Guided tours are also offered.

Of interest, too, is the Redwood Empire Ice Arena on Steele Lane, and the adjacent Snoopy's Gallery and Gift Shop, both owned by cartoonist Charles Schulz—creator of "Snoopy" and "Peanuts," and quite possibly Santa Rosa's most famous resident.

Among other tourist attractions in Santa Rosa is the Sonoma County Museum on Seventh Street, with superb, changing exhibits, centering on the area's history and arts. The museum is open 11-4, Wednesday-Sunday; it also has a gift shop on the premises. Two other museums in the area are the Coddington Museum of Natural History and the Native

American Museum, located on Summerfield Road and Mendocino Avenue, respectively. Both are open to public viewing.

SONOMA VALLEY WINERIES

ADLER FELS WINERY. 5325 Corrick Road, Santa Rosa; (707) 539-3123. Tours, tasting and sales by appointment.

☐ Adler Fels is a small, 5,000-case winery, located high in the Mayacamas Mountains, just east of the Sonoma Valley. The winery is presently devoted to the production of Sonoma County Appellation wines, including Sauvignon Blanc, Chardonnay, Cabernet Sauvignon, Pinot Noir, and a *méthode champenoise* sparkling wine known as "Melange A Deux"—a blend of Johannisberg Riesling and Gewurztraminer. Adler Fels—German for "Eagle Rock"—is named for a local landmark. The winery was founded in 1980.

ARROWOOD VINEYARDS & WINERY. 14347 Sonoma Hwy., Glen Ellen; (707) 938-5170. Open for tours, tasting and sales, Mon.-Fri. 8.30-5, Sat. 10-4.30.

☐ 9600-square-foot winery, situated on a knoll overlooking Sonoma Valley. The winery specializes in varietal Chardonnay and Cabernet Sauvignon. Arrowood Vineyards was founded in 1987 by Richard and Alis Arrowood, present owners.

BUENA VISTA WINERY. 18000 Old Winery Road, Sonoma; (707) 938-1266. Open 10-5 daily. Self-guided tours, wine tasting and sales.

☐ Buena Vista is the oldest winery in California, originally founded in 1857 by Count Agoston Haraszthy, the acknowledged "father" of California viticulture. Buena Vista's picturesque old stone cellar is now a State Historical Landmark, open to public tours; it features a wine museum and ancient aging caves which were dug into the hillside by Chinese laborers in 1862. There is also a visitor center at the winery, with a tasting room and art gallery, and a large, shaded picnic area. The winery is owned by the A. Racke firm of West Germany, which has built a new winemaking facility in the Los Carneros area, and now offers a full line of estate-bottled Sonoma Valley varietal wines, as well as some sparkling wines. The winery schedules music concerts and other events in the summer months.

CARMENET VINEYARD. 1700 Moon Mountain Road, Sonoma; (707) 996-5870. Tours, tasting and sales by appointment, 10-4, Mon.-Fri.

☐ Carmenet Vineyard is located on a 450-acre ranch in the Mayacamas Mountains, at an elevation of approximately 1,200 feet. The winery produces primarily Bordeaux-style wines from its hillside vineyards located at the winery. Wines featured include a Cabernet Sauvignon blend, Sauvignon Blanc Semillon, and a red table wine made from Cabernet Sauvignon, Cabernet Franc and Merlot. The winery also has a 14,000-square-foot cellar, built into the hillside and believed to be among the first underground aging cellars to be constructed since the repeal of Prohibition in 1933. Carmenet is owned by Chalone, Inc., owner of Edna Valley Vineyards and Chalone Vineyards in the San Luis Obispo and Monterey counties, respectively.

CHATEAU ST. JEAN. 8555 Sonoma Hwy., Kenwood; (707) 833-

4134. Open daily 10-4.30. Self-guided tours, tasting and sales.

☐ Chateau St. Jean (pronounced, by the way, "Jean" and not "jawn") is one of the best known and most prestigious wineries in the Sonoma Valley, housed in a splendid chateau-style building, complete with a tower and colonnade, and surrounded by estate vineyards. St. Jean produces high-quality white varietal wines, and a *méthode champenoise* sparkling wine which is bottled at a separate facility, some 25 miles from the winery. The winery features landscaped grounds with picnic facilities; it also offers an excellent self-guided tour that begins in the fermentation cellar and ends in the tower, with beautiful views of valley vineyards to be enjoyed from there. Chateau St. Jean is now owned by Suntory Ltd., a well-known whiskey distiller from Japan. The winery was originally established in 1973.

B.H. COHN. 15000 Sonoma Hwy., Glen Ellen; (707) 938-4064. Tours, tasting and sales by appointment only.

☐ New Sonoma County winery, producing premium Sonoma Valley Chardonnay and and Cabernet Sauvignon.

H. COTURRI & SONS. 6725 Enterprise Road, Glen Ellen; (707) 996-6247. Tours and tasting by appointment, 8-5.30 daily.

☐ Small, family owned and operated winery, established in 1979. Coturri makes wine by the traditional method, from grapes purchased from Sonoma Valley growers. Chardonnay, Cabernet Sauvignon, Pinot Noir, Zinfandel, Riesling and Semillon are the wines produced. Coturri's other labels are Enterprise Cellars, King Wine Company, and The Kings.

GLORIA FERRER CHAMPAGNE CAVES. 2355 Hwy. 121, Sonoma; (707) 996-7256. Open for tours, tasting and sales, 11-5 daily.

☐ Large, newly-built Spanish-style winery, situated on a knoll overlooking estate vineyards, located near Schellville, just south of Sonoma. Gloria Ferrer represents a $12-million investment by Freixenet of Spain, the largest *méthode champenoise* sparkling wine producer in the world. The winery was only recently established, opening to the public in July, 1986. Tours of the facility include a visit to the winery's newly-excavated limestone aging caves, built into the hillside adjacent to the winery. The winery also features a spacious tasting patio, with delightful vineyard views. The winery is named for Freixenet president Jose Ferrer's wife, Gloria Ferrer.

FISHER VINEYARDS. 6200 St. Helena Road, Santa Rosa; (707) 539-7511. Winery visits by appointment.

☐ Fisher makes premium Cabernet Sauvignon and Chardonnay from its 75 acres of estate vineyards located in the Napa Valley and in the Mayacamas Mountains in Sonoma County. The vineyards were originally established in 1973, and the winery was built in 1979, using native firs and redwoods grown on estate hillsides. The winery building, in fact, was chosen by the American Institute of Architects as one of the twelve best buildings designed by California architects since 1975. The winery currently bottles around 7,000 cases of varietal wines annually.

GLEN ELLEN WINERY. 1883 London Ranch Road, Glen Ellen; (707) 996-1066. Open for tasting and sales daily 10-4; tours by appointment.

☐ Glen Ellen is an historic winery, located in the timbered hills adjacent to the Jack London State Historic Park, and situated on property that was originally part of the 122-acre Rancho Petaluma Mexican land grant, dating from the

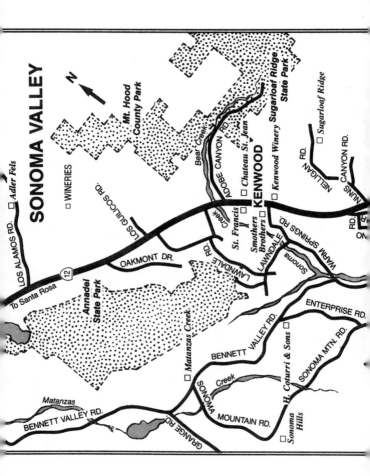

Wineries on This Section of Map -

Adler Fels
Arrowood
Buena Vista
Carmenet
B.H. Cohn
H. Coturri & Sons
Chateau St. Jean
Glen Ellen Winery
Grand Cru
Gundlach-Bundschu
Hacienda
Hanzell
Haywood
Kenwood Winery
La Crema Vinera
Las Montanas
Matanzas Creek
Ravenswood
St. Francis
Sebastiani
Smothers Brothers
Sonoma Hills
Sugarloaf Ridge
Valley of the Moon

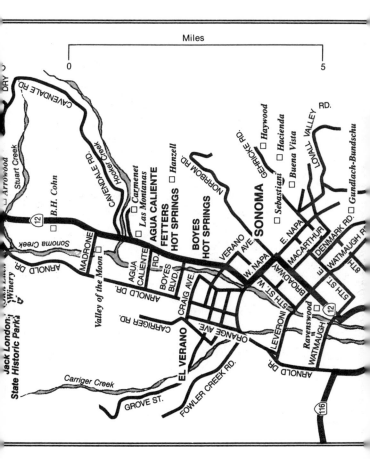

1860s. The vineyard property, which had been largely neglected over the years, was bought and revived by the Benziger family in 1980. The winery now offers estate-grown Sauvignon Blanc, Chardonnay and Cabernet Sauvignon from its 41-acre vineyard located at the winery; some proprietary generic wines are also produced. The winery, interestingly, is housed in an old barn, also dating from the 1860s. There is a shaded picnic area on the premises.

GRAND CRU VINEYARDS. 1 Vintage Lane, Glen Ellen; (707) 996-8100. Wine tasting and sales daily 10-5; tours by appointment only.
☐ Grand Cru is a well-known varietal wine producer, established in 1970. The winery is housed in an A-frame building with a rustic wooden deck, situated on the site of a 100-year-old wine cellar. The winery, in fact, offers a unique contrast between the old and new, utilizing the most modern, scientific equipment and winemaking techniques, together with century-old stone and concrete fermentation tanks. Grand Cru wines include vintage-dated Sauvignon Blanc, Gewurztraminer, Chenin Blanc and Cabernet Sauvignon, all made from grapes purchased on a select vineyard basis. Barbeque and picnic area on premises.

GUNDLACH-BUNDSCHU WINERY. 2000 Denmark Street, Sonoma; (707) 938-5277. Open for tours, tasting and sales, 11-4.30 daily. Picnic area on premises.
☐ Historic, Sonoma Valley winery, originally established in 1858 by pioneer vintner Jacob Gundlach, who was joined in his venture a few years later by his son-in-law Charles Bundschu. The winery flourished for some years, then closed during Prohibition and remained idle for several decades. In 1976, a fifth generation Bundschu, James Bundschu, re-opened the family cellars. Gundlach-Bundschu now offers estate-bottled, vintage-dated varietal wines from its 370 acres of vineyards located in the valley, where some original vines, planted by Jacob Gundlach and Charles Bundschu, are still producing. A specialty of the winery is a little known Sonoma Valley white varietal known as Kleinberger. The winery also produces some sparkling wines.

HACIENDA WINE CELLARS. 1000 Vineyard Lane, Sonoma; (707) 938-3220. Open for wine tasting and sales, 10-5 daily; tours by appointment.
☐ Spanish-style winery, set among oak trees and gardens on the outskirts of the Sonoma township. The winery was established in 1973, and it incorporates in its estate the historic 50-acre Buena Vista Vineyard, originally developed by Agoston Haraszthy in 1862. Hacienda offers vintage-dated Zinfandel, Pinot Noir, Cabernet Sauvignon and Johannisberg Riesling from its estate vineyard. There is a lovely, shaded picnic area located adjacent to the winery, overlooking the Buena Vista vineyard.

HANNA WINERY. 5345 Occidental Rd., Santa Rosa; (707) 575-3330. Visitors by appointment, Mon.-Fri. 8-5.
☐ Small, Sonoma County winery, founded in 1985 by Dr. Elias Hanna, present owner. The winery makes vintage-dated varietal Chardonnay, Sauvignon Blanc and Cabernet Sauvignon, from grapes purchased on a select-vineyard basis; small lots of Semillon and Late Harvest Sauvignon Blanc are also produced. Hanna's 22-acre vineyard is located at the winery.

HANZELL VINEYARDS. 18596 Lomita Avenue, Sonoma; (707) 996-3860. Visitors by appointment only.
☐ Small, 3,000-case winery, producing Chardonnay and Pinot Noir from its

34-acre vineyard located at the winery in the Sonoma Valley. The winery, modeled after a French chateau, was originally built in 1957 by late Ambassador James Zellerbach.

HAYWOOD WINERY. 18701 Gehricke Road, Sonoma; (707) 996-4298. Open for tasting and sales, 11-5 daily.

□ Small, family owned and operated winery, producing premium Sonoma County varietals from its 100-acre vineyard on the slopes of the tiny Chamizal Valley, just above the town of Sonoma. Four wines are featured: Chardonnay, Riesling, Cabernet Sauvignon and Zinfandel. The winery was established in 1980 by present owner Peter Haywood.

KENWOOD VINEYARDS. 9592 Sonoma Hwy., Kenwood; (707) 833-5891. Wine tasting and sales 10-4.30 daily; tours by appointment.

□ Well-known, 40,000-case winery, originally established in the Sonoma Valley in 1906 by the Pagini family. The winery was acquired and modernized in 1970 by its present owners, John Sheela and Martin and Michael Lee. Kenwood offers a complete line of vintage-dated varietal wines, including Pinot Noir, Pinot Noir Blanc, Zinfandel, Cabernet Sauvignon, Chardonnay, Riesling, a dry-styled Chenin Blanc from the Delta region, Gewurztraminer, and Sauvignon Blanc. One or two vintage-dated generic wines are also featured. The winery has a rustic tasting room.

LAS MONTANAS. 4400 Cavedale Road, Glen Ellen; (707) 996-2448. Winery visits by invitation only. Tasting room located in Kenwood, at 8860 Hwy. 12, open 10-5 Thurs.-Mon.

□ Las Montanas is a small, owner-operated winery, located in the Mayacamas Mountains above Sonoma Valley. The winery produces primarily varietal wines from its 16-acre hillside vineyard located at the winery; offerings include a Zinfandel, Cabernet Sauvignon and Gamay. Las Montanas was founded in 1982.

MATANZAS CREEK WINERY. 6097 Bennett Valley Road, Santa Rosa; (707) 528-6464. Visitors by appointment only.

□ Small, family-owned winery, housed in a modern facility in the Bennett Valley, just outside Santa Rosa. The winery specializes in Sonoma County wines, made in the French style. Offerings include Chardonnay, Cabernet Sauvignon, Merlot and Sauvignon Blanc, all made from grapes grown in the estate's 42 acres of vineyards located in the Bennett Valley. The winery was established in 1977 by Sandra and William MacIver, present owners.

RAVENSWOOD WINERY. 21415 Broadway, Sonoma; (707) 938-1960. Winery visits by appointment only.

□ Small, 5,000-case winery, established in 1976. Ravenswood produces four Sonoma County wines: Zinfandel, Cabernet Sauvignon, Merlot and Chardonnay. Wines are generally vineyard-designated, and produced in the unique Ravenswood style—fermented with wild yeast, and aged in oak.

RICHARDSON VINEYARDS. 2711 Knob Hill Rd., Sonoma; (707) 938-2610. Visitors by appointment only.

□ Family owned and operated winery, founded in 1980 by the Richardson family. The winery offers primarily varietal, vintage-dated Chardonnay, Cabernet Sauvignon, Zinfandel, and Pinot Noir, all made from grapes purchased on a select-vineyard basis.

ST. FRANCIS WINERY. 8450 Sonoma Hwy., Kenwood; (707) 833-4666. Open for tasting and sales, 10-4.30 daily; tours by appointment.
□   St. Francis is one of the newest wineries in the Sonoma Valley, founded in 1979 by Joseph Martin, present owner. The winery is housed in a redwood building, surrounded by approximately 100 acres of estate vineyards. St Francis wines include estate-bottled, vintage-dated Chardonnay, Gewurztraminer, Johannisberg Riesling, Merlot, and Pinot Noir.

SEBASTIANI VINEYARDS. 389 4th St. East, Sonoma; (707) 938-5532. Open for tours, tasting and sales, daily 10-5.
□   Sebastiani is an historic Sonoma winery, originally founded in 1904 by Italian immigrant Samuele Sebastiani, and still owned and operated by the founding family. The winery bottles primarily varietal wines: Cabernet Sauvignon, Barbera, Gewurztraminer, Chardonnay, Nouveau Gamay Beaujolais, Zinfandel, Chenin Blanc, and a Proprietor's Reserve Pinot Noir; some generics and jug wines are also offered, and a line of "country" varietals is bottled under the August Sebastiani label. Tours of the winery are conducted daily, highlighting Sebastiani's collection of hand-carved redwood casks, believed to be the largest such collection in North America. Also of interest at the winery are the Indian Artifact Museum and a display of a small, antique crusher and basket press, with which Samuele Sebastiani made his first wine, a Zinfandel, in 1895.

SMOTHERS WINERY (TASTING ROOM). 9575 Hwy. 12, Kenwood; (707) 833-1010. Open for wine tasting and sales, 10-4.30 daily.
□   Famous comedians Dick and Tom Smothers make wine from grapes grown in their Santa Cruz and Sonoma County vineyards; approximately 100 acres, planted to Chardonnay and Sauvignon Blanc, are located in the Glen Ellen area, and another 30 acres or so are in the Santa Cruz Mountains. The Smothers' winery was originally established in the Santa Cruz Mountains in 1977, and the tasting room at the present Kenwood location opened in 1982. Varietal wines offered are Cabernet Sauvignon, Sauvignon Blanc, Zinfandel, Gewurztraminer, and White Riesling.

SONOMA HILLS WINERY. 4850 Peracca Rd., Santa Rosa; (707) 523-3415. Winery open to visitors by appointment only.
□   Small, owner-operated winery, founded in 1983 by the Votruba family, present owners. The only wine produced here is Chardonnay, made from grapes purchased on a select-vineyard basis. Sonoma Hills, interestingly, also has the distinction of being the smallest winery in California.

SUGARLOAF RIDGE WINERY. 2250 Nelligan Rd., Glen Ellen; (707) 833-6535. Winery visits by appointment.
□   Small, Cabernet-only winery. The winery was founded by Richard and Joann Puttbach, present owners.

VALLEY OF THE MOON WINERY. 777 Madrone Road, Glen Ellen; (707) 996-6941. Open for tasting and sales, 10-5 daily.
□   Historic, Sonoma Valley winery, established in 1857. The estate was originally part of the Agua Caliente Mexican land grant, and was owned, at different times, by General "Fighting Joe Hooker" of Civil War fame, Eli Shepard who served as the American Consul to China, and George Hearst, U.S. Senator and father of newspaper tycoon William Randolph Hearst. In 1941, the Parducci family—long associated with California wine—purchased the vineyard property. The winery now offers primarily generic jug wines and a line of

estate-bottled, Sonoma Valley varietal wines, including French Colombard, Semillon, Pinot Noir, Zinfandel, White Zinfandel, Zinfandel Rosé, and Pinot Noir Blanc.

VIANSA WINERY. 25200 Arnold Dr. (Hwy. 121), Sonoma; (707) 935-4700/935-4747. Open for tours, tasting and sales, daily 10-5.
□ New, Italian-style winery, situated on a knoll just south of Sonoma, in the Carneros district, overlooking Sonoma Valley. The winery was established in late 1989 by Sam Sebastiani, of Sonoma's well-known, winemaking Sebastiani family. Wines produced here include Cabernet Sauvignon, Chardonnay and Sauvignon Blanc, all made from grapes purchased from select Napa and Sonoma County vineyards; small lots of Muscat Canelli and Barbera Blanc are also offered. Wine and gift shop on premises; also picnic fare available.

PRACTICAL INFORMATION FOR SONOMA VALLEY

HOW TO GET THERE

Sonoma lies 45 miles northeast of San Francisco. The best and easiest way to reach it is by way of *Highway 101* north from San Francisco to Novato (26 miles), then a combination of *Highways 37, 121* and *12* directly northeast to Sonoma. A slightly longer route from San Francisco is by way of *Interstate 80* east to Vallejo (31 miles), then northwest some 25 miles on *Highways 29, 37, 121* and *12* to Sonoma.

Santa Rosa is located 25 miles northwest of Sonoma, or 58 miles north of San Francisco, at the intersection of *Highways 101* and *12*. It can be reached directly on *101* north from San Francisco, or by way of *Highway 12* from Sonoma.

Santa Rosa also has a commercial airport, the *Sonoma County Airport*, located at 2200 Airport Boulevard (airport phone: 707-542-3139). It is serviced by *United Express* (800-241-6522), which has regularly scheduled flights to Santa Rosa.

TOURIST INFORMATION

Sonoma Valley Chamber of Commerce, 453 First St. East, Sonoma; (707) 996-1033. Visitor information brochures, walking tour maps, visitor guides; also calendar of events and information on area wineries, cheese factories and art galleries.

Sonoma County Convention and Visitors Bureau, 10 Fourth St., Santa

Rosa; (707) 575-1191. Visitor information; maps, brochures, calendar of events, listings of area lodgings and restaurants.

ACCOMMODATIONS

Sonoma

Sonoma Hotel. *$62-$105*. 110 W. Spain St.; (707) 996-2996. Historic hotel on the plaza. 17 antique-filled guest rooms; garden patio, restaurant and bar. Continental breakfast.

El Dorado Inn. *$120-$130*. 405 First St. West; (707) 996-3030. Beautifully restored adobe inn, situated on the plaza. 29 rooms, private baths; excellent Italian restaurant, saloon, fireplace lounge, heated pool. Continental breakfast.

Best Western Sonoma Valley Inn. *$85-$125*. 550 Second St. West; (707) 938-9200. 75 units. TV, phones, pool, spa, complimentary continental breakfast. Located close to downtown Sonoma.

Sonoma Mission Inn & Spa. *$195-$290*. 18140 Sonoma Hwy., Boyes Hot Springs; (707) 938-9000, (800) 862-4945 in Califorina, (800) 358-9022/358-9027 outside California. Luxury resort, located 2 miles out of Sonoma. 160 guest rooms, many with fireplaces and balconies. Facilities include restaurants, pools, tennis courts, and a European-style spa with a bathhouse, whirlpool, aerobics classes, exercise equipment, heated pool, beauty salon and massage room.

El Pueblo Motel. *$45-$60*. 896 W. Napa St.; (707) 996-3651. 39 motel units; TV, phones, pool.

Santa Rosa

Best Western Garden Inn. *$45-$60*. 1500 Santa Rosa Ave., Santa Rosa; (707) 546-4031. 78 rooms, with TV and phones. 2 pools, coffee shop. Some family units.

El Rancho Tropicana. *$60-$75*. 2200 Santa Rosa Ave., Santa Rosa; (707) 542-3655/(800) 248-4747. 300 rooms, with TV, phones. Pool and tennis. Restaurant, cocktail lounge and coffee shop.

Flamingo Resort Hotel. *$66-$146*. 2777 Fourth St., Santa Rosa; (707) 545-8530. 140 rooms; TV, phones. Pool, spa, tennis, restaurant.

Fountaingrove Inn. *$80-$155*. 101 Fountaingrove Parkway, Santa Rosa; (707) 578-6101/(800) 222-6101 in CA. 87 rooms; TV, phones. Pool, jacuzzi, gourmet restaurant.

Holiday Inn. *$62-$120*. 3345 Santa Rosa Ave., Santa Rosa; (707) 579-3000/(800) HOLIDAY. 104 rooms; TV, phones. Pool, tennis, health club with steam rooms, sauna, whirlpools, jogging track, putting green, and aerobics classes. Restaurant on premises.

Los Robles Lodge. *$60-$100*. 925 Edwards Ave., Santa Rosa; (707) 545-6330/(800) 552-1001. 106 rooms, with TV, phones and refrigerators. Also pool and hot tub.

Doubletree Inn. *$80-$110*. 3555 Round Barn Blvd., Santa Rosa; (707) 523-7555/(800) 833-9595 in CA. Five-star hotel, with 252 rooms and suites. Pool, jogging path. Restaurant and bar.

Vintners Inn. *$118-$175*. 4350 Barnes Rd., Santa Rosa; (707) 575-7350.

Spanish-style hotel with plaza and fountains, surrounded by 50-acre vineyard. 44 rooms, some with fireplaces and balconies. Concierge service; gourmet restaurant. Complimentary breakfast served in the dining nook off the lobby. Library.

The Flamingo Resort Hotel. *$76-$176*. 4th St. and Farmers Lane, Santa Rosa; (707) 545-8530. Full-service hotel with 137 guest rooms. Olympic-size pool, jacuzzi, tennis, shuffleboard courts, shopping arcade.

Heritage Inn. *$45-$80*. 870 Hopper Ave., Santa Rosa; (707) 545-9000/(800) 533-1255. 95 rooms; TV, phones. Pool, spa, sauna. Restaurant and cocktail lounge.

BED & BREAKFAST INNS

Sonoma

Trojan Horse Inn. *$75-$100*. 19455 Sonoma Hwy.; (707) 996-2430. 7 antique-decorated rooms in historic, rural mansion, built in 1887. Creekside setting; gardens, patio, spa, and bicycles for guests' use. Gourmet breakfast.

Victorian Garden Inn. *$69-$129*. 316 E. Napa St.; (707) 996-5339. Quiet, 1860s farmhouse-style inn near the Plaza. 4 guest rooms; creekside gardens, pool. Hearty country breakfast.

Overview Farm. *$110*. 15650 Arnold Dr.; (707) 938-8574. Beautifully restored, 1880s Victorian farmhouse. 3 guest rooms, private baths, fireplaces. Full breakfast, served in a formal dining room.

The Hidden Oak. *$85-$95*. 214 E. Napa St.; (707) 996-9863. Centrally-located, early 1900s bungalow, furnished with antiques. 3 rooms with private baths. Hors d'oeuvres, gourmet breakfast. Bicycles for guests' use.

Thistle Dew Inn. *$70-$110*. 171 W. Spain St.; (707) 938-2909. Inn comprises two restored, single-story Victorian homes, decorated with early 1900s furniture pieces. 6 guest rooms, and a country cottage; some phones and fireplaces. Complimentary sherry, fresh-cut flowers; buffet-style continental breakfast.

Chalet. *$70-$100*. 18935 Fifth St. West; (707) 938-3129. Delightful country inn, with 4 guest rooms, some with private baths. Spa. Country breakfast.

Magliulo's Pensione. *$70-$80*. 691 Broadway; (707) 996-1031. Splendid Victorian bed and breakfast inn, located just south of the plaza. 5 well-appointed guest rooms, decorated with fine antiques and fresh flowers; some private baths. Gourmet restaurant on premises.

Glen Ellen

Beltane Ranch. *$75-$90*. 11775 Sonoma Hwy., Glen Ellen; (707) 996-6501. 4 rooms in 1890s ranch house. Private baths, private entrances. Vineyard views; tennis courts.

Gaige House Inn. *$75-$145*. 13540 Arnold Dr., Glen Ellen; (707) 935-0237. Beautifully restored Italian Gothic Victorian residence. 5 guest rooms, all with private bath; some fireplaces and jacuzzi tubs. Full breakfast. Pool.

Glenelly Inn. *$75-$120*. 5131 Warm Springs Rd., Glen Ellen; (707) 996-6720. 6 rooms in restored 1920's inn. Private baths.

Santa Rosa

The Gables. *$90-$115*. 4257 Petaluma Hill Rd., Santa Rosa; (707) 585-7777. Gothic Revival mansion, dating from the 1870s. 5 guest rooms, each with private bath. Full breakfast with freshly squeezed fruit juices and home-made breads and pastries.

Melitta Station Inn. *$70-$90*. 5850 Melitta Station Rd., Santa Rosa; (707) 538-7712. Housed in restored railroad station, dating from the early 1900s. 6 antique-furnished rooms, with private baths. Country breakfast, evening wine.

Pygmalion House. *$55-$65*. 331 Orange St., Santa Rosa; (707) 526-3407. Charming Queen Anne Victorian within walking distance of Railroad Square. 5 rooms with private baths. Country-style breakfast.

SEASONAL EVENTS

March. *Symphony of Food & Wine.* At Santa Rosa; last weekend of the month. Classical music, wine tasting, gourmet food. (707) 544-9480.

May. *Cinco de Mayo.* At the Sonoma State Historic Park; 5th of the month. Events include a parade, music, dancing, and other festivities. For more information, call (707) 938-1578. *Luther Burbank Rose Festival.* Held at Santa Rosa, usually during the 3rd week of the month. Features a parade, barbeque, arts and crafts show, square dancing, and "Run for the Roses." (707) 546-ROSE.

June. *Valley of the Moon Chili Cookoff.* Held during the 1st weekend of June, at the Sonoma Plaza. Features some of the area's best chili cooks, who prepare their championship recipes; also live music. More information on (707) 938-6791. *Art in the Park.* Arts and Crafts show, also at the Sonoma Plaza; 1st weekend. (707) 996-5947. *Annual Ox Roast.* Sonoma Plaza; 1st weekend. Barbeque and live entertainment. (707) 996-1033. *Art Farm Festival.* Held at the Art Farm, 280 Leveroni Rd.; 2nd weekend of the month. Two-day music festival, featuring several well-known performers. For a schedule and information, call (707) 938-4171. *JumbleBerry Jubilee.* At Santa Rosa, on Fourth Street between B and E Streets; 2nd weekend of the month. Fine arts and crafts, live music, berry wines and a variety of berries — blue, black, logan, boysen, olallie, rasp and strawberries — served in every imaginable way. Phone (707) 545-3534. *Bear Flag Day Celebration.* At the Sonoma Plaza; (707) 996-2337. Celebration of Bear Flag Revolt. Events include a flag raising ceremony, barbeque, and entertainment. *Great Chefs of Sonoma.* Popular annual event, hosted by the Buena Vista Winery. 35-40 local chefs prepare and serve their specialties. For a schedule, reservations and information, call (707) 938-8504.

July. *Wine Country Film Festival.* 2nd and 3rd weeks of the month; at the Luther Burbank Center in Santa Rosa and the Palace Theatre, Petaluma. Feature films, documentaries, animated films and foreign films; also seminars and receptions. For reservations and more information, call (707) 996-2536. *Sonoma County Fair.* Held at the Sonoma County Fairgrounds in Santa Rosa. Wine competition, agricultural exhibits, live entertainment, horse racing, carnival and flower show. For a schedule of events, call (707) 528-3247. *Midsummer Mozart Concert.* Open-air concert at historic Buena Vista Winery, with performances by some of Northern California's top musicians. For a program, call the winery at (707) 938-1266. Concerts begin during the 3rd week of July and continue into late August. *Pioneer Days.* Sonoma Plaza; 4th weekend. Colorful festival, with events celebrating the life in 19th century Sonoma; booths with handicrafts, homemade breads, and more. (707) 938-1033.

August. *Annual Wine Showcase and Auction.* Held at the Sonoma Mission Inn & Spa, usually during the third week of the month. Some of Sonoma County's finest wineries offer their wines for auction. For more information, call (707) 579-0577. *Dixieland Jazz Festival.* At the Railroad Square, Santa Rosa; 4th week. Performances by several fine jazz musicians and bands. Call (707) 578-8478 for a schedule.

September. *Shakespeare at Buena Vista.* Buena Vista Winery; (707) 938-1266. Shakespeare performances by the Sonoma Vintage Theatre; first three weeks of the month. *Valley of the Moon Vintage Festival.* Held at the Sonoma Plaza; (707) 938-2021. Festivities include a flower show, gem show, arts and crafts show, and a parade and ball.

October. *Musique Macabre.* Buena Vista Winery; (707) 938-1266. Readings from Edgar Allan Poe, and spooky music. *Federweisse.* Also at the Buena Vista Winery. Traditional harvest festival with wine tasting and Dixieland jazz. Phone (707) 938-8504.

November. *Sonoma County Harvest Fair.* At the Sonoma County Fairgrounds, Santa Rosa; 1st week of the month. Annual fair featuring a variety of events, including an art show, wine competition, jazz festival, 10-kilometer run, and grape stomp. For more information, call (707) 543-4203. *Nouveau Beaujolais Festival.* Hosted by Sebastiani Vineyards, generally around the middle of the month. Celebration of the first wine of the year's harvest. Wine tasting and music. For a schedule of events, call the winery at (707) 938-5532.

December. *Holiday Candlelight Tour of Inns.* Bus tours of selected Sonoma County Bed & Breakfast Inns, offered during the 2nd and 3rd weeks of month; music and refreshments along the way. Sponsored by the Sonoma County Museum; (707) 579-1500.

PLACES OF INTEREST

Sonoma Plaza. Delightful Spanish-style plaza, dating from the Mexican era. Visit old adobes and other historic buildings; among them the *Sonoma Barracks, Sonoma Mission, Toscano Hotel, Swiss Hotel, Sonoma Hotel, El Dorado Hotel*, and the remains of General Vallejo's *Casa Grande*. Most of these old buildings now house charming little shops and restaurants; of particular interest are the famous *Somona Cheese Factory*, home of California's Sonoma Jack cheese, and the *Sonoma French Bakery*. There is also a lovely, tree-shaded park at the center of the plaza, with picnic tables, children's play area, flower bushes, footpaths, a duck pond, and a large bronze statue commemorating the 1846 Bear Flag Revolt. The picture-perfect *Sonoma City Hall*, dating from 1910, is at the southern end of the plaza park, and the *Sonoma Chamber of Commerce*, also housed in a splendid old building, along its east side. (Maps pinpointing Sonoma's historical sites and other places of interest are available from the Chamber of Commerce for a nominal fee of around $1.00.)

Sonoma Mission. Cnr. Spain St. and First St. East. Last and northernmost of California's 21 missions founded by Franciscan fathers, established in 1823. Mission museum has displays of local historical interest, and a splendid collection of paintings of all 21 California missions. Open daily 10-5; admission: $1.00 adults, 50¢ children. Phone (707) 938-1519.

Sonoma Barracks. Spain St. Picturesque old adobe, dating from the 1840s, formerly used to house the troops of General Mariano Vallejo, Mexican Governor of California. The Barracks now contain historic artifacts from Sonoma's three most important eras—Indian, Mexican, and early American. The last of these includes a replica of the original, handmade "Bear Flag" raised at Sonoma in 1846. Lovely courtyard, and balcony with plaza views. Open daily 10-5.

Vallejo Home (Lachryma Montis). Located 3 blocks west of the Mission, off Spain Street. Beautiful redwood house on landscaped grounds, formerly the home of General Mariano Vallejo, built in the early 1850s. Vallejo lived here with his family until his death in 1890. Most of the rooms have been superbly restored to their original state, with the original, antique furnishings and fixtures. Also on display here are Vallejo's 19th century carriage and several old, historical photographs. The home is now part of the Sonoma State Historic Park which also contains in it the Sonoma Mission and Sonoma Barracks. An admission fee of $1.00 adults/50¢ children allows entry to all three historic buildings. Open daily 10-5.

Depot Park. 270 First St. West. Grassy park with picnic and barbeque facilities, children's playground and a well-kept railroad museum. Open daily.

Sonoma Cheese Factory. 2 Spain St.; (707) 938-5225. Makers of famous Sonoma Jack Cheese. Watch the cheese being made in the factory, with pre-taped commentary to explain the process. accompanied by taped commentary. Fully-stocked deli on premises, offering excellent picnic fare. Open daily 9-6.

Vella Cheese Factory. 315 Second St. East; (707) 938-3232. Another good place to observe the cheese-making process. Also variety of cheeses for sale. Open Mon.-Sat. 9-6, Sun. 9-5.

Train Town. 10-acre theme park just south of town on Broadway, featuring short, 20-minute train rides around its premises, passing through tunnels and over bridges. Petting farm for children. Cost of train ride: $2.20 adults, $1.60 children and seniors. Open 10.30-5 daily, June-Sept.; 11-5 on weekends the rest of the year. For more information, call (707) 938-3912.

Stornetta's Dairy. Cnr. Hwy. 121 and Napa Rd.; (707) 938-2354. Well-known Sonoma dairy, open to public tours. Watch the cows being milked, with taped commentary explaining the process. Viewing room open daily 2-4 p.m.

Jack London State Historic Park. London Ranch Rd., Glen Ellen; (707) 938-5216. 800-acre park, comprising novelist Jack London's famous "Beauty Ranch," where the author lived and worked during his latter years, until his death in 1916. Chief attractions in the park are the stone ruins of London's *Wolf House*, and *The House of Happy Walls*—built in 1919 by the author's wife, Charmain London, and now housing a museum with displays of furnishings and other items from London's original study as well as from the Wolf House, and the author's collection of South Pacific art. The park also has good hiking, picnicking, and horseback riding possibilities. Open daily, 8 a.m. until sunset. Admission: $3.00 per car.

Sugarloaf Ridge State Park. 2605 Adobe Canyon Rd., Kenwood. Park in Sonoma Valley setting, with camping, picnicking, hiking and horseback riding. Campsites $10.00 per day; day use $3.00 per car. Open daily, sunrise to sunset. For campsite reservations and information, call (707) 833-5712.

Annadel State Park. 6201 Channel Dr., Santa Rosa; (707) 539-3911. 4,913-acre park with hiking, horseback riding, bicycling and fishing.

Hood Mountain Regional Park. 3000 Los Alamos Dr., Santa Rosa; (707) 539-9903. Hiking trails through 1,450-acre park with excellent views from the top.

Howarth Memorial Park. Summerfield Rd., Santa Rosa; (707) 528-5115. 152-acre park with a small lake. Boating, picnic and barbeque areas, tennis courts, children's playground and petting zoo. Also bicycle and jogging trails.

Spring Lake County Park. Cnr. Summerfield Rd. and Newanga Ave., Santa Rosa; (707) 539-8092. 320-acre park. Swimming, sailing, fishing, picnicking and camping.

Coddington Museum of Natural History. 557 Summerfield Road, Santa Rosa; (707) 539-0556. Exhibits of regional and worldwide natural history. Open Wed.-Sat. 11-4. Admission free.

Luther Burbank Home & Gardens. Santa Rosa & Sonoma Aves., Santa Rosa; (707) 576-5115. Home and gardens of renowned naturalist Luther Burbank. Open Wed.-Sun. 10-3.30; tours every half hour. Tour cost: $1.00 adults, children under 12 free. Gardens open daily; no admission fee.

Robert L. Ripley "Believe It or Not" Memorial Museum. 492 Sonoma Ave., Santa Rosa; (707) 576-5233. Located across from the Luther Burbank Gardens, in the famous "Church Built from One Redwood Tree." Exhibits include historical photos of the church, cartoons and items from Robert Ripley's travels, and other Ripley memorabilia. Open Wed.-Sun. 11-4. Admission fee: $1.00 adults, 50¢ children.

Sonoma County Museum. 425 Seventh St., Santa Rosa; (707) 579-1500. Housed in the Old Post Office Building, the museum has on display various historical exhibits, as well as visiting art exhibits. Museum hours: Wed.-Sun. 11-4; admission fee: $1.00 adults, 50¢ children.

RECREATION

Tours. The following tour companies offer tours of Sonoma and the surrounding wine country, some of them including visits to specific wineries. *Linda Viviani Touring Company,* 500 Michael Drive, Sonoma, (707) 938-2100; *Sonoma Airporter,* (800) 772-7260/(707) 938-4246; *North Bay Tours.* P.O. Box 1809, Santa Rosa, (707) 431-8687; *Sonoma Tours.* 18495 Sonoma Hwy., Sonoma, (707) 938-4248.

Hot Air Ballooning. *Sonoma Thunder,* (707) 996-3665. One-hour balloon flights over the Sonoma Valley, followed by a champagne brunch. Cost: $135.00 per person. *Air Flambuoyant,* 2967 Coors Court, Santa Rosa; (707) 575-1955/(800) 456-4711. Flights over the Sonoma wine country, followed by a champagne brunch. Flight cost is $135.00 per person. *Airborn of Sonoma County,* P.O. Box 4887, Santa Rosa; (707) 528-8133. Champagne balloon flights; also flight instruction. Cost: $140.00 per person.

Scenic Flights. *Aero-Schellville,* 23982 Arnold Drive (at the Schellville Airport), Sonoma; (707) 938-2444. Offers unique scenic flights over the Sonoma Valley in a vintage biplane.

Bicycling. Both the Sonoma township and the Sonoma Valley offer excellent opportunities for bicycling. Scenic *Highway 12*, which journeys through the heart of the valley, is an especially good bicycling route; other good routes include the small countrified roads on the outskirts of Sonoma, many of them leading to wineries. For bike rentals and repair service, contact *Rincon Cyclery*, 4927 Sonoma Hwy., #H, Santa Rosa; (707) 538-0868.

Horseback Riding. *Sonoma Cattle Company,* (707) 996-8566. Guided trail rides in Jack London State Historic Park and Sugarloaf Ridge State Park. Also carriage rides through the Jack London state park. Rates: $15.00 for one hour, $22.00 for two hours. *Oak Hill Ranch,* 3485 Porter Creek Rd., Santa Rosa; (707) 528-6498. Horse rentals, trail rides, breakfast and dinner rides; lessons. *Cloverleaf Ranch,* 3890Y Old Redwood Hwy., Santa Rosa; (707) 545-5906. Trail rides.

Spas and Hot Springs. *The Spa at Sonoma Mission Inn,* Hwy. 12, Boyes Hot Springs; (707) 938-9000/ext. 427. Luxury resort, with full line of spa treatments. Reservations required. *Agua Caliente Mineral Springs.* 17350 Vailetti Dr., Agua Caliente; (707) 996-6822. Facilities include spa, mineral water swimming pool, diving pool, and picnic area. *Morton's Warm Springs,* 1651 Warm Springs Rd., Kenwood; (707) 833-5511. Heated pools, picnic area, and snack bar.

GOLF

Sonoma National Golf Club, 17700 Arnold Dr., Sonoma; (707) 996-0300. 18-hole championship course; 72 Par. Green fees: $15.00 weekdays, $20.00 weekends. Pro shop, lessons.

Oakmont Golf Club, 7025 Oakmont Dr. (off Hwy. 12), Oakmont; (707) 539-0415. Two 18-hole championship courses; 72 Par and 63 Par. Green fees: $18.00 weekdays, $25.00 weekends. Lessons, and pro shop.

Bennett Valley Golf Course, 3330 Yulupa, Santa Rosa; (707) 528-3673. 18-hole public golf course; Par 72. Pro shop, lessons. Green fees: $9.00 weekdays, $12.00 weekends.

Fairgrounds Golf Course and Driving Range, Sonoma County Fairgrounds (inside the race track), Santa Rosa; (707) 546-2469. 9 holes, Par 29. Lessons available. Green fees: $5.00 weekdays, $6.00 weekends.

Fountaingrove Country Club, 1525 Fountaingrove Parkway, Santa Rosa; (707) 579-4653. 18-hole private course, Par 72. Pro shop, lessons. Green fees: $40.00 weekdays, $60.00 weekends; fees include cart rental.

Mountain Shadows Golf Courses, 100 Golf Course Drive, Rohnert Park; (707) 584-7766. Two 18-hole championship courses, both Par 72. Driving range, cart rentals, pro shop, free lessons, snack bar and cocktail lounge. Green fees: North Course $12.00 weekdays/$17.00 weekends; South Course $24.00 weekdays/$30.00 weekends. Green fees on South Course include mandatory cart rental.

Santa Rosa Golf & Country Club, 5110 Oak Meadow Drive, Santa Rosa; (707) 546-3485. Private 18-hole golf course. Par 72.

Wickiup Golf Course, 5001 Carriage Lane, Santa Rosa; (707) 546-8787. 9-hole public course. Pro shop, lessons, snack bar. Green fees: $7.00 weekdays, $8.00 weekends.

RESTAURANTS

(Restaurant prices—based on full course dinner, excluding drinks, tax and tips—are categorized as follows: *Deluxe,* over $30; *Expensive,* $20-$30; *Moderate,* $10-$20; *Inexpensive,* under $10.)

Sonoma

The Grille. *Moderate-Expensive.* At the Sonoma Mission Inn, Hwy. 12, Boyes Hot Springs; (707) 938-9000. Features pasta specialties, and items from the mesquite grill. Open for breakfast, lunch and dinner; brunch on Sundays. Reservations advised.

Sonoma Hotel. *Moderate.* 110 Spain St. (on the Plaza); (707) 996- 2996. Historic hotel-restaurant, with delightful garden patio and antique mahogany bar. House specialties include fresh pasta and seafood, and homemade desserts. Menu changes weekly. Open for lunch and dinner Fri.- Tues.; brunch on Sundays.

La Casa. *Inexpensive-Moderate.* 121 E. Spain St.; (707) 996-3406. Authentic Mexican restaurant, emphasizing traditional Mexican foods. Homemade specialties; multi-flavored margaritas and Mexican beer. Open daily.

Magliulo's Restaurant. *Expensive.* 691 Broadway; (707) 996-1031. Established Sonoma restaurant, housed in a charming, antique-decorated cottage. Superb Country French cuisine; wine list features California and French vintages. Brick patio for outdoor dining. Lunch and dinner daily; Sunday brunch. Reservations advised.

L'Esperance. *Expensive-Deluxe.* 464 First St. East (behind the French Bakery); (707) 996-2757. Fine French dining; elegant setting. Lunch and dinner daily; brunch on Sundays. Reservations required.

Marioni's *Expensive.* 8 W. Spain St.; (707) 996-6866. Menu emphasizes steaks and seafood. Contemporary Southwestern decor; multi-level dining rooms. Open for lunch and dinner, Tues.-Sun. Reservations suggested.

Ma Stokeld's. *Inexpensive-Moderate.* 464 First St. East; (707) 935-0660. Casual pub-style restaurant in the Place des Pyrenees, specializing in authentic English pies and pasties. Open for lunch and dinner daily.

Swiss Hotel. *Moderate.* 19 W. Spain St.; (707) 938-2884. Restored historic hotel, located on the Plaza. Features Italian, Chinese and American fare; informal setting. Open daily.

Les Arcades Restaurant. *Expensive.* 133 E. Napa St., Sonoma; (707) 938-3723. Traditional French cuisine. Extensive wine list, featuring Napa and Sonoma County wines as well as French wines. Open for dinner, Wed.-Sun. Reservations required.

Ranch House. *Moderate.* 20872 Broadway; (707) 938-0454. Authentic Mexican cooking, with emphasis on foods from the Yucatan region. Casual atmosphere. Lunch and dinner daily.

El Dorado Inn. *Moderate-Expensive.* 405 First St. West; (707) 996-3030. Elegantly restored 19th-century hotel, specializing in Continental and American cuisine. Shaded courtyard for outdoor dining; live entertainment. Open for lunch and dinner daily. Reservations recommended.

T.J's Sonoma Grill *Inexpensive.* 529 First St. West; (707) 938-2122. Casual eatery, serving omelettes, salads and burgers. Indoor and outdoor dining; expresso bar, soda fountain. Open for breakfast, lunch and dinner daily.

Sonoma Cheese Factory. *Inexpensive.* Located on the Plaza on Spain St.; (707) 996-1000. Popular deli-cum-cafe; home of the famous Sonoma Jack cheese. Large variety of sandwiches and salads, cheeses and Sonoma County wines. Excellent picnic lunches. Outdoor patio. Open daily 9.30 a.m.-5.30 p.m.

Glen Ellen

The Grist Mill Inn Restaurant. *Moderate-Expensive.* 14301 Arnold Dr., Glen Ellen; (707) 996-3077. Delightful Sonoma Valley restaurant, housed in historic building with working water wheel. Seafood, poultry and lamb, mesquite charcoal grilled; comprehensive wine list, featuring local wines. Open for lunch Wed.-Sat., dinner Tues.-Sun.; also Sunday brunch. Reservations recommended.

Santa Rosa

Russian River Vineyards Restaurant. *Moderate-Expensive.* 5700 Gravenstein Hwy. North, Forestville; (707) 887-1562. Greek and California cuisine; specialties include Spanakopita and Souvlaki. Delightful garden patio. Open for lunch and dinner, daily (except Tuesday) in summer, Fri.-Sun. in winter. Sunday brunch.

W.H. Frazier's. *Moderate-Expensive.* 3785 Cleveland Ave., Santa Rosa; (707) 579-9550. Art deco style restaurant, serving seafood, pasta, and specialties from the mesquite grill. Piano bar. Open for lunch Mon.-Fri., dinner daily.

Restaurant Matisse. *Moderate-Expensive.* 620 Fifth St., Santa Rosa; (707) 527-9797. Small, intimate restaurant decorated with fresh flowers and Matisse prints. Features French and American cuisine, with emphasis on local produce and poultry. Menu changes daily. Open for lunch and dinner, Mon.-Sat.

John Ash & Co. *Expensive.* At the Vintners Inn, 4330 Barnes Rd., Santa Rosa; (707) 527-7687. Well-appointed restaurant, specializing in Nouveau-French cuisine, prepared with fresh local produce and seasonally available ingredients. Delightful outdoor courtyard. Open for dinner daily.

La Province. *Moderate.* 525 College Ave., Santa Rosa; (707) 526-6233. Well-known Santa Rosa restaurant, specializing in French and Continental cuisine. Extensive wine list. Open for lunch, Tues.-Fri., dinners daily from 5.30 p.m.

PICNIC FARE

Deli Depot. 555 W. Fifth St., Sonoma; (707) 996-5832. Sandwiches, salads, meat and cheese trays, barbeque specialties.

Sonoma Cheese Factory. 2 W. Spain St., Sonoma; (707) 996-1931. Sandwiches and salads, meats and cheeses. Open daily.

Good Stuff Market & Deli. 1760 Piner Rd., Santa Rosa; (707) 544-6067. Hors d'oeurves, meat and cheese trays, sandwiches and salads; also health foods, and wine. Open daily.

Maison Gourmet. At Petrini's Market, 2751 4th St., Santa Rosa; (707) 545-2252. Domestic and imported meats and cheeses, sandwiches, chicken and ribs. Also freshly-baked sourdough bread. Open daily.

THE RUSSIAN RIVER REGION

Sun-drenched Valleys and Quiet Byways

The Russian River region is one of the newest and most exciting parts of the California wine country. It is vast, varied, and unhurried. It has in it nearly 100 wineries, mostly smaller than those in the Napa Valley, a majority of them family owned and operated, and largely scattered, in small clusters, across a much greater area.

The Russian River region is made up of primarily three valleys— The Russian River Valley, the Dry Creek Valley and the Alexander Valley. The Dry Creek and Alexander valleys run north-south, located adjacent to one another, with the Dry Creek Valley lying to the west of the Alexander Valley; and the Russian River Valley adjoins to the south of both the Alexander and Dry Creek valleys, itself extending south and west. There are, in addition, three or four smaller viticultural areas in the Russian River region, tacked on to the three major valleys: the Green Valley, for one, adjoins to the south of the Russian River Valley; Chalk Hill adjoins to the south of Alexander Valley; Knights Valley is located just east of the Alexander Valley; and the tiny Lytton Springs area lies in the small hills separating the Dry Creek Valley from the Alexander Valley.

The Russian River region can be reached more or less directly on Highway 101 north from San Francisco, with most major towns in the area — Healdsburg, Windsor, Geyserville, Asti and Cloverdale — located on the highway. Guerneville, of course, lies westward, on Highway 116, which, too, goes off 101.

THE RUSSIAN RIVER VALLEY

The Russian River Valley is a loosely defined viticultural area comprising the low-lying, flat plain to the south and southwest of Healdsburg, and following the course of the Russian River as it turns sharply westward to Guerneville, where the coastal hills finally close off the valley. The valley encompasses roughly 7,500 acres of planted vineyards (and more than a hundred microclimates!), with much of the acreage, largely along the river, devoted to the noble Pinot Noir grape, which makes the area all the more attractive to sparkling wine producers.

Healdsburg, at the top end of the valley, is of course the largest town here, and one of the best centers for visitors to the area. It has good accommodations, including several excellent bed and breakfast lodgings, and some worthwhile restaurants. Besides which, the town also has at the center of it an historic, century-old Spanish-style plaza, surrounded by old and lovely buildings, mostly dating from the 19th and early 20th centuries, and many of them restored to their former glory, especially interesting to history buffs. There is also a museum just off the plaza, with displays of local historical interest; and four ancient churches — Methodist (1870), First Baptist (1868), Episcopal (1888) and Christian (1892) — all located within easy distance of the plaza, add to the interest. The Healdsburg Historical Society publishes a tour book entitled *Historic Homes of Healdsburg*, available at local bookstores, with details and descriptions of several other historic buildings and homes in Healdsburg.

For wine enthusiasts, too, Healdsburg has much of interest. There are, in fact, at least a dozen or so wineries in and around town, most with visitor facilities. Just off the Healdsburg Plaza, for instance, is the William Wheeler Winery tasting room, offering primarily Sonoma County varietal wines; and on Fitch Street, a little to the southeast of the plaza, is the Clos du Bois winery, noted for its barrel-fermented white wines and one or two proprietary red wines. Another, the White Oak Winery, is also located on Fitch Street, quite close to Clos du Bois, and northwest of town on Grove Street is the historic Seghesio Winery, dating from 1902. Seghesio features primarily estate-bottled varietal wines.

Also try to visit Foppiano Vineyards, just south of Healdsburg on the Old Redwood Highway, originally established in 1896 by Italian immigrant John Foppiano, and still owned and operated by the Foppiano family. Two other wineries of interest, southeast of town on Grant Avenue, are J.W. Morris and Domaine St. George. The latter of these, Domaine St. George, formerly Cambiaso Vineyards, dates from 1934 and has on its premises the old residence of founders Giovanni and Maria Cambiaso, dating from 1852. The winery is now owned by the Four Seas Corporation of Thailand.

South still, nearer the small, rural town of Windsor, on the Old Redwood Highway, is the French-style sparkling wine producer, Piper-Sonoma, owned in part by France's Piper-Heidsieck. Piper-Sonoma is housed in a modern facility, built in 1980, which features a delightful terrace where you can sample Piper-Sonoma wines. A small restaurant on the premises, serving light luncheons, is also open to the public. The winery, besides, has daily tours of its facility, highlighting the *méthode champenoise* sparkling wine-making process.

Adjacent to Piper-Sonoma, and also of interest, is Windsor Vineyards, with its associations to Rodney Strong, a well-known contemporary figure in the California wine industry. The winery is housed in a most interesting, cross-shaped building, with each of the four wings of the cross housing a different phase of the winemaking process, enabling the visitor to view the entire operation from the tasting room directly above. The winery features vineyard-designated, estate varietal wines under the Windsor Vineyards label.

Among other wineries in the area are Jimark and Sotoyome, situated off Limerick Lane which goes off Los Amigos Road, just north of Windsor, and Landmark Vineyards, located on Los Amigos Road itself. This last is of particular interest to first-time visitors to the area, housed in a lovely, Spanish villa, and reached by way of a dramatic cypress-lined driveway, featured on Landmark's wine label.

Although more remains to be seen in the Russian River Valley, especially westward toward Guerneville, it is easiest, for touring purposes, to journey south from Windsor on the Old Redwood Highway to the small viticultural area of Green Valley, adjoining to the south of the Russian River Valley, and named for the enchanting little Green Creek that meanders through it. It has as its chief towns, Forestville, Fulton, Graton and Sebastopol, with a half-dozen or so wineries lying just on the outskirts of these. Fulton, situated on Fulton Road, just off the Old Redwood Highway, is quite possibly the best starting point for exploring the region. From Fulton, you can journey west on River Road, which has upon it the small Fulton Valley and Z Moore wineries, the latter housed in a picturesque old hop hiln, with a small picnic area adjacent to it. Z Moore, of course, specializes in dry Gewurztraminer and Chardonnay, made from Sonoma County grapes.

West from Z Moore, about a mile, and we are at the intersection of Olivet Road. Detour south on Olivet Road, a short distance, to arrive on Guerneville Road, remembering to visit the family-owned De Loach Vineyards, situated at the bottom end of Olivet, which offers estate-grown table wines from its 140-acre vineyard estate located at the winery. On Guerneville Road, westward another mile or so, is the small, 7,000-case Dehlinger Winery, with its entrance on Vine Hill Road, and with a lovely picnic area on the premises. Above Dehlinger, a brief detour north on Laguna Road—which goes off the Guerneville Road—will lead you to Martini & Prati, the largest winery in the area, primarily a bulk wine producer, with a capacity of 2.5 million cases a year, originally established in 1951. Also of interest, north of Martini & Prati on the Trenton-Healdsburg Road (which is more or less a continuation of Laguna Road after it crosses over River Road), are the Mark West Vineyards, named for the tiny creek that borders on the estate, and overlooking the Russian River Valley. Mark West offers estate-bottled varietal wines from its 60-acre vineyard. It also has a picnic area, with views of valley vineyards.

Returning to our main route of travel, however, and continuing westward, Guerneville Road merges with Guerneville Highway (116), and a little past the intersection, off on the tiny Ross Station Road, is Iron Horse, a *méthode champenoise* sparkling wine producer, perched on a plateau overlooking its 110 acres of estate vineyards. Just to the north of there on the Guerneville Highway, and also worth visiting, is Topolos at Russian River Vineyards, housed in a most unique wooden structure which borrows heavily from both the typical, old hop kiln buildings and the Russian Orthodox Church at Fort Ross, with its characteristic wooden towers. The winery makes small lots of vintage-dated Chardonnay and some oaky, varietal red wines. There is also a delightful little restaurant here, specializing in Greek and Continental food.

Westward still, on the Guerneville Highway, then north on Martinelli Road, is Domaine Laurier, one of the smallest wineries in the area, producing around 5,000 cases of wine annually, mostly estate-bottled varietals. Domaine Laurier—French for "Home of the Laurel"—derives its name from a 150-year-old laurel tree which stands on the estate and which is featured on the winery label.

There remains yet another winery. Korbel Champagne Cellars, the gem of them all, is situated to the northwest of Domaine Laurier — some 2 miles or so east of Guerneville—reached by way of Martinelli Road north from Domaine Laurier to River Road, then northwest on River Road, across the Russian River, directly to Korbel. Korbel is the largest bottle-fermented champagne and brandy producer in the county, and with an excellent, educational tour of its facility. It was originally founded in 1882 by the Korbel brothers, Anton, Joseph and Francis, and is now owned by the Heck family. The winery itself is housed in an attractive old red-brick building, gabled and ivy-covered, overlooking rich Russian River bottomland vineyards and redwood-covered hills.

Beyond Korbel, of course, there is Guerneville, a small resort town on the Russian River, surrounded by luxuriant woods, and with abundant outdoor recreational opportunities, including camping, kayaking, bicycling and hiking. Be sure to visit the Armstrong Redwood State Reserve, a splendid, 752-acre park, just to the north of Guerneville, which has in it some of the oldest and loveliest of Sonoma County's redwoods. It also has several hiking trails and nature walks, and adjoining to the northwest of the park is the larger Austin Creek State Recreation Area, encompassing some 4,236 acres of unspoiled wilderness. Austin Creek offers some camping possibilities, and fishing and horseback riding.

Farther still, westward on Highway 116 lies the Sonoma Coast—where you can explore Jenner, Bodega Bay and Fort Ross—not part of the wine region, but nevertheless with visitor interest.

THE DRY CREEK VALLEY

The Dry Creek Valley, adjoining to the northwest of the Russian River Valley and west of the Alexander Valley, is one of the loveliest of California's wine regions, with rolling, vine-covered hills, criss-crossed by small, twisty country roads, and with the enchanting little Dry Creek meandering through the midst of it. The valley itself is approximately 12 miles long, extending northwest from the confluence of Dry Creek and the Russian River, south of Healdsburg, to the Warm Springs-Dry Creek confluence at the closed, northern end. It has in it a score or more most interesting wineries, mostly small, rustic, and tucked away among vineyards devoted largely to Zinfandel—a grape that ripens almost to perfection on the sunny hillsides of Dry Creek, producing full-bodied wines, with rich varietal flavors.

The best place to begin a tour of the Dry Creek Valley, however, we might suggest, is at its southern end, on Westside Road—which can be reached from River Road, southwest of Healdsburg, by crossing over the Russian River on the tiny Wohler Road. Alternatively, from Healdsburg it is possible to go directly east on Westside Road to emerge at an approximate midway point in the valley, north of which—just to confuse the matter—Westside Road becomes West Dry Creek Road until it reaches the top end of the valley. In any case, most of the wineries are located on the Westside and West Dry Creek roads, with brief detours leading to one or two of the out-of-the-way wineries.

Southernmost in the valley, of course, on Westside Road, are the Porter Creek Vineyards and Davis Bynum Winery, the latter especially to be recommended to visitors, situated on a hillside, and with a picnic area and tasting facilities. Bynum offers primarily vintage-dated varietal wines and—for the stout of heart—wine futures.

A mile or so above Davis Bynum is the rustic, redwood J. Rochioli Winery, nestled amid estate vineyards. It has ongoing art shows, and wine tasting; and adjoining to its north, of supreme tourist interest, is the picture-perfect Hop Kiln Winery, housed in an old hop-drying barn, dating from 1905 and restored, by owner Marty Griffin, in 1975. Hop Kiln has an historic tasting room where you can sample such estate bottlings as "Marty Griffin's Big Red" and "A Thousand Flowers." It also has a picnic area on the premises, with valley views, and both the winery and the adjacent Griffin Vineyards are now a State Historic Landmark. Hop Kiln, interestingly, has also provided the setting for several motion pictures, including the much-loved *Lassie*.

Just to the north on Westside Road, and also with a measure of tourist interest, is Belvedere Winery, specializing in vineyard-designated wines from such well-known area vineyards as Robert Young and Bacigalupi; and farther still, a mile or so distant, are the Mill Creek Vineyards, where you can visit a charming little wood-frame winery with a real, working waterwheel. Not far from Mill Creek, off on a short detour east on Westside Road—toward Healdsburg—and south again on Kilney and Magnolia Drive, is Alderbrook, a small and relatively new, 17,000-case winery, offering primarily estate-grown

Chardonnay and Sauvignon Blanc, and with good visitor facilities.

North of Mill Creek, of course, West Dry Creek Road begins, and upon it are the Bellerose Vineyard, a specialist in "Bordeaux style" wines, situated on an historic vineyard estate dating from 1857; and the Lambert Bridge Winery, a small varietal wine producer, named for the bridge located a half-mile or so to the north of the winery, built in the 1800s by pioneer C.L. Lambert. Interestingly, the view of the winery from the bridge is the same as that depicted on the Lambert Bridge wine label.

North of the Lambert Bridge Winery, another mile, Lambert Bridge Road branches off West Dry Creek Road, eastward across Dry Creek, offering a worthwhile detour to visitors, for it has on it not only the tiny, ancient bridge of the same name, but also two small wineries of importance, Robert Stemmler and Dry Creek, both with visitor interest, and situated more or less directly across the street from one another. Robert Stemmler has a delightful little patio overlooking hillside estate vineyards, where you can enjoy estate-bottled Sonoma varietal wines; and at Dry Creek Vineyard—a largely white varietal wine producer—it is possible to meet the winery's owner-winemaker, David Stare, a graduate of the University of California, Davis. Dry Creek also has a shaded picnic area for visitors.

Returning to West Dry Creek Road, however, northward is the A. Rafanelli Winery, small, family owned and operated, specializing in varietal Zinfandel; and north of there, some two or three miles, along a winding section of the road, are the Meeker Vineyard and Preston Vineyards & Winery. Preston is of course the more interesting of the two, comprising a 120-acre vineyard estate which formerly was a pear orchard. The winery offers two classic Dry Creek Valley wines, Sauvignon Blanc and Zinfandel.

Other wineries of interest in the area, in upper Dry Creek Valley, include the Ferrari Carano Vineyards, situated at the top end of Dry Creek Road (which runs parallel to West Dry Creek Road), and the J. Pedroncelli Winery, eastward on Canyon Road, and which dates from 1904, originally founded by Italian immigrant Giovanni Pedroncelli. Both wineries offer estate-grown Sonoma County varietal wines.

Also of interest, northwest of the Dry Creek Valley, and reached on the Dry Creek Road itself, is the newly-developed Lake Sonoma Recreation Area, open to the public. It has boating, fishing, and camping facilities.

THE ALEXANDER VALLEY

The Alexander Valley, lying to the east of Dry Creek Valley, is a largely flat, landlocked valley, and one of Sonoma County's largest and most important wine growing areas, accounting for nearly half of the county's total vineyard acreage—approximately 15,000 acres. It extends from just southeast of Healdsburg, directly above Chalk Hill, northward to Geyserville, Asti and Cloverdale, with the wine varieties grown here ranging from Zinfandel and Cabernet Sauvignon—grown largely in the Geyserville area and the eastern parts of the valley—to Gewurztraminer, Johannisberg Riesling and Chardonnay, which thrive in the fertile bottomlands of the Russian River, in the cooler, southwestern corner of the valley, near Healdsburg. There are also, we might add, some 40 or so notable wineries here, mostly scattered in small groups, and which can be toured quite at random, criss-crossing Highway 101 and the Old Redwood Highway, and occasionally the Russian River.

The valley, of course, can quite easily be approached from the north, especially if you are in the upper Dry Creek Valley or journeying south on Highway 101 from Mendocino County. However, as most visitors arrive in the Alexander Valley from the south, directly from San Francisco and the Bay Area or the nearby Napa and Sonoma valleys, we have chosen to begin our tour in the southeast corner of the valley—its southernmost part. The southeast corner of the valley can be reached either on Chalk Hill Road which goes off Highway 101 northeastward, passing through the small viticultural area of the same name, and where you can visit one or two wineries; or by way of Route 128 northwestward from the Napa Valley, journeying over the Mayacamas ridge and past Knights Valley—another small viticultural area, with roughly 1,000 acres of Zinfandel and Chardonnay vineyards—descending directly into the Alexander Valley. Alternatively, if you are already in Healdsburg, it is possible to go north on Healdsburg Avenue a short distance, then northwestward on the Alexander Valley Road, and so to the southeast corner of the valley.

In any event, southernmost in the valley on Route 128 is the small but unique Field Stone Winery, built largely underground, using native stones from nearby fields, and surrounded by some 800 acres of estate vineyards. The winery offers mainly estate varietal wines, and one or two proprietary red wines. It also has a large, shaded picnic area for visitors, and it features music concerts and other events in the summer months.

North of Field Stone, a little way, are the Alexander Valley Vineyards, comprising a 120-acre estate, originally homesteaded in the 1840s by pioneer Cyrus Alexander, for whom the estate and indeed the valley itself are named. The winery, of course, is housed in a most historic stone and timber building, dating from the 1800s and nestled among estate vineyards. Alexander Valley Vineyards offers primarily varietal wines from its estate; it also has informal tours of its facility.

Farther up the valley, a half-mile or so, are other wineries of interest, among them Johnson's Alexander Valley Wines and Sausal Winery—both established in the 1950s—and Toyon Vineyards, a smaller, owner-operated winery, founded in 1973. All have good visitor facilities, and offer, for the most part, estate-grown Sonoma County varietal wines. At Johnson's you can also view a restored, 1924 pipe-organ.

Northwestward from the southeast corner of the valley, journeying toward Geyserville—which lies more or less at the heart of the Alexander Valley—we again have a choice of routes. The first, Route 128, continues up the valley some 20 miles directly to Geyserville, passing by the Alexander Valley Fruit & Trading Company, which has daily wine tasting and sales and occasional vineyard walks, and the small, newer Murphy-Goode Winery, located just to the north of the Alexander Valley Fruit & Trading Company. Alternatively, you can follow Alexander Valley Road westward from 128 to the intersection of Healdsburg Avenue and the Old Redwood Highway, then directly north on the Old Redwood Highway—which parallels Highway 101—to Geyserville. This latter route is quite possibly the more rewarding of the two, for it has on it some important wineries, most with visitor interest. Just to the south of the Healdsburg Avenue intersection, for instance, is Simi Winery, the best known and most prestigious of them all, housed in a picturesque old stone cellar dating from 1876. The winery was originally established by Italian immigrants Pietro and Guiseppe Simi, and is now owned by Möet-Hennessy of France, makers of Champagne Möet & Chandon, Hennessy Cognac and Dior perfumes. Simi has public tours of its facility, highlighting its state-of-the-art winemaking equipment. It also has wine tasting and sales, a gift shop, and a lovely, shaded picnic area.

Above Simi, northwestward, is the small, notable viticultural area of Lytton Springs, nestled in the hills that separate the Alexander Valley from the adjacent Dry Creek Valley, and reached on the tiny Lytton Springs Road which dashes off westward beneath Highway 101 and into the hills. The Lytton Springs area is devoted almost entirely to the Zinfandel variety, and it has in it the small, family owned and operated Lytton Springs Winery, specializing, quite naturally, in Sonoma County Zinfandel. The winery features a 50-acre hillside estate vineyard, where you can see some gnarled 80-year-old vines—still producing! Also on Lytton Springs Road are the Mazzocco Vineyards, a family-owned varietal wine producer.

Among other wineries strung along the Old Redwood Highway, north toward Geyserville, are the family-owned-and-operated Trentadue Winery, situated on a 200-acre vineyard estate and producing largely estate varietal wines; and Nervo, housed in a classic, turn-of-the-century stone building, and with a picnic area and grape arbor on the premises. Across from Trentadue and Nervo, reached on Independence Lane which crosses westward beneath Highway 101, is the grand old Chateau Souverain, which sits hugely on a rise of ground, overlooking valley vineyards. Souverain is one of the largest and most important wineries in the area, housed in a chateau-style building with two identical towers, reminiscent of early-day hop kilns, and a large, open courtyard with a fountain at the center of it. The winery has an excellent public tour, which leads along elevated walkways from where you can view the entire winemaking operation. There is also a popular little restaurant here, with high ceilings and vineyard views, open to the public for lunch and dinner.

Two miles or so above Souverain, reached on Geyserville Avenue (which is really a continuation of the Geyserville Road), is the small, rural town of Geyserville, dating from the 1800s, and situated at the center of a geothermal region which is ideally suited to the cultivation of Zinfandel and other heat-loving winegrape varieties. The town itself has very little of interest to the visitor, with the exception of a handful of well-appointed bed and breakfast inns and a restaurant or two. Just to

Picturesque Hop Kiln Winery, housed in a turn-of-the-century hop-drying barn in the Dry Creek Valley

Mill Creek Vineyards, Dry Creek Valley

Cabernet Sauvignon grapes

Korbel Champagne Cellars, Sonoma County's largest sparkling
wine producer

the northeast of town, however, some 4 or 5 miles on Geysers Road, you can visit some old geysers, which in the mid-1800s made the town famous as a spa resort, and from which, in fact, the town derives its name. Also of interest, to the northwest of town on Chianti Road—which runs parallel to Highway 101, to its west —is the Geyser Peak Winery, dating from 1880 and claimed to be the oldest winery in the Geyserville area. It features a unique tasting room, constructed from old redwood tanks, and with beautiful stained-glass windows; it also has a small patio overlooking the Russian River valley. Among other wineries here are Vina Vista, just above the Geyser Peak Winery, and Pastori, small, family owned, and located on Geyserville Avenue, east of 101.

North of Geyserville, approximately 4 miles, is the tiny village of Asti, named for the Italian winegrowing region of the same name. The Asti village itself comprises only a shop or two, a picnic area, and a tasting room for the Pat Paulsen Vineyards—founded in 1980 by former comedian (of TV's "Laugh In" fame) and perennial Presidential candidate, Pat Paulsen.

North still, some 10 miles on Highway 101, is Cloverdale, the northern terminus of the Alexander Valley, and important, also, as the gateway to the Mendocino wine country to the north. Cloverdale itself has a few bed and breakfast lodgings, some shops, and a tasting room for the area's Bandiera Winery, one of Sonoma County's northernmost wineries, notable for its colorful wine labels featuring California wildflowers. The Bandiera tasting room is located on Cloverdale Boulevard, adjacent to the Cloverdale Chamber of Commerce, and just to the southwest of town on Dutcher Creek Road are the Fritz Cellars, another winery of interest, enjoying a scenic country setting. Both Bandiera and Fritz offer California table wines.

Beyond Cloverdale, of course, Highway 101 heads out directly north toward the Mendocino County winegrowing regions of Hopland, Talmage, Ukiah, and the Porter Valley; while Route 128 branches northwestward and into the delectable Anderson Valley, with its half dozen or so small, family wineries, offering the wine country visitor yet another worthwhile detour.

RUSSIAN RIVER WINERIES

ALDERBROOK VINEYARDS. 2306 Magnolia Drive, Healdsburg; (707) 433-9154. Tasting and sales daily 10-5; tours by appointment.
□ Alderbrook is a newer, 17,000-case winery, established in 1982 by Mark Rafanelli, John Grace and Philip Staley. The winery's two principal offerings are Sauvignon Blanc and Chardonnay, both made from grapes grown in the estate's 55-acre vineyard located in the Dry Creek Valley, west of Healdsburg. Small lots of Semillon are also produced. Picnic facilities.

ALEXANDER VALLEY FRUIT & TRADING. 5110 Hwy. 128, Geyserville; (707) 433-1944. Tasting and sales daily 10-5; vineyard tours by appointment. Picnic area.

☐ Small, family owned and operated winery, specializing in vintage-dated varietal wines and custom gift packs. Wines produced are Cabernet Sauvignon, Chardonnay, Sauvignon Blanc, Chenin Blanc and White Zinfandel. The winery was established in 1984 by present owners Candace and Steve Sommer.

ALEXANDER VALLEY VINEYARDS. 8644 Hwy. 128, Healdsburg; (707) 433-7209. Wine tasting and sales 10-5 daily; tours by appointment. Picnic area on premises.

☐ One of the best-known family-owned wineries in the area, established in 1975 on property that was originally homesteaded in the 1840s by pioneer Cyrus Alexander—for whom both the winery and the valley are named. The winery is housed in an historic stone and timber building, situated at the center of the estate-owned 240-acre vineyard. Wines produced are estate-grown varietal Chardonnay, Johannisberg Riesling, Gewurztraminer, Dry Chenin Blanc, Cabernet Sauvignon, Pinot Noir, and Zinfandel. Wines are also offered under a second label, Sin Zin.

BALVERNE VINEYARDS. 10810 Hillview Road, Windsor; (707) 433-6913. Open for sales, daily 9-4; tours and tasting by appointment only.

☐ Located in the foothills just south of Healdsburg, Balverne offers oak-aged Chardonnay and Sauvignon Blanc from its 250-acre vineyard. Three other white and two red varietal wines are also produced. The winery has picnicking facilities and some hiking trails which are open in the spring and fall. The winery was established in 1979.

BANDIERA WINERY (TASTING ROOM). 555 So. Cloverdale Blvd., Cloverdale; (707) 894- 4298. Wine tasting and sales 10-5 daily.

☐ Bandiera is one of Sonoma County's northernmost wineries, originally founded in 1937 and re-opened in 1977 after a forty-year hiatus. The winery produces around 100,000 cases of varietal and generic wines annually, mostly from the estate's 600 acres of vineyards located in Sonoma and Napa counties and in Mendocino's Potter Valley. Wines produced include Cabernet Sauvignon, Sauvignon Blanc, White Zinfandel, Rosé of Zinfandel, Johannisberg Riesling, Chenin Blanc, and Chardonnay, with some of the wines also being bottled under a second label, John B. Merrit. Bandiera is especially notable for its colorful wine labels, featuring illustrations of California wildflowers.

BELLEROSE VINEYARD. 435 West Dry Creek Road, Healdsburg; (707) 433-1637. Tours and sales by appointment only.

☐ Bellerose is a 10,000-case, owner-operated winery, located on an historic vineyard estate where, in 1887, Captain Everett Wise built a winery from stones hauled from nearby Mill Creek. Bellerose, of course, was established in 1979, with the winery building incorporating part of the old stone winery which burned down in the 1930s. The estate's 52-acre vineyard, located at the winery, is planted to five traditional Bordeaux varieties—Cabernet Sauvignon, Cabernet Franc, Merlot, Petite Verdot, and Malbec—from which owner-winemaker Charles Richard makes a "Medoc" style wine, Cuvée Bellerose Cabernet Sauvignon. Two other blended wines offered are "Rosé du Val" and "Rouge du Val." Small lots of Barbera and Grignolino are also produced.

BELVEDERE WINE COMPANY. 4035 Westside Road, Healdsburg; (707) 433-8236. Tasting and sales, daily 10-4.30; tours by appointment.

☐ Small Healdsburg area winery, producing limited quantities of varietal wines from such well-known individual vineyards as Robert Young Vineyard, Bacigalupi Vineyard, York Creek Vineyards, Winery Lake Vineyards, and Spring Mountain. The winery was established in 1979.

BLACK MOUNTAIN VINEYARD. 101 Grant Avenue, Healdsburg; (707) 431-7015. Wine tasting and sales, Thurs.-Sun. 10-4; tours by appointment.

☐ Originally established as the J.W. Morris Winery, a Port specialist, in 1975, the winery was purchased by the owners of the Black Mountain Vineyard of Alexander Valley in 1983. The winery now offers estate-grown Cabernet Sauvignon, Chardonnay and Sauvignon Blanc under the J.W. Morris label, and varietal, vintage-dated Chardonnay, Sauvignon Blanc and Zinfandel under the Black Mountain Vineyard label. Late Bottled Vintage Port is also produced under both labels. The winery's 275-acre estate vineyard is located in the Alexander Valley.

BRENNER CELLARS. 35 Executive Ave., Rohnert Park; (707) 584-5522. Visitors by appointment only.

☐ Small winery, founded in 1979. Owner-winemaker Allan Brenner produces vintage-dated Zinfandel, Cabernet Sauvignon and Chardonnay from grapes purchased on a select vineyard basis.

CASWELL VINEYARDS. Tasting room located at 8860 Hwy. 12, Kenwood; (707) 874-2517. Open for tasting and sales, Thurs.- Mon. 12-5. Art gallery.

☐ Turn of the century winery, originally established by the Pieroni family and re-established by the Caswells, present owners, in 1982. Estate-bottled varietal wines featured here include Chardonnay, Zinfandel, Petite Sirah, and Claret, all made by traditional winemaking methods. A spiced honey wine and fermented cider are also offered. The Caswells' second label is Winter Creek.

CHALK HILL WINERY. 10300 Chalk Hill Road, Healdsburg; (707) 838-4306. Visitors by appointment only.

☐ Prominent Chalk Hill area winery, established in 1980 on a century-old 780-acre vineyard property. Chalk Hill offers primarily estate-grown varietal Chardonnay and Cabernet Sauvignon from its 180-acre vineyard located at the winery. Other wines, Sauvignon Blanc, Semillon, Merlot, Pinot Noir and Cabernet Franc, are made in small lots. The winery features Mozart and other music and wine festivals in summer.

CHARIS VINEYARDS. 7850 Dry Creek Rd., Geyserville; (707) 433-3533. Visitors by appointment, daily 8.30-4.30.

☐ Small, owner-operated winery, founded in 1981 by John and Fran Florence. The winery offers vintage-dated, varietal Cabernet Sauvignon and Sauvignon Blanc from its estate vineyard located in the Dry Creek Valley. Picnic area on premises.

CHATEAU DeBRAUN. 1160 Hopper Ave., Santa Rosa; (707) 544-1600. Visitors by appointment, Mon.-Fri. 9-4.

☐ New Santa Rosa area winery, housed in a 6,000 square-foot French chateau with a courtyard and a fountain at the center of it. The winery specializes in the production of wines from the unique, new California hybrid varietal, Symphony, developed by the School of Viticulture at the University of California, Davis, from Muscat of Alexandria and Grenach Gris. Four estate-bottled varietal wines and two champagnes are produced from the Symphony grape—Overture, Prelude, Theme, Finale, Romance and Rhapsody. The winery was established in 1989.

CHATEAU DIANA. 6195 Dry Creek Rd., Healdsburg; (707) 433-6992. Retail sales Mon.-Sat., 10-4.30; no tours or tasting.
□ Family owned and operated winery, founded in 1977 by Diana Manning, for whom it is named. The winery buys wine in bulk, and finishes it at its Dry Creek Valley facility. Varietal, vintage-dated wines bottled under the Chateau Diana label include Cabernet Sauvignon, Petite Sirah, Chardonnay, Gewurztraminer and Chenin Blanc. Some generic wines are also offered. Wine sales in case lots only. Picnic area on premises.

CHATEAU SOUVERAIN. Independence Lane, at Hwy. 1, Geyserville; (707) 433-8281. Tours, tasting and sales, 10-4.30 daily; last tour at 3 p.m. Restaurant on premises; for reservations, call (707) 433-3141.
□ Souverain is a large, 500,000-case winery, situated on a knoll in the Alexander Valley, surrounded by estate vineyards. The winery itself is housed in an imposing chateau-style building with two identical towers, reminiscent of early-day hop kilns, and a large, open courtyard with a fountain at the cneter of it. It was originally built in 1973 by the Pillsbury Company, and in 1976 it was acquired by its present owners, a consortium of some 300 North Coast grape growers, who produce 100% varietal, North Coast Appellation wines under the Souverain label. The winery also has an excellent tour of its facility, leading along elevated walkways, and a small restaurant at the winery serves lunch, dinner and Sunday brunch. There is a gift shop on the premises, and art shows, concerts, theater and fairs are scheduled throughout the year.

CLOS DU BOIS. 5 Fitch Street, Healdsburg. Open for wine tasting and sales, 10-5 daily; tours by appointment.
□ Well-known Healdsburg winery, established in 1974. The winery offers estate-grown varietal wines from its 650 acres or so of estate vineyards located in Sonoma County's Dry Creek and Alexander valleys. Offerings include Chardonnay, Sauvignon Blanc, Johannisberg Riesling, Gewurztraminer, Pinot Noir, Merlot, and Cabernet Sauvignon. Also featured is a proprietary red wine, Marlstone, blended from Cabernet Sauvignon and Merlot. Clos du Bois' second label is River Oaks Vineyard.

DAVIS BYNUM WINERY. 8075 Westside Road, Healdsburg; (707) 433-5852. Open for tasting and sales daily 10-5; tours by appointment.
□ Davis Bynum's winery is situated on a hillside in the Russian River Valley, overlooking valley vineyards. The winery was originally established in 1965 in Berkeley, and moved to its present location in 1975. Bynum produces primarily vintage-dated varietal wines from Sonoma County grapes. Offerings include Zinfandel, White Zinfandel, Pinot Noir, Cabernet, Gewurztraminer, Fumé Blanc, Chardonnay, and a Sonoma Chablis. Wines are also bottled under a second label, River Bend. Picnic facilities are available at the winery.

DEHLINGER WINERY. 6300 Guerneville Road (entrance off Vine Hill Rd.), Sebastopol; (707) 823-2378. Tasting and sales Mon.-Fri. 10-4.30, Sat.-Sun. 10-5; tours by appointment.
□ Dehlinger is a reputable small winery, producing approximately 7,000 cases of premium Sonoma County varietal wines annually, including Chardonnay, Cabernet Sauvignon, Zinfandel and Pinot Noir. Some of the wines are estate-bottled, with the grapes coming from Dehlinger's 31-acre vineyard located in

the lower reaches of the Russian River Valley. The winery was founded in 1976 by present owner Tom Dehlinger.

DE LOACH VINEYARDS. 1791 Olivet Road, Santa Rosa; (707) 526-9111. Wine tasting and sales daily, 10-4.30; tours by appointment.
☐ Small, family-owned operation, with 140 acres of estate vineyards located at the winery in the Russian River Valley. Founders Cecil and Christine De Loach originally established their vineyards in 1975 and sold grapes to other wineries for some years. In 1982, the winery was launched. Current annual production is in the 18,000-case range, with Zinfandel and White Zinfandel leading the list of estate-grown table wines. Other vintage-dated varietal wines produced are Pinot Noir, Chardonnay, and Gewurztraminer. The winery has a picnic area located adjacent to the vineyards.

DE LORIMIER WINERY. 2001 Hwy. 128, Geyserville; (707) 433-7718. Tours, tasting and sales by appointment, Mon.-Fri. 9-5.
☐ De Lorimier produces three proprietary white wines—Spectrum, which is a blend of Semillon and Sauvignon Blanc, and Prism (Chardonnay) and Lace (Late Harvest Sauvignon Blanc). The winery was founded by Dr. A. deLorimier, present owner.

DIAMOND OAKS VINEYARD. 26900 Dutcher Creek Rd., Cloverdale; (707) 894-3191. Visitors by appointment only.
☐ Diamond Oaks was founded in 1978. The winery offers primarily varietal Chardonnay, Sauvignon Blanc and Cabernet Sauvignon, made from grapes grown in its 153 acres of estate vineyards located in the Napa Valley and the Wild Horse Valley; grapes are also purchased on a select-vineyard basis. The winery's second label is Thomas Knight.

DOMAINE LAURIER. 8075 Martinelli Road, Forestville; (707) 887-2176. Visitors by appointment only.
☐ Small, 5,000-case winery. Domaine Laurier—French for "Home of the Laurel"—derives its name from a 150-year-old laurel tree which stands on the estate and is featured on the winery label. The winery itself is situated in the Forestville area of the Russian River Valley, along Green Valley Creek, with 30 acres of estate vineyards located at the winery. Vintage-dated, estate-bottled Cabernet Sauvignon, Sauvignon Blanc, Chardonnay and Pinot Noir are the wines produced here. The winery was founded in 1978.

DOMAINE MICHEL. 4155 Wine Creek Rd., Healdsburg; (707) 433-7427. Winery tours and tasting by appointment.
☐ Small Russian River winery, producing varietal Chardonnay and Cabernet Sauvignon. Picnic area on premises.

DOMAINE ST. GEORGE WINERY. 1141 Grant Ave., Healdsburg; (707) 433-5508. Open for sales 10-4, Mon.-Fri.; no tasting. Tours by appointment only.
☐ Domaine St. George, formerly Cambiaso, is a 60,000-case winery, situated on a hillside overlooking the Russian River. It is located near an old country house, dating from 1852, which once was the residence of the Cambiaso family. The winery was of course founded in 1934 by Giovanni and Maria Cambiaso, to produce Burgundy, Chablis and Vin Rosé—all of which are still produced under the "1852 House Wine" label. The winery now also offers varietal vintage-dated Chardonnay, Chenin Blanc, Fumé Blanc, Cabernet Sauvignon, Petite Sirah, and Barbera. Domaine St. George is owned by the Four Seas Corporation

of Thailand.

DRY CREEK VINEYARD. 3770 Lambert Bridge Road, Healdsburg; (707) 433-1000. Open for tasting and sales daily 10.30-4.30; tours by appointment.
☐ Established Dry Creek Valley winery, founded in 1972 by present owner-winemaker David Stare, a graduate to the University of California, Davis. The winery is devoted to the production of 100% varietal vintage-dated wines, including Chardonnay, Fumé Blanc, Gewurztraminer, a dry-styled Chenin Blanc, Sauvignon Blanc, Zinfandel, Petite Sirah, Merlot and Cabernet Sauvignon, with white varietals accounting for more than three-quarters of the winery's annual, 70,000-case output. The winery is housed in an ivy-covered, gray-stone building, situated on a 70-acre vineyard estate. Shaded picnic area on premises.

EAGLE RIDGE WINERY. 111 Goodwin Ave., Penngrove; (707) 664-9463. Open for tours, tasting and sales, daily 11-4. Picnic area on premises.
☐ Housed in an historic, 1880s building, surrounded by estate vineyards and situated on a hill overlooking Petaluma Valley. The only wine produced here is Sauvignon Blanc. Wines are also bottled under a second label, Chu Tai. The winery was established in 1985.

FERRARI-CARANO VINEYARDS & WINERY. 8761 Dry Creek Rd., Healdsburg; (707) 433-6700. Tasting and sales daily 10-5; tours by appointment.
☐ Family owned and operated winery, situated on a vineyard estate bordered by the Dry Creek. The winery produces primarily varietal Cabernet Sauvignon, Chardonnay, Sauvignon Blanc and Merlot, all from grapes grown in five estate-owned vineyards located in the Alexander and Dry Creek valleys. The winery and vineyards were founded in 1981 by Don and Rhonda Carano, present owners.

FIELD STONE WINERY. 10075 Hwy. 128, Healdsburg; (707) 433-7266. Tasting and sales daily 10-5; tours by appointment.
☐ Field Stone is a unique winery, built largely underground, using native stones from nearby fields. The winery is family owned and operated, situated on an 800-acre vineyard estate in the Alexander Valley. It produces primarily estate-grown varietal wines, led by a Cabernet Sauvignon and Petite Sirah, and a Rosé of Cabernet labeled "Spring Cabernet." A proprietary Cabernet Sauvignon, "Hoot of the Owl," is also produced. The winery features music concerts and other events in summer; it also has a large, shaded picnic area for winery visitors.

FOPPIANO WINE COMPANY. 12707 Old Redwood Hwy., Healdsburg; (707) 433-7272. Open for tasting and sales daily 10-4.30; tours by appointment.
☐ The Foppiano Wine Company was originally founded in 1896 by immigrant John Foppiano, and is still owned and operated by the Foppiano family. The winery produces nearly 200,000 cases of varietal and barrel-aged generic wines annually, all from its 200-acre estate vineyard located adjacent to the winery. Wines are bottled under both the Foppiano label and a secondary label, Riverside Farm. Picnic area on premises.

FRICK WINERY. 23072 Walling Rd., Geyserville; (415) 362-1911.

Visitors by appointment only.
□ Small, owner-operated winery, founded in 1976 by Bill and Judith Frick, present owners. Vintage-dated, varietal wines produced here are Pinot Noir, Petite Sirah, Zinfandel, Chardonnay, and Grenache, all made from grapes purchased on a select-vineyard basis.

FRITZ CELLARS. 24691 Dutcher Creek Rd., Cloverdale; (707) 894-3389. Open for wine tasting and sales, 12-4.30 daily; tours by appointment.
□ Fritz Cellars is situated on a hillside in upper Dry Creek Valley, with a picnic area overlooking a small lake. The winery produces estate-grown varietal wines primarily, including Chardonnay, Fumé Blanc and Pinot Noir Blanc. Vintage-dated Cabernet Sauvignon and Zinfandel are also offered. The winery was established in 1981.

FULTON VALLEY WINERY. 875 River Rd., Fulton; (707) 578-1744. Wine tasting and sales daily 10-5 in summer; tours by appointment. Picnic area and deli on premises.
□ Fulton Valley Winery makes varietal Cabernet Sauvignon, Sauvignon Blanc, Chardonnay, Gewurztraminer and Pinot Noir Blanc from its 40-acre estate vineyard. The winery was established in 1983.

GAUER ESTATE WINERY & VINEYARD. 18700 Geyserville Ave., Geyserville; (707) 433-4402. Visitors by appointment only.
□ New Alexander Valley winery, with 500 acres of estate vineyards, planted to Chardonnay and Cabernet Sauvignon. First vintage was released in 1989.

GEYSER PEAK WINERY. 22281 Chianti Avenue, Geyserville; (707) 433-6585/(800) 255-WINE in CA. Open for tasting and sales daily 10-5; tours by appointment.
□ Geyser Peak is the oldest winery in Geyserville, named—much like the town of Geyserville—for the many natural geysers once found in the area. The winery was originally established in 1880 by August Quitzow, as the Quitzow Winery. It is now owned by the Trione family, who own approximately 1,100 acres of planted vineyards in Sonoma County. The winery bottles a full line of varietal, vintage-dated wines, as well as a Chablis and Burgundy, and Blanc de Noir and Brut California Champagne. Wines are also bottled under the Summit and Trione labels. There is a picnic area on the premises, and a tasting room constructed from old redwood tanks.

HOP KILN WINERY. 6050 Westside Road, Healdsburg; (707) 433-6491. Open for tasting and sales daily 10-5; tours by appointment.
□ Picturesque old winery, housed in a former hop-drying barn, dating from 1905 and restored, by owner Marty Griffin, in 1975. Estate-grown varietal wines produced here include Cabernet Sauvignon, Petite Sirah, Napa Gamay, Zinfandel, Chardonnay, Gewurztraminer, and Johannisberg Riesling. Three proprietary wines are also featured: A Thousand Flowers, Weihnachten and Marty Griffin's Big Red. The winery and its adjoining 65-acre Griffin Vineyard—which was originally established in 1880—are now a State Historic Landmark. Picnic area at winery.

IRON HORSE VINEYARDS. 9786 Ross Station Road, Sebastopol; (707) 887-1507. Winery visits by appointment only.
□ Small, notable *méthode champenoise* sparkling wine producer, established in 1976. The winery is housed in a renovated old barn, situated on a plateau

overlooking the estate's 110 acres of vineyards, planted primarily to Chardonnay and Pinot Noir. An additional 30 acres of estate vineyards are located in the Alexander Valley, planted to Cabernet Sauvignon and Sauvignon Blanc. Sparkling wines produced here are Brut, Blanc de Blanc and Blanc de Noirs. Some estate-grown varietal wines are also offered, including Chardonnay, Cabernet Sauvignon, Pinot Noir, and Blanc de Pinot Noir. Picnic area at winery, with a gazebo and flower garden.

JIMARK WINERY. 602 Limerick Lane, Healdsburg; (707) 433-3118. Open for tasting and sales by appointment only.
☐ Small, 12,000-case winery, producing vintage-dated Chardonnay and Cabernet Sauvignon from its 140-acre vineyard in the Alexander Valley. The winery was founded in 1982 by winemaker James Wolner and Mark Michtour, and aptly named "Jimark."

JOHNSON'S ALEXANDER VALLEY WINES. 8333 Hwy. 128, Healdsburg; (707) 433-2319. Wine tasting and retail sales daily 10-5; tours by appointment.
☐ Small, family owned and operated winery, housed in a wooden barn, situated in the southwest corner of the Alexander Valley. The winery was originally established in 1952 by James Johnson, and sold to his sons Jay, Tom and Will Johnson, in 1972. Johnson's produces vintage-dated Chardonnay, Gewurztraminer, Johannisberg Riesling, Cabernet, Zinfandel and Pinot Noir, all from grapes grown in its 70-acre vineyard located at the southern end of the valley. A pear wine is also offered. As added interest, the winery has on display a restored 1924 pipe organ. Organ concerts are featured at the winery once a month. Picnicking possibilities.

JORDAN VINEYARD AND WINERY. 1474 Alexander Valley Road, Healdsburg; (707) 433-6955. Wine sales Mon.-Fri. 8-5; no tasting. Tours by appointment only.
☐ Jordan is housed in a traditional Bordeaux-style chateau, situated on a 275-acre vineyard estate. It offers two classic Sonoma County wines—Cabernet Sauvignon and Chardonnay. The winery was established in 1976.

KORBEL CHAMPAGNE CELLARS. 13250 River Road, Guerneville; (707) 887-2294. Winery hours: 9-5 daily May-Sept., 9-4.30 Oct.-Apr.; tours 9.45-3.45 May-Sept.; 10-3 Oct.-Apr. Wine tasting and sales.
☐ Korbel is the largest producer of bottle-fermented champagne in Sonoma County, with annual production in the 500,000 case range. It also produces approximately 400,000 cases of brandy annually. The winery was originally founded in 1880 by Anton, Joseph and Francis Korbel, natives of Czechoslovakia, and is now owned by the Heck family. The winery itself is housed in a splendid, ivy-covered red-brick buiding, surrounded by lavish flower gardens. Korbel also has one of the best champagne-cellar tours, where you can view the entire champagne-making process, and then gaste the finished product. Korbel offerings include Brut, Blanc de Blanc, Blanc de Noirs, Extra Dry, Demi-Sec, Natural, Rouge and Rosé.

LA CREMA VINERA. 971 Transport Way, Petaluma; (707) 762-0393. Visitors by appointment only.
☐ Small, 7,000-case winery, producing varietal vintage-dated Chardonnay and Pinot Noir from grapes grown in the Carneros district and western Sonoma County. The winery was founded in 1979.

LAKE SONOMA WINERY. 9990 Dry Creek Rd., Geyserville; (707) 431-1550. Open for tours, tasting and sales daily 10-5. Picnic area.

☐ The Lake Sonoma Winery was originally established in 1977 at Benicia, California, by the Robert Polson family. The Polson's vineyard estate at the head of Dry Creek Valley, however, was developed in 1982, with a new wine tasting facility located on a hillside on the estate, overlooking the Warm Springs Dam and Dry Creek Valley. The winery features primarily Dry Creek and Alexander Valley wines; offerings include Cabernet Sauvignon, Chardonnay, Merlot Zinfandel, and Chenin Blanc. There is also a deli and shaded picnic area on the premises.

LAMBERT BRIDGE. 4085 West Dry Creek Road, Healdsburg; (707) 433-5855. Tasting and sales daily 10-4.30; tours by appointment.

☐ Small Dry Creek Valley winery, established in 1975 and named for the nearby Lambert Bridge—which was originally built in the late 1880s by pioneer C.L. Lambert. The winery view depicted on the Lambert Bridge wine label, quite interestingly, is the same as that seen from the bridge. The winery itself is housed in a wood-frame structure, featuring an aging cellar with a fireplace and chandeliers. The winery offers estate-bottled, vintage-dated varietal Chardonnay, Cabernet Sauvignon and Merlot from its 76-acre vineyard located in the valley.

LANDMARK VINEYARDS. 9150 Los Amigos Road, Windsor; (707) 838-9466. Open for tasting and sales, Thurs.-Sun. 10-5; tours by appointment.

☐ Small, family owned and operated winery, established in 1974 by the William R. Mabey family, present owners. The winery is housed in a lovely Spanish villa, situated at the end of a dramatic driveway lined with century-old cypresses; both the winery and driveway are featured on the wine label. Landmark produces primarily Sonoma County Chardonnay and Petite Sirah from its estate vineyards in Windsor and the Alexander and Sonoma valleys. There is a picnic area with tables at the winery.

LYETH VINEYARD & WINERY. 24625 Chianti Rd., Geyserville; (707) 857-3562. Tasting and sales Mon.-Fri. 11-4, daily in summer.

☐ Small, Bordeaux-style winery, originally established in 1973 as the Brignole Ranch. The winery produces two proprietary wines: Lyeth, which is a blend of Cabernet Sauvignon, Cabneret Franc, Merlot and Malbec; and Lyeth Blanc, a blend of Sauvignon Blanc and Semillon. Lyeth's 100-acre estate vineyard is located in the Alexander Valley.

LYTTON SPRINGS WINERY. 650 Lytton Springs Road, Healdsburg; (707) 433-7721. Open for tasting and sales daily 10-4; tours by appointment.

☐ Lytton Springs specializes in premium Sonoma County Zinfandel, made from grapes grown on the estate's 50-acre vineyard located at the winery, which has some vines that are more than 80 years old and still producing. The winery was established in 1977.

MARK WEST VINEYARDS. 7000 Trenton-Healdsburg Road, Forestville; (707) 544-4813. Open for tours, tasting and sales, daily 10-5.

☐ Mark West Vineyards was established in 1976 by Robert and Joan Ellis, present owners, and named for the tiny creek that borders on the estate. 60 acres of family vineyards are located at the winery, overlooking the lovely Russian River Valley. The winery's current 15,000-case production consists of estate-

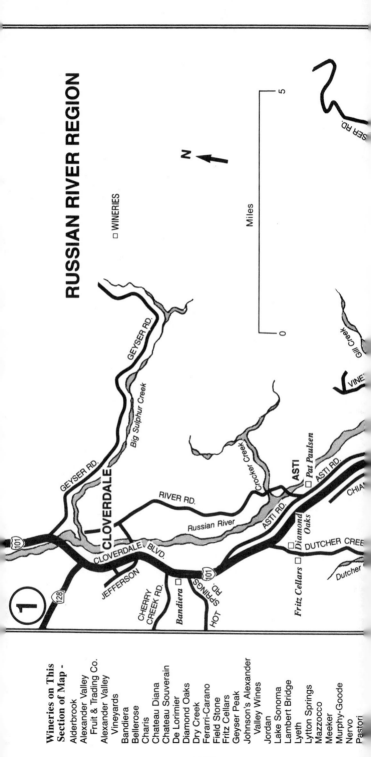

RUSSIAN RIVER REGION

☐ WINERIES

N

Miles

0   5

GEYSER RD.

Big Sulphur Creek

GEYSER RD.

CLOVERDALE

RIVER RD.

Russian River

Crocker Creek

ASTI

Pat Paulsen ☐ ASTI RD.

CHIA

ASTI RD.

☐ *Diamond Oaks*

DUTCHER CREE

101

CLOVERDALE BLVD.

JEFFERSON

CHERRY CREEK RD.

Bandiera ☐

HOT SPRINGS RD.

Fritz Cellars ☐

Dutcher

101

128

1

VINE

Gill Creek

SER RD.

Wineries on This Section of Map -

Alderbrook
Alexander Valley Fruit & Trading Co.
Alexander Valley Vineyards
Bandiera
Bellerose
Charis
Chateau Diana
Chateau Souverain
De Lorimier
Diamond Oaks
Dry Creek
Ferarri-Carano
Field Stone
Fritz Cellars
Geyser Peak
Johnson's Alexander Valley Wines
Jordan
Lake Sonoma
Lambert Bridge
Lyeth
Lytton Springs
Mazzocco
Meeker
Murphy-Goode
Nervo
Pastori

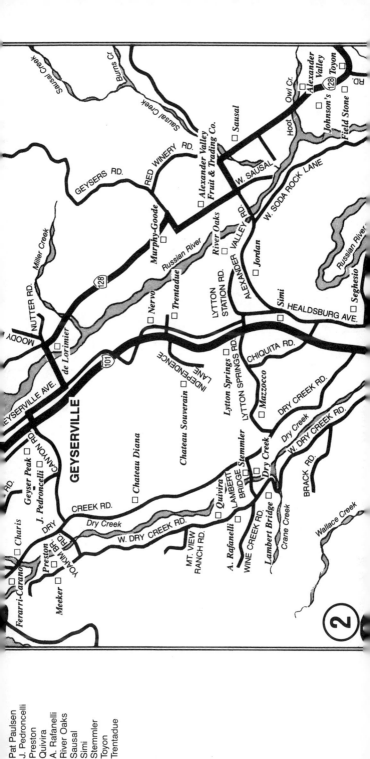

Pat Paulsen
J. Pedroncelli
Preston
Quivira
A. Rafanelli
River Oaks
Sausal
Simi
Stemmler
Toyon
Trentadue

107

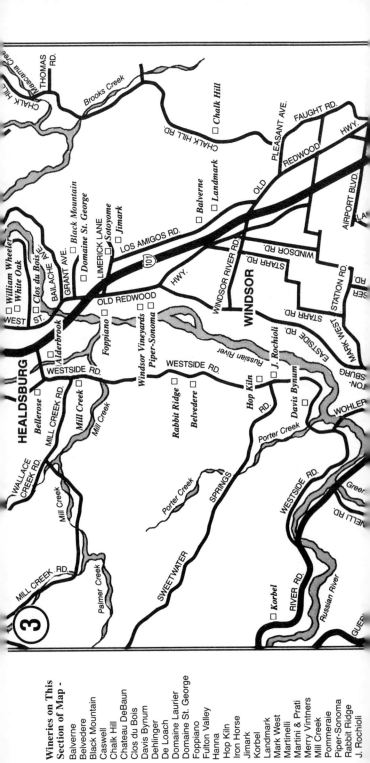

Wineries on This
Section of Map –

Balverne
Belvedere
Black Mountain
Caswell
Chalk Hill
Chateau DeBaun
Clos du Bois
Davis Bynum
Dehlinger
De Loach
Domaine Laurier
Domaine St. George
Foppiano
Fulton Valley
Hanna
Hop Kiln
Iron Horse
Jimark
Korbel
Landmark
Mark West
Martinelli
Martini & Prati
Merry Vintners
Mill Creek
Pommeraie
Piper-Sonoma
Rabbit Ridge
J. Rochioli

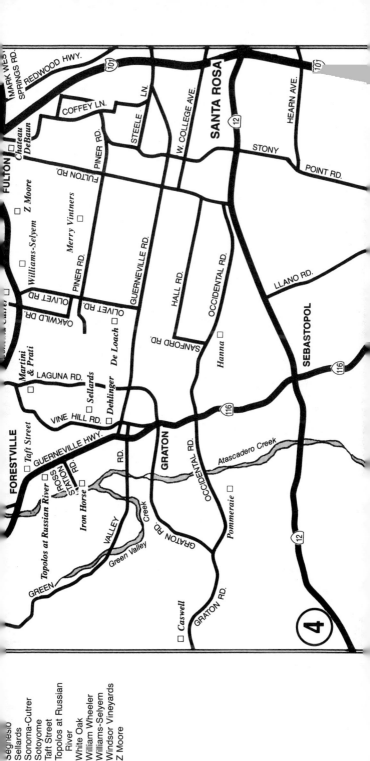

grown varietals, led by Chardonnay. Mark West offers picnicking opportunities to visitors, and special catered luncheons for organized functions. It also has a gift shop on the premises.

MARTINELLI ORCHARDS & VINEYARDS. 3360 River Rd., Windsor; (707) 525-0570. Wine tasting and sales daily 10-5.
□ Housed in an historic hop-drying barn, in the heart of the Russian River Valley. The orchards and vineyards were founded by the present owners, the Martinelli family—apple and grape-growers for more than three generations. The Martinellis offer primarily Sonoma County wines. Picnic area adjacent to vineyards.

MARTINI & PRATI WINES. 2191 Laguna Road, Santa Rosa; (707) 823-2404. Open for tasting and sales, Mon.-Fri. 9-4.
□ Martini & Prati is a well-known producer of bulk wines, with a 2.5-million case capacity. Nearly 90% of its wines are sold to other large wineries, with only some 25,000 cases or so being bottled under the Martini & Prati label, much of it devoted to jug wines and a line of varietal and generic wines. The winery was established in 1951 by Elmo Martini and Edward Prati, present owners.

MATANZAS CREEK WINERY. 6097 Bennett Valley Road, Santa Rosa; (707) 528-6464. Visitors by appointment only.
□ Small, family-owned winery, housed in a modern facility in the Bennett Valley, just outside Santa Rosa. The winery specializes in Sonoma County wines, made in the French style. Offerings include Chardonnay, Cabernet Sauvignon, Merlot and Sauvignon Blanc, all made from grapes grown in the estate's 42 acres of vineyards located in the Bennett Valley. The winery was established in 1977 by Sandra and William MacIver, present owners.

MAZZOCCO VINEYARDS. 1400 Lytton Springs Rd., Healdsburg; (707) 433-9035. Tasting and sales daily 10-4; tours by appointment.
□ Small, family-owned winery, located in the Lytton Springs area, adjacent to Alexander Valley. Chardonnay is the only wine produced here, made from grapes grown on the estate's 18-acre vineyard in the Alexander Valley. The winery was established in 1984.

THE MEEKER VINEYARD. 9711 West Dry Creek Road, Healdsburg; (707) 431-2148. Winery visits by appointment only.
□ Meeker Vineyard is situated on a 215-acre hillside estate in the Dry Creek Valley area, with approximately 54 acres planted to wine grapes. Estate-grown varietal wines produced are Chardonnay, Cabernet Sauvignon and Zinfandel. The winery was established in 1983 by present owners Charles and Molly Meeker.

THE MERRY VINTNERS. 3339 Hartman Rd., Santa Rosa; (707) 526-4441. Winery visits by appointment only.
□ Small, family operation, established in 1984. Owner-winemaker Merry Edwards mades varietal Chardonnay, from grapes purchased on a select-vineyard basis.

MILL CREEK VINEYARDS. 1401 Westside Road, Healdsburg; (707) 431-2121. Open for wine tasting and sales, daily 10-4.30 Apr.-Dec., Fri.-Mon. 12-4.30 Jan.-Mar.
□ Small, family-owned winery, established in 1975 by the Charles Kreck family, present owners. The winery is housed in a charming little woodframe

structure, with a real, working waterwheel on its side. Varietal, vintage-dated wines produced here are Cabernet Sauvignon, Chardonnay, Cabernet Blush, Merlot, Gamay, Pinot Noir and Gewurztraminer, all made from grapes grown on the estate's 65-acre vineyard located at the winery. Wines are also bottled under a second label, Feltz Springs. Picnic area on premises.

MURPHY-GOODE VINEYARDS. 4001 Hwy. 128, Geyserville; (707) 431-7644. Winery visits by appointment only.

□ Small, Alexander Valley winery, founded in 1985 by Tim Murphy and Dale Goode, grape growers for over 20 years. Estate-bottled varietal wines produced are Fumé Blanc, Chardonnay, Cabernet Sauvignon and Merlot.

NERVO WINERY. 19550 Geyserville Avenue, Geyserville; (707) 857-3417. Open for tasting and sales, 10-5 daily.

□ Nervo is housed in a classic turn-of-the-century stone building, with a grape arbor and picnic area on the premises. The winery offers mainly "young" wines, sold only at the winery. The winery was originally established in 1888, and is now owned by the Trione family of Geyser Peak Winery.

PASTORI WINERY. 23189 Geyserville Avenue, Cloverdale; (707) 857-3418. Open for tasting and sales daily 9-5.

□ 10,000-case, family-owned winery, producing primarily generic wines from its 60-acre estate vineyard located at the winery. Pastori was originally established in 1914, and revived in 1975.

PAT PAULSEN VINEYARDS. 25510 River Road, Cloverdale; (707) 894-3197. Tasting room located at the Asti Village on Highway 101; open daily 10-6.

□ Founded in 1980 by comedian Pat Paulsen, of TV's "Laugh In" fame, and perennial candidate for the President of the United States. The winery and a 40-acre vineyard are situated on a 600-acre ranch just outside Cloverdale, with a tasting room located in the tiny village of Asti, just to the south of the The Winery at Asti. Estate-bottled varietal wines produced at the winery include Chardonnay, Sauvignon Blanc, Cabernet Sauvignon, Gewurztraminer and Muscat Canelli. Wines are also bottled under a second label, Matrose.

J. PEDRONCELLI WINERY. 1220 Canyon Road, Geyserville; (707) 857-3531. Open for tasting and sales daily 10-5.

□ Originally established in 1904, the winery was acquired by Italian immigrant John Pedroncelli in 1927, and is still owned and operated by the Pedroncelli family. The winery bottles a full line of varietal, vintage-dated wines, made from Sonoma County grapes; offerings include Cabernet Sauvignon, Zinfandel, Gamay Beaujolais, Johannisberg Riesling, Gewurztraminer, Chardonnay, Chenin Blanc, Sauvignon Blanc, French Colombard, White Zinfandel, and Pinot Noir. Some jug wines are also offered under the J. Pedroncelli label. Pedroncelli's 135-acre estate vineyard is located at the winery in upper Dry Creek Valley.

PIPER-SONOMA CELLARS. 11447 Old Redwood Hwy., Healdsburg; (707) 433-8843. Open daily 10-5; wine tasting and retail sales, tours every half-hour. Restaurant.

□ French-style, *méthode champenoise* sparkling wine producer, housed in a modern facility near Windsor in the Russian River Valley, with lovely, landscaped grounds. The winery offers three types of sparkling wines: Brut, Blanc de Noirs, and Tete de Cuvée. It also has a small restaurant on the premises, Café de Chai, serving light luncheons. The winery was established in 1980, and is owned in part by Piper-Heidsieck of France.

POMMERAIE VINEYARDS. 10541 Cherry Ridge Rd., Sebastopol; (707) 823-9463. Visitors by appointment. Picnic area on premises.
☐ Small, Russian River winery, producing primarily Sonoma County Chardonnay and Cabernet Sauvignon. The winery was established in 1979 by Ken and Arlene Dalton and Robert and Norma Wiltermood, present owners.

PORTER CREEK. 8735 Westside Rd., Healdsburg; (707) 887-1150. Tasting and sales, Thurs.-Sun. 10-4.30.
☐ Owner-operated winery, specializing in estate-grown Chardonnay and Pinot Noir from its 22-acre vineyard located at the winery. The winery was founded in 1982.

PRESTON VINEYARDS & WINERY. 9282 West Dry Creek Road, Healdsburg; (707) 433-3372. Tasting and sales Mon.-Fri. 11-3; tours by appointment.
☐ 20,000-case, family-owned winery, situated on a 120-acre vineyard estate which was formerly a pear orchard. Preston's winemaking operation is in fact housed in the old pear dehydrator, converted into a winery. The winery offers premium, estate-bottled varietal Sauvignon Blanc, Cabernet Sauvignon, Zinfandel, Gamay Beaujolais, Sirah-Sirah, Dry Chenin Blanc, and a Late Harvest Zinfandel. Also produced are a red table wine, and a vintage-dated proprietary wine, Cuvée de Fumé. The winery was established in 1975 by Louis and Susan Preston, present owners.

QUIVIRA. 4900 West Dry Creek Rd., Healdsburg; (707) 431-8333. Winery visits by appointment only.
☐ New Healdsburg area winery, established in 1987 by Holly and Henry Wendt, present owners. The winery offers estate-bottled Zinfandel, Cabernet Sauvignon and Sauvignon Blanc from its 76-acre vineyard located in the Dry Creek Valley.

RABBIT RIDGE VINEYARDS. 3291 Westside Rd., Healdsburg; (707) 431-7128. Winery visits by appointment only.
☐ Small, owner-operated winery, situated on a 45-acre hillside vineyard estate in the Russian River Valley. Estate-bottled varietal wines produced are Cabernet Sauvignon, Cabernet Franc, Chardonnay and Zinfandel. The winery was established in 1985 by Erich and Catherine Russell, present owners.

A. RAFANELLI WINERY. 4685 West Dry Creek Road, Healdsburg; (707) 433-1385. Visitors by appointment.
☐ Small, 3,000-case, family owned and operated winery, established in 1974. Rafanelli offers varietal, vintage-dated Zinfandel and Gamay Beaujolais from its 25-acre vineyard located at the winery. Sales in case quantities.

RIVER OAKS VINEYARDS. Lytton Station Rd., Healdsburg; (707) 433-5576. Tours, tasting and sales by appointment, daily 10-5. Wines may also be tasted at the winery's tasting room at 5 Fitch St. in Healdsburg.
☐ 50,000-case winery, with 600 acres of estate vineyards located in the Alexander Valley. The winery bottles a full line of estate-grown varietal wines. Also produced is a line of inexpensive table wines. The winery was established in 1964.

J. ROCHIOLI WINERY. 6192 Westside Road, Healdsburg; (707) 433-2305. Open for wine sales daily 10-5; tours by appointment.
□ The winery was founded in 1985 by the Rochioli family, grape growers for over 60 years. The redwood winery building is situated among estate vineyards in the Dry Creek Valley, adjacent to historic Hop Kiln, overlooking the valley vineyards. Estate-grown varietal Chardonnay, Sauvignon Blanc, Cabernet Sauvignon and Pinot Noir are the wines featured here.

SAUSAL WINERY. 7370 Hwy. 128, Healdsburg; (707) 433-2285. Open for tasting and sales daily 10-4; tours by appointment. Picnic area.
□ The winery is situated on a 125-acre vineyard estate located in the Alexander Valley, bordered on its north by the Sausal Creek, for which it is named. The acreage was originally planted to apples and prunes, until in 1956 Leo Demostene purchased the property and slowly began replanting the acreage to wine grapes, with plans to convert the old prune dehydrator to a winery. The winery was finally established in 1973 by the next generation of the Demostenes. Sausal now produces approximately 30,000 cases of estate-grown Zinfandel, White Zinfandel, Cabernet Sauvignon and Chardonnay, as well as a blended white, Sausal Blanc.

SEA RIDGE WINERY. P.O. Box 287, Cazadero; (707) 847-3469. Tasting room and art gallery located at 935 Hwy. 1, Bodega Bay; open daily 11-7. Winery visits by appointment only.
□ Established in 1980, Sea Ridge derives its name from its location—on a sea ridge, just 3 miles inland from the Pacific coast, at an elevation of 1,200 feet. The winery specializes in Pinot Noir made from its 14-acre estate vineyard located at the winery. Small lots of Chardonnay, Sauvignon Blanc and Zinfandel are also produced. The winery's second label is Wild Boar Cellars.

SEGHESIO WINERY. 14730 Grove Street, Healdsburg; (707) 433-3579. Open Mon.-Fri. 8-5; retail sales only.
□ The winery was originally founded in 1902 by Italian immigrant Edoardo Seghesio, and is still owned and operated by the Seghesio family. The Seghesios produce primarily estate-grown, vintage-dated varietal wines, including Cabernet Sauvignon, Zinfandel, Chenin Blanc, White Zinfandel, and French Colombard.

SELLARDS WINERY. 6400 Sequoia Circle, Sebastopol; (707) 823-8293. Winery visits by appointment only.
□ Small, owner operated winery, established in 1981 by Thomas Sellards. The winery makes small lots of Sonoma County Cabernet Sauvignon, Sauvignon Blanc and Chardonnay, all from grapes purchased on a select-vineyard basis. Wines are aged in oak. Sales by mailing list.

SIMI WINERY. 16275 Healdsburg Avenue, Healdsburg; (707) 433-6981. Open for tours, tasting and sales, 10-4.30 daily; tours at 11 a.m. and 1 and 3 p.m.
□ Prestigious Alexander Valley winery, housed in an historic stone cellar, originally built in 1876 by Italian immigrants Pietro and Guiseppe Simi. The winery is now owned by Möet-Hennessy of France, makers of Champagne Möet & Chandon, Hennessy Cognac and Dior perfumes. The winery was extensively remodeled and modernized in 1979, and now features state-of-the-art winemaking equipment and facilities,. Varietal, vintage-dated wines bottled under the Simi label include Chardonnay, Sauvignon Blanc, Cabernet Sauvignon,

Rosé of Cabernet Sauvignon, and Chenin Blanc. Gift shop and shaded picnic area on premises.

SONOMA-CUTRER VINEYARDS. 4401 Slusser Road, Windsor; (707) 528-1181. Visitors by appointment only.

☐ Cutrer's is a large 900-acre vineyard estate, with a small and relatively new winemaking operation. Estate-grown, barrel-fermented Chardonnay is the only wine produced here. The winery was established in 1973.

SOTOYOME WINERY. 641 Limerick Lane, Healdsburg; (707) 433-2001. Tours, tasting and sales, Fri.-Sun. 11-5.

☐ Small, family owned and operated winery, established in 1974. Sotoyme produces limited quantities of Cabernet Sauvignon, Zinfandel, Petite Sirah and Chardonnay from its 10-acre vineyard located at the winery. The winery derives its name from Rancho Sotoyme, a Mexican land grant of 1840, on part of which the Sotoyme vineyard is now located.

ROBERT STEMMLER WINERY. 3805 Lambert Bridge Road, Healdsburg; (707) 433-6334. Open for tours, tasting and sales, daily 10.30-4.30

☐ Situated in the scenic Dry Creek Valley, the winery was founded in 1977 by Robert Stemmler, a native of Germany and formerly winemaker at Charles Krug, Inglenook and Simi wineries. Stemmler makes vintage-dated Chardonnay, Sauvignon Blanc, Pinot Noir and Cabernet Sauvignon from his 4-acre estate vineyard located at the winery, as well as from grapes purchased on a select-vineyard basis. Wines are also bottled under the Bel Canto label. Shaded picnic area and tasting patio overlooking estate vineyards.

RODNEY STRONG WINES/WINDSOR VINEYARDS. 11455 Old Redwood Hwy., Windsor; (707) 433-6511. Open for tasting and sales, daily 10-5; winery tours 11-4.

☐ Large, modern winery, with a 3.4-million-gallon capacity, and over 1,200 acres of estate-owned vineyards located in Sonoma County. The winemaking operation is housed in a unique, architect-designed cross-shaped building, set among estate vineyards in the Russian River Valley. Each of the four wings of the cross house a different phase of the winemaking operation, enabling the visitor to view the entire operation from the tasting room directly above. The winery bottles a full line of premium vineyard-designated varietal wines, including Chardonnay, Cabernet Sauvignon, Merlot, Pinot Noir, Fumé Blanc, Johannisberg Riesling, Gewurztraminer, Chenin Blanc, French Colombard, Petite Sirah, Zinfandel, and Brut and Blanc de Noirs sparkling wines. Some wines are also bottled under the Windsor Vineyards and Tiburon Vintners labels. The winery was established in 1961 by Rodney Strong, reputed winemaker and well-known figure in the California wine industry.

TAFT STREET WINERY. 6450 First St., Forestville; (707) 887-2801. Visitors by appointment only.

☐ Taft Street offers varietal, vintage-dated Chardonnay, Sauvignon Blanc, and Cabernet Sauvignon. Also produced are "House Wines," both Red and White. The winery was established in 1982.

TOPOLOS AT RUSSIAN RIVER VINEYARD. 5700 Gravenstein Hwy., Forestville; (707) 887-2956/887-1562. Open for tasting and sales daily 11-5.

☐ Small, 5,000-case winery, owned and operated by the Topolos family, originally established in 1964. The winery is housed in a most unique wooden structure, which borrows heavily from both the typical old hop kiln buildings and the Russian Orthodox Church at Fort Ross, with its characteristic wooden towers. The Topolos winery sits amid 25 acres of family vineyards, with an additional 50 acres or so of estate-owned vineyards located in the Glen Ellen area in Sonoma Valley. The Topolos roster features a vintage-dated Chardonnay, and some ripe,oaky reds, including Zinfandel, Pinot Noir, Petite Sirah, and Cabernet Sauvignon. There is also a popular little restaurant at the winery, devoted to Greek and Continental cuisine.

TOYON VINEYARDS. 9643 Hwy. 128, Healdsburg; (707) 433-6847. Visitors by appointment only.

☐ Small, owner-operated winery, founded in 1973. Vintage-dated varietal wines produced are Chardonnay, Sauvignon Blanc, Gewurztraminer, Zinfandel, and an estate-bottled Cabernet Sauvignon. Toyon's vineyard is located in the Alexander Valley.

TRENTADUE WINERY. 19170 Redwood Hwy., Geyserville; (707) 433-3104. Wine tasting and sales daily 10-5; tours by appointment.

☐ Family owned and operated winery, established in 1969 by Leo and Evelyn Trentadue, present owners. The winery produces primarily estate-grown varietal wines from its 200-acre estate vineyard located at the winery in the Alexander Valley. Offerings include Chardonnay, Johannisberg Riesling, Chenin Blanc, Sauvignon Blanc, Cabernet Sauvignon, Zinfandel, Merlot, Petite Sirah, Gamay, French Colombard, and Semillon. Gift shop and picnic area on premises.

VINA VISTA VINEYARDS. 24401 Chianti Rd., Geyserville; (707) 857-3722. Visitors by appointment only.

☐ Small Alexander Valley winery situated on a hillside near Asti. The winery makes tiny lots of Cabernet Sauvignon, Chardonnay, Merlot and Sauvignon Blanc. Wines are also produced under a second label, Warnelius Vineyards. The winery was founded in 1972.

WEINSTOCK CELLARS. 231 Center St., Healdsburg; (707) 433-3186. Winery hours: Mon.-Fri. 8-5; tours by appointment.

☐ Family owned and operated winery, specializing in Kosher wines, produced under rabbinical supervision. The winery bottles approximately 4,500 cases of estate-grown, Kosher varietal wine annually, made from grapes grown on the family's 50-acre vineyard located in the Dry Creek Valley and a 40-acre vineyard located in the Alexander Valley. Offerings include White Zinfandel, Pinot Chardonnay, Johannisberg Riesling, Sauvignon Blanc and Zinfandel. The winery was founded in 1985 by the Robert Weinstock family.

WILLIAM WHEELER WINERY. 130 Plaza Street, Healdsburg; (707) 433-8786. Tasting, tours and sales, Thurs.-Mon. 10-4 in summer, Mon.-Fri. 12-4 in winter.

☐ 18,000-case Healdsburg winery, with tasting room located in the center of town. The winery produces mainly varietal Chardonnay, Sauvignon Blanc, Zinfandel, and an estate-grown Cabernet Sauvignon from its 30-acre hillside vineyard located some 5 miles from the winery, overlooking Dry Creek Valley. The winery was established in 1981.

WHITE OAK VINEYARDS. 208 Haydon Street, Healdsburg; (707) 433-8429. Tours, tasting and sales, daily 10-4.

☐ Owner William Myers designed and built this modern, 10,000-case wine-making facility in Healdsburg in 1981, to produce limited quantities of primarily oak-aged varietal white wines — hence the name, "White Oak." The winery now offers an estate-grown Chardonnay from its 6-acre vineyard in the Alexander Valley, as well as Sauvignon Blanc, Johannisberg Riesling, Chenin Blanc, Zinfandel, and Cabernet Sauvignon. A generic red table wine is also produced. The winery's second label is Fitch Mountain Cellars.

WILLIAMS-SELYEM WINERY. 850 River Rd., Fulton; (707) 887-7480. Visitors by appointment.
☐ Owner-operated winery, founded in 1981 by winemaker Burt Williams and Ed Selyem. Wines produced are Pinot Noir, Zinfandel, Cabernet Sauvignon and Chardonnay. A dry-styled Late Harvest Zinfandel is also offered.

Z MOORE. 3364 River Rd., Windsor; (707) 544-3555. Tasting and sales, Wed.-Sun. 10-5.
☐ Small, owner-operated winery, housed in a picturesque old hop kiln. The winery specializes in Chardonnay and a dry-styled Gewurztraminer. Picnic area on premises.

PRACTICAL INFORMATION FOR THE RUSSIAN RIVER REGION

HOW TO GET THERE

Healdsburg lies approximately 75 miles north of San Francisco, reached on *Highway 101* directly north from San Francisco. Geyserville lies another 9 miles and Cloverdale 16 miles north of Healdsburg, also on *Highway 101*.

Guerneville, the other important town in the Russian River region, is situated 23 miles to the west of Santa Rosa on *Highway 116*. It can be reached by way of *Highway 101* north from San Francisco to Santa Rosa, then *12* and *116* northwestward to Guerneville.

TOURIST INFORMATION

Healdsburg Chamber of Commerce, 217 Healdsburg Ave., Healdsburg; (707) 523-0388. Information on area lodgings and dining; also calendar of events, and literature on touring and bicycle routes.

Geyserville Chamber of Commerce, 21030 Geyserville Ave., Geyserville; (707) 433-6935. Variety of tourist literature.

Russian River Chamber of Commerce, 14034 Armstrong Woods Rd., Guerneville; (707) 545-1414. Maps and brochures; information on canoeing, hiking, camping, accommodations and local events.

ACCOMMODATIONS

Windsor

Redwood Royale Hometel. *$45-$55.* 8900 Bell Rd., Windsor; (707) 838-9771. 80 units, each with bedroom and kitchenette. Pool.

Healdsburg

Best Western Dry Creek Inn. *$60-$80.* 198 Dry Creek Road, Healdsburg; (707) 433-0300/(800) 222-5784. 104 rooms; TV, phones, pool and spa. Complimentary continental breakfast, and wine.

Fairview Motel. *$45-$55.* 74 Healdsburg Ave., Healdsburg; (707) 433-5548. 18 rooms, with TV and phones. Pool, spa.

Guerneville

Brookside Lodge & Motel. *$72-$94.* Cnr. Hwy 116 and Brookside Lane; Guerneville; (707) 869-2470. Newly-remodelled lodge. Rooms with fireplaces and wet bars; some kitchenettes. Also cabins overlooking adjoining vineyards. Pool, sauna, hot tub.

BED & BREAKFAST INNS

Windsor

Country Meadow Inn. *$75-$105.* 11360 Old Redwood Hwy., Windsor; (707) 431-1276. 1890's Queen Anne Victorian overlooking vineyards, trees and gardens. 5 guest rooms with private baths. Full country breakfast; evening wine and cheese. Heated pool.

Healdsburg

Belle de Jour Inn. *$85-$130.* 16276 Healdsburg Ave., Healdsburg; (707) 433-7892. Individual cottages on 6-acre retreat. Fireplaces, whirlpool tubs.

Camellia Inn. *$55-$95.* 211 North St., Healdsburg; (707) 433-8182. Italianate Victorian townhouse, dating from 1869. 9 guest rooms, many with private baths. Full breakfast, served in formal dining room. Pool.

Frampton House. *$70-$85.* 489 Powell Ave., Healdsburg; (707) 433-5084. 3 rooms with private baths. Gardens, pool, spa, sauna. Full country breakfast; also champagne brunch on Sundays. Bicycles available for guest use.

Grape Leaf Inn. *$70-$90.* 539 Johnson St., Healdsburg; (707) 433-8140. Beautifully restored Queen Anne Victorian home. 7 guest rooms, with private baths. Full breakfast; afternoon wine and cheese.

The Haydon House. *$60-$75*. 3321 Haydon St., Healdsburg; (707) 433-5228. Charming Queen Anne Victorian with 6 guest rooms, each with private bath and whirlpool tub. A separate 2-room cottage is also available. Country breakfast.

Healdsburg Inn on the Plaza. *$95-$135*. 116 Matheson St., Healdsburg; (707) 433-6991. Elegant, turn-of-the-century inn, with an art gallery and lounge on the ground floor, and 9 antique-decorated guest rooms upstairs, all with private baths with clawfoot tubs. Breakfast is served in the rooftop solarium; also afternoon wine and cheese, and weekend champagne brunch.

Lytton Springs Inn. *$65-$90*. 17698 Healdsburg Ave., Healdsburg; (707) 431-1109. Mediterranean ranch-style home on hilltop overlooking picturesque Alexander Valley. Three antique-furnished rooms; hot tub. Breakfast served on deck.

Madronna Manor. *$115-$175*. 1001 Westside Rd., Healdsburg; (707) 433-4231. Elegant, full-service country inn, situated on secluded 8-acre estate. 20 rooms, with private baths; some fireplaces. Also restaurant on premises, serving dinner daily and brunch on Sundays. Pool.

The Raford House. *$75-$125*. 10630 Wohler Rd., Healdsburg; (707) 887-9573. Historic Victorian farmhouse overlooking valley vineyards, located between Windsor and Forestville. 7 guest rooms, 5 with private baths. Some fireplaces.

Geyserville

Campbell Ranch Inn. *$90-$110*. 1475 Canyon Rd., Geyserville; (707) 857-3476. Modern ranch-style home on 35-acre estate. Vineyard views. 5 guest rooms. Tennis court, pool, hot tub, spa. Full breakfast.

Hope-Bosworth House. *$60-$85* 21232 Geyserville Ave., Geyserville; (707) 857-3356. Beautifully restored Victorian, with 5 guest rooms, some with private baths.

Hope-Merrill House. *$90-$115*. 21253 Geyserville Ave., Geyserville; (707) 857-3356. 5 rooms in delightful Victorian home. Private baths; pool.

Isis Oasis. *$60-$100*. 20889 Geyserville Ave., Geyserville; (707) 857-3524. 12-room lodge, just outside town, situated on 10-acre estate. Also one cottage, restored farmhouse and several yurts. Pool, spa, sauna; dinner theater performances on most weekends. Small menagerie on property.

Cloverdale

Abrams House Inn. *$60-$100*. 314 N. Main St., Cloverdale; (707) 894-2412. 4 guest rooms, including one suite with private bath.

Vintage Towers. *$70-$110*. 302 N. Main St., Cloverdale; (707) 894-4535. Queen Anne Victorian, with turreted towers. 7 guest rooms, 5 with private baths, including 3 tower suites. Generous breakfast.

Guerneville

Creekside Inn & Resort. *$30-$50*. 16180 Neeley Rd., Guerneville; (707) 869-3623. Comfortable bed and breakfast inn with 6 rooms. Also 9 housekeeping cottages. Pool.

The Estate Inn. *$100-$150*. 13555 Hwy. 116, Guerneville; (707) 869-9093. Historic Mission Revival mansion, set amid redwoods. 10 rooms with private baths, TV and phones. Also pool and spa for guests' use. Full breakfast.

Ridenhour Ranch House Inn. *$65-$115*. 12850 River Rd., Guerneville; (707) 887-1033. Turn-of-the-century redwood ranch house, located close to Korbel Champagne Cellars. 8 rooms with antiques and quilts; hot tub, croquet, Gourmet breakfast; dinner available on some Saturdays.

Santa Nella House. *$80-$85*. 12130 Hwy. 116, Guerneville; (707) 869-9488. Delightful little country inn, dating from the 1870s, formerly the Santa Nella Winery. 4 antique-decorated rooms. Hot tub. Champagne brunch.

SEASONAL EVENTS

March. *Russian River Wine Barrel Tasting.* Scheduled for the 1st weekend in month. Russian River Wine Road members offer a sampling of wines directly from the cask. For list of participating wineries, send $1.00 to the Russian River Wine Road, P.O. Box 127, Geyserville, CA 95441. More information on (707) 433-2917.

May. *Russian River Wine Fest.* Held during the 3rd weekend of the month, at the Healdsburg Plaza in Healdsburg. 50 participating Russian River Valley wineries offer tasting of their wines; also featured are jazz, an arts and crafts fair, and food stalls. For festival information, call (707) 433-6935/(800) 648-9922 in California. *Stumpdown Days.* Guerneville. Events include a barbeque, parade, and two-day rodeo. (707) 869-9009.

June. *Clos du Bois Annual Summer Celebration.* Hosted by the Clos du Bois Winery in Healdsburg, generally during the 3rd weekend of the month. Features music, entertainment, food and wine tasting. For a schedule of events and more information, call the winery at (707) 433-5576.

September. *Russian River Jazz Festival.* Two-day event, held at the Johnson's Beach in Guerneville; 1st weekend of the month. for a schedule and more information, call (707) 887-1502. *Cloverdale Grape Festival.* Cloverdale. (707) 894-5790.

PLACES OF INTEREST

Armstrong Redwoods State Reserve, 17000 Armstrong Woods Rd. (off Hwy. 116), Guerneville; (707) 869-2015/865-2391. Walking trails through the last grove of virgin redwoods in Sonoma County which is open to the public. 752-acre park; picnicking facilities. Admission: $3.00 per car.

Austin Creek State Recreation Area, 17000 Armstrong Woods Rd. (above Armstrong Redwoods State Reserve), Guerneville; (707) 869-2015. 4,236-acre park with camping, hiking, fishing and horseback riding facilities.

Lake Sonoma/Warm Springs Dam. Dry Creek Rd., Healdsburg; (707) 433-9483. 17,600-acre recreation area with lake surrounded by meadows and forests. Warm Springs Dam, at 319-feet high, is the largest structure ever built in Sonoma County. Visitor center, boating, hiking and fishing.

Windsor Waterworks and Slides, 8225 Conde Lane, Windsor; (707) 838-7760. 4 water slides, swimming and wading pools, picnic area and snack bar.

Fort Ross State Historic Park, Hwy. 1 at Fort Ross Rd., Jenner; (707)

847-3286. Stockade, restored Russian Orthodox Church, museums depicting the Russian presence in California in the 1800s are housed in the former Commandante's office and block houses. 1,065-acre park with hiking trails, fishing and picnicking.

Healdsburg Memorial Beach Park, Healdsburg Ave. (near Front St.), Healdsburg; (707) 433-1625. Sandy beach on the Russian River, with lifeguards on duty. Picnic area, snack bars, boat launching facilities.

Healdsburg Plaza. Healdsburg. Plaza bordered by Healdsburg Ave., Plaza, Center and Matheson Sts. Lawns, shade trees, fountain at the center. Gazebo where concerts take place during summer.

Healdsburg Museum, 221 Matheson St., Healdsburg; (707) 431-3325. Exhibits of local historical interest, depicting the Indian, Mexican and early American periods of Healdsburg area history. Thousands of original historical photographs, local newspapers dating back to 1878. Open Tues.-Sat., 12-5; free admission.

Isaac E. Shaw Museum, 215 North Cloverdale Rd., Cloverdale; (707) 894-2246/894-2067. Museum housed in a turn-of-the-century home, with each room decorated in an individual historical theme, such as an old-time general store, a Victorian living room, etc. Museum hours: 9-4, Mon.-Fri. Free admission.

RECREATION

Horseback Riding. *Armstrong Woods Pack Station,* Armstrong Redwoods State Reserve, Guerneville; (707) 887-2939. Trail rides through the redwoods; also 2- and 3-day pack trips into nearby Austin Creek Wilderness.

Golf. *Tayman Park Golf Course,* 927 S. Fitch Mountain Rd., Healdsburg; (707) 433-4275. 9-hole public golf course; Par 35. Pro shop and lessons; green fees: $7.00 weekdays, $8.00 weekends.

Boat Cruises. Lake Sonoma-based *Sailing in the Wine Country* offers scenic as well as sunset cruises on the lake; lunch is also available on board. For reservations and more information, call (707) 431-7245.

Canoeing. Kayaking and canoeing are quite popular on the Russian River, especially from Healdsburg southwestward, or from Guerneville. For guided canoe trips on the river, contact: *W.C. "Bob" Trowbridge Canoe Trips,* at 20 Healdsburg Ave. in Healdsburg, (707) 433-7247, or *Burke's Russian River Canoe Trips,* 8600 River Road, Forestville, (707) 887-1222.

Bicycling. The Russian River region offers excellent bicycling opportunities. Good bicycle routes in the area include the *Alexander Valley* and *Chalk Hill roads,* the *Old Redwood Highway,* and the *Dry Creek* and *West Dry Creek roads.* Organized bicycle tours are offered by the following Bay Area tour operators: *Backroads Bicycle Tours,* P.O. Box 1626, San Leandro 94577, (415) 895-1783; *On the Loose Adventure Vacations,* P.O. Box 55, Berkeley 94709, (415) 527-4005; *One of a Kind Bicycle Tours,* 484 Lake Park Way, Suite 314, Oakland 94610, (415) 763-6231; and *California Bicycle Cruises,* 1362 Pacific Ave., Suite 4, Santa Cruz 95060, (800) 222-0072. Also, in the area, full day bicycle tours are offered by *Daybreak Tours,* Healdsburg, (707) 433-3919; and for bicycle rentals and repair service contact *Spoke Folk Cyclery,* 249 Center Street, Healdsburg, (707) 433-7171.

Tours. *Five Oaks Farm,* 15831 Chalk Hill Rd., Healdsburg; (707) 433-2422. Tours of Alexander Valley wineries, in a horse-drawn carriage; lunch included. *Stage-A-Picnic,* P.O. Box 536, Geyserville; (707) 857-3619. Horse-drawn stagecoach, touring two or three wineries in the Geyserville area, with picnic lunch in the grape arbor at Trentadue Winery.

RESTAURANTS

(Restaurant prices—based on full course dinner, excluding drinks, tax and tips—are categorized as follows: *Deluxe*, over $30; *Expensive*, $20-$30; *Moderate*, $10-$20; *Inexpensive*, under $10.)

Healdsburg

Jacob Horner. *Moderate.* 106 Matheson St. (on the Plaza), Healdsburg; (707) 433-3939. Continental and California cuisine, with emphasis on pasta and seafood. Dinner Tues.-Sat., lunch Mon.-Sat.; reservations suggested.

Madrona Manor. *Expensive.* 1001 Westside Rd., Healdsburg; (707) 433-4231. Well-regarded restaurant, located at teh Madrona Manor Inn, specializing in creative California cuisine. Open for dinner Wed.-Sun.; brunch on Sunday. Reservations recommended.

Forty Karrots Diner. *Inexpensive.* 109 Plaza St., Healdsburg; (707) 431-8181. 50's style diner serving burgers, sandwiches and salads. Also soda fountain. Open for breakfast and lunch daily, dinner Wed.-Fri.

Plaza Grill. *Expensive.* 109A Plaza St., Healdsburg; (707) 431-8305. Mesquite-broiled steak, chicken and seafood. Good selection of local wines. Open for lunch Tues.-Fri., dinner Tues.-Sat. Reservations suggested.

Compadres Mexican Restaurant. *Inexpensive.* 125 Healdsburg Ave., Healdsburg; (707) 433-1687. Authentic Mexican cooking. Restaurant open for lunch and dinner daily.

New China Restaurant. *Inexpensive-Moderate.* 336 Healdsburg Ave., Healdsburg; (707) 433-4122. Mandarin and Cantonese dishes. Open for lunch and dinner daily.

Geyserville

Catelli's the Rex. *Moderate.* 21047 Geyserville Ave., Geyserville; (707) 857-9904. Italian restaurant, family owned and operated for over 50 years. House specialties are homemade ravioli and scampi. Dinner daily, lunch Mon.-Fri.

Chateau Souverain. *Expensive.* 400 Souverain Rd., Geyserville; (707) 433-3141. Well-liked restaurant at the Chateau Souverain winery, with spacious dining room and outdoor patio, overlooking hillside vineyards. Menu features primarily California cuisine. Lunch daily, dinner Thurs.-Sat.; also Sunday brunch. Reservations suggested.

The Hoffman Farm House. *Expensive.* 12712 Geyserville Ave., Geyserville; (707) 857-3264. Specializing in California cuisine; also prime rib and seafood. Open for lunch and dinner daily (except Tues.), brunch on Sundays. Reservations recommended.

Guerneville

Burdon's. *Moderate-Expensive.* 15405 River Rd., Guerneville; (707) 869-2615. Fresh seafood, prime rib, and chicken and lamb dishes. Dinner

Thurs.-Mon. Reservations recommended.

Little Bavaria. *Moderate-Expensive.* 17123 Hwy. 116, Guerneville; (707) 869-0121. Authentic Bavarian cuisine, as well as steaks, seafood and Continental selections. Extensive wine list, featuring local and imported wines and beers. Open for lunch and dinner daily, brunch on Sundays. Reservations recommended.

PICNIC FARE

Salame Tree Deli. 304 Center St., Healdsburg; (707) 433-7224. Sandwiches and salads, meat and cheese trays, selection of local wines. Open daily.

Dry Creek General Store. 3495 Dry Creek Rd., Healdsburg; (707) 433-4171. Sandwiches and groceries; local wines. Open daily.

Warm Springs Station & Deli. 520 Dry Creek Rd., Healdsburg; (707) 433-7766. Sandwiches, meats and cheeses; also Sonoma County wine. Open daily.

Nello's Italian Deli. 8872 Lakewood Dr., Windsor; (707) 838-6669. Meat and cheese platters, sandwiches and salads, wine. Open daily.

The Asti Store. 26155 Asti Store Rd., Asti; (707) 894-5266. Sandwiches, salads, ice-cream and desserts.

The Midway Deli. 15045 River Rd., Guerneville; (707) 869-0501. Sandwiches, meats and cheeses.

Perry's Delicatessen. 16337 Main St., Guerneville; (707) 869-2393. Wide selection of meats and cheeses; also sandwiches. Open daily.

WINE TASTING

Wine tasting is essentially the appreciation or judging of wine—by sight, smell and taste. Wines vary—within each class or variety—in winemaking style, grape quality, cooperage, and other such variables. Each wine has its unique characteristics and subtleties, and tasting, then, is simply the distinguishing of one wine from another and the analyzing and identifying of the discernible qualities of the wine. For newcomers, of course, such analysis of a wine is generally expressed as a simple like or dislike.

Wines may be tasted in any order of class, variety or vintage. Although, when tasting several different wines, it is suggested that dry white wines be sampled first, followed by rosés and red wines, then sweet wines—such as dessert wines—and finally sparkling wines.

For newcomers to the world of wine, the following is a basic guide to tasting and analyzing wine:

APPEARANCE. The first impression of a wine is its appearance. Hold up the wine glass, preferably by the stem or base, and look at the wine. The wine should be clear to brilliantly clear. The color of the wine is equally important, and should be appropriate for the type of wine. Typically, white wines range from a pale to golden yellow, rosés are pink to orange-pink, and red wines vary from a light crimson to garnet and even deep hues of ruby.

SMELL. The next step is smell, or analyzing the aromas and bouquet of the wine. Gently swirl the wine in the glass, thereby mixing it with air and releasing its aromas, then bring the glass to your nose and inhale. The aroma of a wine is directly related to the winegrape from which the wine is made, and it should be pleasing and identifiable with the specific grape variety. The bouquet of a wine results from cooperage, and is especially pronounced in long-aging red wines and appetizer and dessert wines.

TASTE. Finally, it is time to taste the wine. Taste, quite simply, is sweet, sour, bitter, and salty. Sip the wine and swish it around your mouth. The taste of the wine should, in fact, be an extension of your perception of the wine's aromas and bouquet, and should add new information about the wine's texture and balance. Dry (which denotes the absence of sweetness) white wines are generally tart or acidic, indicating the presence of naturally occuring fruit acids; young red wines, typically, tend to be more astringent, indicating the presence of tannin, a mouth-puckering compound derived from grape skins; while dessert wines are largely sweet, and high in alcohol—which is recognizable as a warming sensation at the back of the throat.

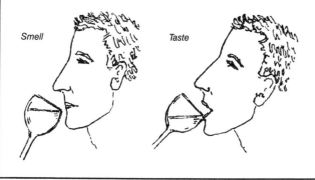

Smell   Taste

HOW TO READ
A CALIFORNIA WINE LABEL

1. BRAND NAME. The brand name is either the name of the bottling winery, or a winery label (i.e. special label, secondary label, etc.) under which the wine is bottled.

2. VINTAGE DATE. A vintage date on a wine label is optional. When it appears, however, it indicates that at least 95% of the grapes used in the wine were harvested in the stated year.

3. GEOGRAPHIC ORIGIN. The region of origin is required by law to be shown on the label. To use an AVA (Approved Viticultural Area), such as "Napa Valley," at least 85% of the grapes must come from such AVA; to use the name of a county, such as "Sonoma County," a minimum of 75% of the grapes should come from the stated county; and to be labeled "California," 100% of the grapes used must be grown within the state.

4. TYPE OF WINE. When a varietal name such as "Cabernet Sauvignon" or "Chardonnay" appears on a wine label, it is required that 75% or more of the wine be made from such varietal. If an appellation is used in conjuction with the varietal name, the minimum 75% of the varietal grapes used must come from the stated appellation. For generic—Burgundy, Rosé, Chablis, etc.— and proprietary wines, there is no specific requirement governing the use of the wine name on the label.

5. SPECIFIC CHARACTER. Any of several different terms may be used to describe the qualities or character of a wine, such as "Estate Bottled," "Bottle-fermented," "Late Harvest," etc. This is voluntary information, however. Typically, the use of "Estate Bottled" requires that the vineyard and winery be located within the stated geographic area or appellation, and that the vineyard be under the control of the bottling winery.

6. SPECIFIC VINEYARD. The use of an individual vineyard name on a label, such as in a "vineyard-designated" wine, requires that a minimum of 95% of the grapes used in the wine come from such stated vineyard.

7. BOTTLER. A wine label must bear the name of the bottling winery—which may or may not be the same as the "Brand Name"—and its business location. The use of "Produced and Bottled by" indicates that 75% or more of the grapes used in the wine were fermented by the bottler; "Made and Bottled by" indicates that at least 10% of the grapes were fermented by the bottler; while "Cellared and Bottled by," "Vinted and Bottled by," and other such terms have no specific requirement as to their use.

8. ALCOHOL CONTENT. The alcohol content of a wine—expressed as "% by volume"—is required to be shown on the label. The permissible amount for table wines is 7%-13%; for sparkling wines, 10%-13.9%; for appetizer wines, 17%-20%; and for dessert wines, 18%-20%. A 1.5% variation is allowed either way. Occasionally, the term "Table Wine" may appear instead of the alcohol content, which simply indicates that the wine contains between 7% and 13.9% alcohol. (Some wine labels also offer voluntary information on residual sugar, total acid, pH, etc.)

California Winery

ESTATE BOTTLED

1982

NAPA VALLEY

Zinfandel

Hilltop Vineyard

PRODUCED AND BOTTLED BY
CALIFORNIA WINERY, NAPA VALLEY, CALIFORNIA
ALCOHOL 13.5% BY VOLUME

WINE

Red Wines

CABERNET SAUVIGNON. The most prestigious varietal wine in California, originally from France's Bordeaux region. The wine, quite typically, is a deep ruby-red in color, exhibiting rich varietal flavors and good aging potential. Young Cabernet Sauvignons are generally tannic, but soften with age.

MERLOT. A softer, less tannic varietal red wine, also from Bordeaux. The wine is generally medium red in color, with distinctive aromas and some of the flavor characteristics of Cabernet Sauvignon. Merlot is also used as a blending wine for the more tannic Cabernets.

PINOT NOIR. The principal vinifera grape grown in the Burgundy region of France, Pinot Noir, characteristically, produces full-bodied wines with complex flavors, which benefit immensely from aging in oak. Pinot Noir is also the predominant varietal grape used in most California sparkling wines.

ZINFANDEL. Frequently referred to as California's own varietal, Zinfandel is produced in several different styles, both as a red wine and as a "blush" wine. The red varietal is of course robust, dark red in color, and with intense, spicy flavors—akin to ripe raspberries or blackberries.

PETITE SIRAH. A deep red, full-bodied varietal wine, often described as robust and spicy. Because of its intense character, both in body and color, the wine is frequently used for blending with lighter red wines; it also benefits greatly from bottle aging. Petite Sirah is originally from the Rhone Valley of France.

GAMAY. Light, fruity wine, commonly known as Napa Gamay. The wine's origins are unclear, although it is believed to be derived from two or three different grape varieties. Gamays, typically, are meant for early drinking.

GAMAY BEAUJOLAIS. A light, fresh, fruity red varietal wine, very similar to Gamay. Gamay Beaujolais is one of the many sub-varieties of Pinot Noir.

BARBERA. Originally from Italy's Piedmont district, Barbera is traditionally a robust, full-bodied wine, which benefits enormously from long aging. In California, however, it is also offered as a light, fruity wine, in a mildly off-dry style.

CHARBONO. Another old-style Italian wine, tannic and full-bodied, benefitting greatly from long aging. Charbono's varietal flavors resemble, closely, those of Barbera.

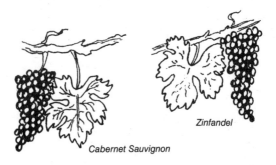

Zinfandel

Cabernet Sauvignon

VARIETIES

White Wines

CHARDONNAY. The world's most prestigious white varietal wine, originally from France's Champagne and Burgundy regions. In California, Chardonnay is produced in several different styles, ranging from a rich, full-bodied wine to a very elegant, delicate wine. The wines are generally aged in small oak barrels and may be fermented in oak as well. Chardonnay is also one of the principal varietals used in California sparkling wines.

CHENIN BLANC. A characteristically fruity, light-bodied wine, light to medium straw in color, meant for early drinking. The wine is offered in a range of styles, from dry to off-dry and even slightly sweet. Chenin Blanc is originally from the Loire Valley of France.

SAUVIGNON BLANC. The principal white varietal grape grown in France's Saùterne district, also known as Fumé Blanc. Sauvignon Blanc wines are typically crisp and fruity, although they may be produced in either a dry or sweet style. Wines labeled Fumé Blanc are generally drier.

PINOT BLANC. A dry varietal wine, with flavor characteristics similar to those of Chardonnay—but subtler, and somewhat more tart.

SÉMILLON. Dry to slightly off-dry wine, with varietal flavors resembling those of Sauvignon Blanc. Sémillon is sometimes offered as a sweet wine. It may also be blended with Sauvignon Blanc.

GREY RIESLING. A slightly sweet, light-bodied wine, mildly spicy, meant for drinking young. Grey Riesling originates in France, under the name Chauche Gris.

GEWURZTRAMINER. An extraordinarily flavorful wine, aromatic and spicy. It is produced in several different styles, ranging from dry to sweet, and given the right climatic conditions it may also be produced as a very sweet, botrytised wine. Gewurztraminer is originally from the French Alsace region.

FRENCH COLOMBARD. The most extensively grown white varietal grape in California. Colombard is typically high in acid, ideally suited to blending with dry white wines, and for bulk champagne production. It is also bottled as an inexpensive jug wine. As a varietal, it may be produced as either a dry or sweet wine.

JOHANNISBERG RIESLING. The premier varietal grape of Germany, named for the great Schloss Johannisberg winery located in the German Rheingau region. Johannisberg Riseling's botanic name, however, is White Riesling, and in California it is generally produced in a slightly sweet to medium sweet style to enhance its fruity character. Johannisberg Riesling may also be produced as a sweet, luscious dessert wine, known as Late Harvest.

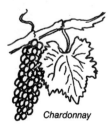

Chardonnay

Gewurztraminer

HOW WINE IS MADE

Winemaking, in its simplest form, is a natural process in which grape juice is converted into alcohol by fermenting with naturally occuring yeast—found on grape skins—when grapes ripen and the grape skins crack or burst. However, with the proper guidance and control, this natural phenomenon becomes a fine art, in which crucial choices must be made at every step of the process, with careful attention paid to the countless variables that will affect the final product.

Thus, in a controlled environment, wine is made in the following manner:

CRUSHING. Ripened grapes are picked and stemmed, then placed in a *crusher*, where grape juice is freed from the berries. The grape juice combines with the crushed skins and seeds to form a pulpy mass known as *must*.

CLARIFICATION AND FERMENTATION. The *must* is clarified, partially, by settling in a tank, or in a centrifuge. It then goes to a *fermentor*—a closed, temperature-controlled vessel, usually a stainless steel tank or wooden cask. Closed vessels are used in order to prevent oxidation, and during fermentation heat is generated, requiring careful control of temperatures. Fermentation temperatures for white wines are usually 45°F-65°F (7°C-18°C), and for reds 70°F-90°F (21°C-32°C). Also, in white wines, grape skins are removed at the start of fermentation, by *pressing*; therefore, white wine grapes go first to a *press*, before fermentation. In pink or rosé wines, some skin contact is allowed during fermentation, although the skins are removed early in the process; and in red wines, typically, grape skins are allowed to remain, to impart color to the wine during fermentation.

FERMENTATION. Fermentation occurs naturally as the yeast acts on the grape juice to convert grape sugars into equal parts of alcohol and carbon dioxide. Fermentation is stopped earlier—frequently by "fortifying" with brandy or neutral spirits—to keep a wine sweet. In dry wines, fermentation ends naturally when all the grape sugar has been converted.

RACKING. After fermentation, the wine is *racked*, or moved from one cooperage to another—generally into a clean tank or cask—thus aiding in the clarification process. The wine may be filtered or centrifuged during racking; it may also be racked again—as in the case of red wines—both for further clarification and to expose the wine to different types of wood—oak, etc.—for flavor.

AGING AND FINING. As the wine ages, or matures, gravity helps clarify the wine further by settling left-over grape and yeast particles to the bottom. To expedite the settling process, such natural substances or fining agents as *bentonite* (fine clay) and *albumen* (egg whites) may be added.

BLENDING. After aging, two or more wines may be blended to obtain the desired characteristics of different grapes or vintages. Merlot, for instance, is blended with young Cabernet Sauvignons for smoothness; and Petite Sirah is often blended with lighter reds for both body and color.

BOTTLING. Finally, when the wine is deemed ready for drinking, it is usually filtered or centrifuged once again for further clarity, then bottled. Bottles, which are vacuum-filled to keep out oxygen, are filled with wine, corked and capped, fitted with a foil or plastic cover over the cap, and then labeled. Typically, in larger wineries, bottling is accomplished on assembly lines that can process approximately 8,500 bottles an hour.

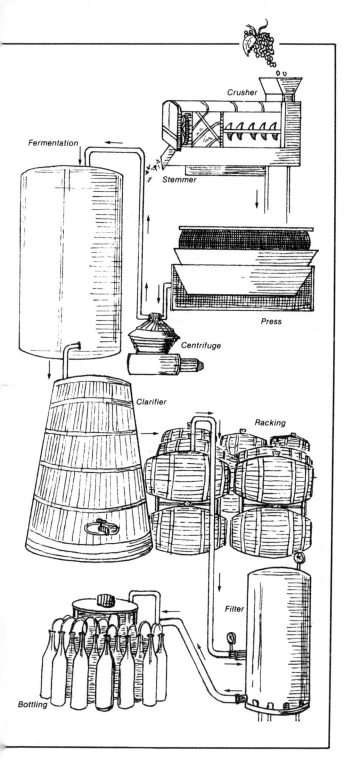

Crusher

Stemmer

Fermentation

Press

Centrifuge

Clarifier

Racking

Filter

Bottling

HOW SPARKLING WINE IS MADE

Sparkling wine- or champagne-making dates from the late 1600s, when Dom Perignon, a Benedictine monk, made the first effervescent wine. The process, principally, is based on the fact that fermentation is the conversion of grape sugars by yeast into roughly equal parts of alcohol and carbon dioxide; and that a second fermentation of a wine in a tightly corked bottle—which may be started by adding small amounts of sugar and yeast—results in the accumulation of additional carbon dioxide, producing bubbles, or an effervescent wine.

All sparkling wines begin with a young, low-alcohol table wine or a *cuvée*—a blend of still wines—and to achieve the effervescence, winemakers may use any of three different methods—*méthode champenoise*, Transfer process, or the Bulk or Charmat process—each of which is identified on the label of the finished wine.

MÉTHODE CHAMPENOISE. This is the traditional method of making champagne or sparkling wine, and the only permitted method in France. Typically, a mixture of yeast and sugar is added to each bottle of still wine, which is then corked and stored on its side. The secondary fermentation occurs within a few weeks, and after all the sugar has been converted, the yeast sediment settles to the bottom of the bottle, where it is allowed to remain for several months, or even years. When the wine is finally deemed ready for drinking, the yeast sediment is worked down into the neck of the bottle in a process known as "riddling." The bottle neck is then frozen in brine or another such solution, and the bottle is uncapped. The small amount of wine lost in this process of "disgorging" is immediately replaced with a mixture of sweet syrup and wine called "dosage," which eventually determines the level of sweetness in the finished wine. The bottle is then corked, and wired to hold the cork in place. The wine label, in all cases, will read *"méthode champenoise"* or "fermented in this bottle."

TRANSFER PROCESS. In the transfer process, wines are bottle-fermented in the same manner as in *méthode champenoise*, but instead of riddling, the wine is transferred from the bottles to a tank, then filtered, under pressure, and rebottled. The label on the finished wine generally reads "Bottle Fermented."

BULK PROCESS. In the bulk process, also known as "Charmat" process, wines undergo secondary fermentation in tanks rather than bottles, with the yeast sediment being removed by filtration before bottling. The wine labels on bulk process wines read "Bulk Process" or "Charmat Process."

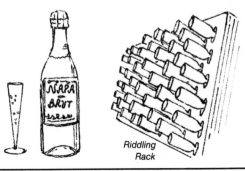

Riddling Rack

WINE GLOSSARY

ACIDITY. Term used to describe the tartness in a wine, indicative of naturally occurring fruit acids. Acidity is important for protecting a wine from spoilage during fermentation and aging, and equally critical in achieving a balanced wine. Among the most common acids in wine are tartaric, malic, lactic, and citric.

AGING. A process by which wine develops smoothness, texture, flavor and character, bringing the wine to a point where it is deemed marketable. In aging, oxygen must act on wine at a very slow, controlled rate, and wine must "breathe" through the container, often taking on the fragrance and flavor characteristics of the cooperage. Wines may be aged in small oak barrels, redwood casks, stainless steel tanks, concrete tanks, or any other appropriate container. Further aging takes place in the bottle.

ALCOHOL. The most important preservative of wine, responsible for transforming perishable grape juice into long-lived, storable wine. The primary alcohol in wine is ethanol, recognizable as a little warming sensation at the back of the throat. Alcohol content of a wine is generally stated on its label, expressed as a numerical percentage of the volume.

APPELLATION. The geographic origin of a wine is referred to as an appellation. An appellation may comprise an area as small or even smaller than the Napa Valley, or as large as the United States. The appellation of a wine is generally indicated on the wine label, and law requires that at least 85% of the grapes that go to make the wine come from such appellation. Also *Viticultural Area*.

AROMA. The smell or fragrance of wine that is directly related to the grape from which the wine is made. (Also see *Bouquet*.)

ASTRINGENCY. Term used to describe the puckery feel in the mouth, caused by the tannins contained in the skins and seeds of grapes. Tannins are also a source of color in fruit, and are therefore more pronounced in red wines than in white wines.

BARREL FERMENTED. Wine fermented either wholly or partially in small oak barrels, rather than in large steel or wood tanks, is referred to as barrel fermented.

BIG. Term used to describe full-bodied wines with rich, full flavors, usually high in glycerine and alcohol. Big red wines are generally also tannic.

BODY. The fullness of a wine, as experienced on the palate, usually derived from a combination of alcohol, glycerine and sugar, is referred to as the "body."

BOTRYTIS CINEREA. Also known as the "noble rot," Botrytis Cinerea is essentially a mold or fungus that affects grapes under certain warm, humid conditions. When Boyrytis occurs late in the season, just before the grapes reach maturity, it causes the grape skins to shrivel, concentrating both natural sugars and fruit acids in the grapes. The resulting wines are sweet, luscious, and unique in their varietal flavors and aromas. Boyrytis wines cannot be achieved under any other conditions.

BOTTLE FERMENTED. A term referring to a method of champagne-making, indicating that the secondary fermentation took place in the bottle. The term can be applied to either *méthode champenoise* or the "transfer process," although it is more likely to be used to describe the latter.

BOUQUET. The smell or fragrance of a wine that results from the cooperage and aging, as distinguished from the "aroma" of a wine.

BRIX. A standard measurement, expressed in degrees, used to determine the percentage of soluble solids, or sugar, in grapes. Brix may be multiplied by .55 to obtain the potential alcohol content of a finished wine.

BRUT. A dry to nearly dry sparkling wine, with 1.5% or less residual sugar.

BULK PROCESS. A method of making champagne in which the secondary fermentation of wine occurs in large tanks, and the yeast is then removed by filtration before bottling. Also known as the "Charmat process."

CELLAR. An area of the winery where wines are made, stored and aged. Also used as a verb: to cellar a wine is to store the bottled wine for aging.

CHARACTER. Term used to describe the integrated features of a wine, such as smell, taste and appearance, which distinguish that wine from any other wine.

COMPLEXITY. A term combining several discernible characteristics in a wine, such as fruit flavor, aroma, bouquet, winemaking style, balance, and overall sensation. A well-balanced wine combining several aroma and flavor elements is referred to as complex.

COOPERAGE. Term used for containers in which wine is stored and aged before bottling. It includes barrels, casks and tanks of any size or material.

CRUSH. The activity following immediately after the harvest, when grapes are transported to the winery, crushed and made into wine. "Crush" and "harvest" are frequently interchangeable, both indicating the culmination of a growing season.

CUVÉE. A French term for the specific blend of still wines used in the secondary fermentation. Applicable primarily to sparkling wines and Champagne.

DECANTING. A process of pouring wine slowly and carefully from the original bottle into a decanter. Decanting is generally used for sedimented wine, in order to guarantee clarity in the serving.

DEMI-SEC. An off-dry to sweet sparkling wine, with 2% or more residual sugar. Also Sec and Extra-Dry.

DESSERT WINE. A term denoting wines with an alcohol content of 17%-24% by volume, usually obtained by adding brandy or neutral spirits to the wine. Such wines are also described as "fortified." Good examples of dessert wines are Port, Muscatel, Sherry, Tokay and Madeira.

DOSAGE. Usually a mixture of sweet syrup and wine, used to replace the small amount of wine lost when removing the yeast sediment from a bottle-fermented sparkling wine. The "dosage" generally determines the level of sweetness in the final product.

DRY. Term used to describe the absence of sweetness in wine. Sweetness in a wine is dependent upon the amount of residual sugar. Wines with less than 0.5% residual sugar are generally referred to as "dry." Most red wines and some whites fall into the dry category.

ENOLOGY. The science of winemaking.

ESTATE BOTTLED. A term used on the wine label to indicate that the wine was made entirely from grapes grown on a vineyard or vineyards owned by the winery and located in the same Viticultural Area as the winery. Law also requires that the entire winemaking process for an estate-bottled wine be carried out at the single winery facility.

FERMENTATION. A process by which the enzymes in yeast transform fresh grape juice into alcohol. Most winemakers today use cultured yeast, although a few continue to ferment wines with wild yeast.

FILTRATION. A process in which wine is clarified by passing through a porous material at various stages of development, in order to remove any suspended residues or other natural solid particles.

FINING. A technique of clarifying wine by introducing fining materials such as clay, gelatin or raw egg whites. The fining materials settle to the bottom of the barrel or tank, taking with them the suspended particles.

FREE RUN. The portion of grape juice which escapes without pressing, prior to fermentation.

GENERIC WINE. A wine not made primarily from a specific grape variety, and whose name indicates that it is part of a general category or type, as distinguished from both varietal and proprietary wines. Good examples of generic wines are Burgundy, Chablis, Claret and Rosé.

GONDOLA. An open trailer used for transporting grapes from the vineyard to the winery for crushing.

JUG WINE. Generally low-priced, low-quality generic wines, sold in large jug bottles. Occasionally, some varietal wines are also sold in jug containers.

LATE HARVEST. When appearing on the wine label, the term "Late Harvest" indicates that the wine was made from grapes harvested at a higher Brix or sugar level, resulting, typically, in a wine finished sweet to some degree. Late Harvest wines may be served after meals as unfortified dessert wines.

MALOLACTIC FERMENTATION. A secondary fermentation which occurs naturally in some wines, converting malic acid into the softer lactic acid and carbon dioxide, thus making the wine less tannic and softer. The fermentation is frequently accompanied by the release of unpleasant odors as the gas escapes into the air.

MÉTHODE CHAMPENOISE. The traditional method of making champagne and sparkling wine, in which the second fermentation occurs in the same bottle in which the wine is sold. In France, it is the only permitted method for champagnes.

MICROCLIMATE. A defined, generally small, winegrowing area, distinguished by its climate, topography, soil and other such environmental factors. Winegrapes grown in such area possess singular characteristics, unique to that particular microclimate.

MUST. The combined mass of grape juice, pulp, seeds and skins, after they leave the crusher.

NOSE. The overall fragrance of a wine, which includes the aroma derived directly from the grape, as well as the bouquet that results from the cooperage and aging.

pH. A chemical measurement, used by winemakers to determine the activity of acid in grapes and ultimately the wine quality. pH is an important factor in winemaking, which can affect a wine's color, taste, textural feel on the palate, and longevity.

PHYLLOXERA VASTATRIX. A root louse that attacks grapevine roots, eventually destroying them. It was widespread in California and Europe in the 1870s and 1880s, until growers developed a phylloxera-resistant rootstock, grafting *vitis vinifera* onto native American roots. Most vines now grow on phylloxera-resistant rootstock.

POMACE. The combined mass of grape skins, seeds and pulp, left over after a wine has been pressed.

PRESS. The most basic winemaking equipment, used to recover the grape juice after crushing or the wine from the fermented must.

PRIVATE RESERVE. A term which, in its strictest sense, applies to special, long-aged wines. There is, however, no law governing the use of this on wine labels.

PRUNING. An activity entailing the trimming of dormant grapevines during winter.

PUMPING OVER. The term refers to the pumping of red wine from the bottom of a fermentation tank into the top of the tank, in order that it may develop even color extraction. Pumping over also aerates the wine as it ferments, thus aiding in the fermentation process.

RACKING. A process of clarifying wine by transferring the wine from one cooperage to another.

REFRACTOMETER. An instrument used to measure the sugar content of grapes, expressed in degrees of Brix.

RESIDUAL SUGAR. The unfermented grape sugars in a finished wine, indicating the sweetness of a wine. Residual sugar may be indicated on a wine label.

ROOTSTOCK. The root and wood stem of non-fruiting grapevine, onto which selected winegrape varieties are grafted. Rootstock is selected on the basis of its resistance to such pests as phylloxera, its adaptability to certain soil types, its affinity for the grape variety to be grown, and its growth characteristics.

SKIN CONTACT. Generally refers to the crushed grape skins left with the fresh grape juice prior to pressing. The amount of time allowed for skin contact can affect such aspects as the color or tannins in a finished wine.

SPARKLING WINE. Wine fermented a second time, either in the bottle or in pressurized containers, resulting in effervescence.

SWEET WINE. Wine with a perceptible amount of residual sugar, usually 1% or more. Sweetness in a wine is generally perceptible at 0.5%-0.7% residual sugar.

TANNIN. A mouth-puckering compound derived from grape skins, seeds and stems. Tannin is also a source of color in fruit and flowers, and is therefore more pronounced in red wines than in white wines. (Also see *Astrigency.*)

TRANSFER PROCESS. A method of making champagne, in which the secondary fermentation occurs in the bottle but the wine is then poured into pressurized tanks and filtered before re-bottling. Wines labeled "bottle fermented" are generally made by the Transfer Process.

VARIETAL WINE. A wine made wholly or primarily from, and named after, a specific grape variety, such as Cabernet Sauvignon, Zinfandel, Chardonnay, etc. Law requires that a wine bearing a varietal name on its wine label contain at least 75% of the named varietal.

VERAISON. A term used to describe the beginning of ripening, when grapes turn from green to purple, as in the case of red varieties, or from green to yellow or translucent green, as in the case of the white varieties. It is also a time when the sugar levels in the grapes begin to increase.

VINTAGE-DATED. A vintage-dated wine is one that bears a vintage date—or year—on the wine label, indicating that at least 95% of the wine was made from grapes harvested in the stated year. A vintage date is important in determining the freshness and aging potential of a wine.

VINTNER. Generally the principal of a winery who is involved to some degree in the winemaking process.

VITICULTURAL AREA. See *Appellation*.

VITICULTURE. The practice and science of grape-growing.

VITIS VINIFERA. A highly-regarded species of Old World or European grapevine, cultivated throughout Europe, and responsible for the world's best wines. Vinifera was first introduced in California in the mid-1800s. Vinifera varieties include Cabernet Sauvignon, Chardonnay, Sauvignon Blanc, Pinot Noir, Riesling and Gewurztraminer.

WINE TYPES

TABLE WINES

Varietals

Red

Cabernet Sauvignon
Cabernet Franc
Merlot
Pinot Noir
Zinfandel
Petite Sirah
Barbera
Charbono
Syrah
Gamay
Gamay Beaujolais

White

Chardonnay
Sauvignon Blanc
Chenin Blanc
Pinot Blanc
Gewurztraminer
Johannisberg Riesling
Grey Riesling
French Colombard
Green Hungarian
Moscato de Canelli

Generics

Red

Burgundy
Claret
Chianti
Rosé

White

Chablis
Sauterne
Rhine
Moselle

APPETIZER WINES

Sherry
White Vermouth
Madiera

DESSERT WINES

Angelica
Marsala
Muscat de Frontigan
Muscatel

Cream Sherry
Port
Tokay

SPARKLING WINES

Natural (Very Dry)
Brut (Dry)
Extra Dry (Off-dry)

Sec (Slightly Sweet)
Demi-Sec (Sweet)

INDEX

The abbreviation NV stands for Napa Valley.
The abbreviation SV stands for Sonoma Valley.
The abbreviation RR stands for the Russian River Region.

WINE NOTES

Winery
Wine Type
Year
Comments

Winery
Wine Type
Year
Comments

Winery
Wine Type
Year
Comments

Winery
Wine Type
Year
Comments

Winery
Wine Type
Year
Comments

WINE NOTES

Winery
Wine Type
Year
Comments

Winery
Wine Type
Year
Comments

Winery
Wine Type
Year
Comments

Winery
Wine Type
Year
Comments

Winery
Wine Type
Year
Comments

WINE NOTES

Winery
Wine Type
Year
Comments

Winery
Wine Type
Year
Comments

Winery
Wine Type
Year
Comments

Winery
Wine Type
Year
Comments

Winery
Wine Type
Year
Comments

WINE NOTES

Winery
Wine Type
Year
Comments

Winery
Wine Type
Year
Comments

Winery
Wine Type
Year
Comments

Winery
Wine Type
Year
Comments

Winery
Wine Type
Year
Comments